# The Jubilee Mandate

Andrew D. Asare

CIBUNET
Publishing

The Jubilee Mandate
Copyright © 2020, Andrew D. Asare

ISBN: 978-0-9964590-6-8

All rights reserved. No part of this book may be reproduced, stored in retrieval system, or transmitted in any form or by any means: electronic, mechanical, photocopies, recording, scanning or other-except for brief quotations in critical reviews or articles, without the prior written permission of the publisher except as provided by the United States of America copyright law. Unless otherwise noted, all Scripture quotations are from the King James version of the Bible.
This work was written from the writer's personal experience and knowledge. Any resemblance to any other work would be purely coincidental.

Printed in the United States of America

Cibunet Publishing
Email: admin@cibunet.com
Website: www.cibunet.com

# TABLE OF CONTENTS

Dedication ........................................................................................... 9

Acknowledgment ............................................................................ 10

Foreword ........................................................................................ 11

Preface ........................................................................................... 13

Chapter 1: Introduction – The Year of Jubilee ............................... 17

Chapter 2: Jubilee and the Lord's Sabbaths .................................... 21

    The Sabbath Rest ..................................................................... 23

    The Sabbath of Sabbaths ......................................................... 25

    The Sabbatical Year ................................................................. 26

    The Jubilee ............................................................................... 27

Chapter 3: The Year of Jubilee ....................................................... 29

Chapter 4: Jesus Our Jubilee – He is the Lord of the Sabbath ....... 55

    The Pre-Existence of Jesus as God .......................................... 56

    Jesus, The Creator ................................................................... 57

    Jesus, The Promised Messiah and Savior ............................... 59

    Jesus' Miraculous Life ............................................................. 69

    Jesus, The Executor of a New and Better Covenant ............... 76

    Jesus, The Temple of God ....................................................... 78

    Jesus, The Fulfilment of the Law and the Prophets ................ 80

    Jesus, The Sabbath Fulfilled .................................................... 85

Chapter 5: Jesus Our Jubilee – The Feasts of Israel (The Lord's Feasts). 89

Chapter 6: Jesus Our Jubilee – Unveiled in the Spring Feasts of Israel .... 97

    The Passover ............................................................................ 97

    The Feast of Unleavened Bread ............................................ 105

    Firstfruits ................................................................................ 110

    The Feast of Pentecost ............................................................................ 116

Chapter 7: Jesus Our Jubilee – Unveiled in the Fall Feasts of Israel ...... 123

    The Feast of Trumpets .......................................................................... 123

    The Feast of Atonement ....................................................................... 127

    The Feast of Tabernacles ..................................................................... 134

    Other Jewish Holidays: Purim and Hanukkah ................................. 140

Chapter 8: Jesus Our Jubilee – Unveiled in the Seven Redemptive Names of God ........................................................................................................ 145

Chapter 9: Jehovah Tsidkenu – The Lord Our Righteousness ............... 149

Chapter 10: Jehovah Nissi – The Lord Our Victory / Banner ................. 155

Chapter 11: Jehovah Shammah – The Lord is There ............................... 169

Chapter 12: Jehovah Shalom – The Lord Our Peace ............................... 175

Chapter 13: Jehovah Rapha / Rophe – The Lord Our Healer ................. 181

Chapter 14: Jehovah Rohi / Raah – The Lord Our Shepherd ................. 187

Chapter 15: Jehovah Jireh – The Lord Our Provider ............................... 193

Chapter 16: The Ultimate Name of Jesus .................................................. 203

Chapter 17: The Proclamation of the Jubilee ........................................... 215

Chapter 18: The Spirit of the Lord is Upon Me ........................................ 219

Chapter 19: Jesus Anointed to Preach the Gospel .................................. 225

    The Gospel of the Kingdom ................................................................ 225

    Repentance ............................................................................................. 229

    Love ......................................................................................................... 230

    Forgiveness ............................................................................................ 232

    Prayer ...................................................................................................... 233

    Faith ........................................................................................................ 235

    Giving ..................................................................................................... 237

His Second Coming .................................................................................. 239

Chapter 20: Jesus Preaches the Gospel / Good News to the Poor ........ 241

Chapter 21: Jesus Sent to Heal the Brokenhearted ................................. 255

Chapter 22: Jesus Preaches Deliverance to the Captives ........................ 261

Chapter 23: Jesus Preaches Recovering of Sight to the Blind ................ 271

Chapter 24: Jesus, Setting at Liberty Them that are Bruised .................. 277

Chapter 25: Jesus Preaches the Acceptable Year / The Year of the Lord's Favor .................................................................................................... 283

    1. The Day of Salvation ................................................................. 284

    2. The Year of the Lord's Favor ................................................... 288

    A. Jacob ........................................................................................ 289

    B. Hannah .................................................................................... 290

    C. Esther ...................................................................................... 292

    D. Daniel ..................................................................................... 295

    E. Mary, the Mother of Jesus .................................................... 296

    F. The Church ............................................................................. 300

    3. Wrapping it all Up ..................................................................... 303

Chapter 26: The Jubilee Mandate ............................................................. 305

    The Jubilee Mandate of Jesus ..................................................... 309

    The Jubilee Mandate of the Disciples ....................................... 312

    The Jubilee Mandate of the Apostle Paul ................................. 315

    The Jubilee Mandate of the Church .......................................... 322

Chapter 27: Jubilee Mandate Keys – Be Full of the Holy Ghost ............ 333

Chapter 28: Jubilee Mandate Keys – Corporate Prayer in the Church ... 343

Chapter 29: Jubilee Mandate Keys – Boldness of the Church ................ 349

Chapter 30: Jubilee Mandate Keys – Unity in the Church ...................... 359

Chapter 31: The Jubilee Mandate – Yours to Enjoy, Enforce, and Transmit Forever! ................................................................................................ 373

## DEDICATION

This book is dedicated to the precious Members of OMEGA CHURCH CENTRE, Brampton, Ontario, Canada. You have shown incredibly steadfast support and loyalty, and have been relentless in prayer and devotion. Your demonstration of immoveable faithfulness to the kingdom dream and purpose of God for OMEGA in Canada and elsewhere in the world has been unqualified, and really inspiring to me.

Having participated in the OMEGA dream, may you also enjoy the release of the dew of heaven and the fatness of the earth. May the Lord command His blessing on you and your storehouses, and cause you to abound always in every good work. May the Lord exponentially anoint your heads with the oil of Jubilee, and cause His goodness and mercy to follow you all the days of your lives.

Unstoppable blessings on you and your generations.

# ACKNOWLEDGEMENTS

All the praise, glory, honor and thanks to Jesus, our Jubilee! My deep appreciation goes to my loving wife, Dr. Ama Asare, whose indefatigable encouragement and support inspired me to finish "The Jubilee Mandate." With commitment, dedication and skill, she edited the manuscript to make it easily accessible to the reader. My dear, you are one of a kind, virtuous, tenacious, full of God and grace. May all generations call you blessed. Great is your reward here on earth and hereafter, for always being there for me, our family, and for the Church family. Boundless blessings to you.

To Rev. Dr. Kenneth Walley of CIBUNET, my dear friend and publisher, I express my profound gratitude. Thank you ever so much for your invaluable advice and encouragement. Your hard work on this material helped shape this product into a beautiful piece. Jehovah God will surely remember you for your devotion, for the selfless sacrifices you have made for this generation. May He increase you and enlarge your coast, and may you be blessed beyond measure in every way.

To the worldwide OMEGA family, unending thanks for your encouragement and love. You have always inspired me to refuel to fight the good fight of faith. May Jesus, our Jubilee, be your exceeding great reward.

# FOREWORD

Andrew Asare has made a great contribution to the Body of Christ. As an author of 14 books, I can imagine the numerous hours that Andrew spent researching and studying, in order to present the vast amount of Biblical knowledge found in this book "The Jubilee Mandate".

He continually reveals that Jesus is the ultimate fulfillment of all that God gave Israel to be and to do. That includes all the feasts, the tabernacle, the year of Jubilee, and the names of God. Jesus fulfilled the old covenant by establishing the new covenant through His death on the cross, buried but resurrected on the third day, then ascended to heaven and sent the Holy Spirit to birth the Church on the Day of Pentecost.

Jesus commissioned the Church with the Jubilee Mandate. Jesus came to earth to take on a mankind body. The Body of Jesus was commissioned to fulfill many things while here on earth. Jesus came from heaven, but could not return to heaven until He had fulfilled the numerous purposes that God had planned for Him to accomplish during His time as a mortal on Earth. After Jesus had fulfilled all things that the Father God had commissioned Him to do, He ascended to heaven and sat down at the right hand of the Father.

Jesus then birthed the Church and began building His Church. Now Jesus has commissioned the Church to fulfill and accomplish many things while being the mortal Church on Earth. Acts 3:21 declares that Jesus cannot return from heaven to resurrect and translate His Church into immortality until the Church has fulfilled its predestined prophetic purposes. Jesus is held in the heavens until … all these things are accomplished.

As you read this book, discover all that Christ Jesus has done for you and me as members of the one and only universal, many-membered, corporate Body of Christ. Discover how you can become a co-laborer with Jesus Christ in fulfilling His eternal plan for redeemed mankind.

This book should be read by every minister and individual Christian, and then kept handy as a reference to continually appropriate all the truths presented in this tremendous book. God bless you, Apostle Asare, for making this book available to Christ's Church.

**By: Bishop Bill Hamon**
**Bishop: Christian International Apostolic-Global Network**
**Author**: The Eternal Church; Prophets & Personal Prophecy; Prophets & the Prophetic Movement; Prophets, Pitfalls, & Principles; Apostles/Prophets & the Coming Moves of God; The Day of the Saints; Who Am I & Why Am I here; Prophetic Scriptures Yet to be Fulfilled (3rd Reformation); 70 Reasons for Speaking in Tongues; How Can These Things Be?; God's Weapons of War; Your Highest Calling.

# PREFACE

Jubilees are recognized in most cultures and traditions, and are celebrated by individuals, families, communities, organizations and entire nations. They commemorate pivotal and significant events such as births, anniversaries, turning points, major events in history, the emergence of various groups or businesses, and the founding or independence of nations.

The Jubilees of nations and kingdoms are marked by national holidays and periods of peace and reflection, where there is no work and no stress. Monarchs, presidents, prime ministers and leaders assemble their populace on national parks and in huge coliseums to deliver great speeches about their history, heritage and accomplishments, and map out how far they have come as a nation and kingdom. Jubilees are a time of optimism, and leaders move to inspire and motivate their people to have hope for greater things yet to come, and they celebrate the past, present and future with faith and anticipation.

Jubilees, as conceived by God Almighty, even Yahweh, are all these and more, and are loaded with even more significance and reality, both materially and spiritually. He templated, through the nation of Israel, what Jubilees are all about, and how the Jubilee Mandate would be disseminated, through Jesus, the Messiah, to all of humanity.

In the nation of Israel, Jubilees were not low-key productions. The trumpet of Jubilee would sound through the land, publicizing the festivities, and the people of God would celebrate, in an atmosphere of jollification and conviviality, not only what God had done, but what He was yet to do. They would honor, praise and glorify God from whom all blessings flow, the source of every good and perfect gift. It was always a special time, a special season, and the dawning of a new day.

The Jubilee atmosphere was always electrified with liberty, freedom, debt relief, restoration, joy and laughter. There were recounts of emotional journeys from trials to triumph, challenges to victories, battles to conquests, weaknesses to strength, and from pain to major interventions through God.

The Church, even the Body of Christ, has been engrafted into the Jubilees of Israel through Jesus Messiah, the eternal Son of God and Son of man. He is the reality of the Jubilees and Feasts of Israel, and the reality of all the Christ-types in the Old Testament narratives, like Moses, Joshua, David, Samson, Deborah, Esther, and all the great heroes of faith who brought salvation, redemption and deliverance to Israel.

He was foreordained, before the foundation of the world, and anointed by the Father God, to preach the gospel to the poor, to heal the broken hearted, to preach deliverance to the captives, and the recovering of sight to the blind, to set at liberty them that are bruised, and to preach the acceptable year of the Lord, which is the Jubilee.

Jubilee is embodied in the person of Jesus Messiah, who is the author and finisher of our faith, the very Alpha and Omega, Yahweh, the horn of our salvation, our strength, our rock, our shield and buckler, our healer, deliverer, provider and banner of victory. He came into the world and declared the Jubilee and its fulfilment in Himself.

He is still sounding through His Bride, the Church, that trumpet of liberty, emancipation, salvation, healing and deliverance, proclaiming Jubilee to all who believe. He has placed, in the hands of the Church, the honorable JUBILEE MANDATE, commissioning and equipping her to proclaim Jubilee to the entire world.

To Him be all glory and praise forevermore!

# Chapter 1

## INTRODUCTION - THE YEAR OF JUBILEE

Jehovah God (Yahweh) is, has always been, and will forever be, the God of Jubilee. Biblical Jubilee was instituted by Him, and He established the commandment that it must be observed and celebrated every 50 years in the nation of Israel, when they came to the promised land (Leviticus 25:1-4).

The English word "Jubilee" is synonymous with the Hebrew word "Yovel", which is rendered by the Septuagint as a "trumpet-blast of liberty". Many therefore assume that the English word "Jubilee" was derived from the Hebrew, but this may be a misconception as the word appears to have stemmed rather from the Latin word "jubilo", which means "shout". The word in ancient Greek is "iuzo".

Jubilee is also likely to have developed from the English word "yowl". The English word "jubilation" means a feeling or expression of joy or exultation, a joyful or festive celebration, joyousness, euphoria, or being in a state of elation. The various renditions suggest shouting joyfully, emitting a shout, a victory cry.

Biblical Jubilee is all of these and more. It is the culmination and epitome of special sacred Sabbaths and Feasts of Israel running through the Hebrew calendar.

The Jubilee year begins on the Day of Atonement in the 49th year, when the priests blow the ram's horn, and these celebrations run into the 50th year. This is the sound of the trumpet of freedom, liberty, emancipation and deliverance to all of Israel. Lands are left fallow; possessed lands are returned to their original owners; bond servants are set free; debts are cancelled. This is the Lord's Jubilee, the acceptable year of the Lord, the year of the Lord's favor.

Through the Jubilee, God shows His people that, despite all the enormous responsibilities of life, and in spite of the battles, storms, struggles and bondage, there remains a joyous rest for them.

This is the whole message – that Jesus, the Son of God, is our Jubilee. He was sent by the Father God to fulfill a predestined and foreordained Jubilee agenda of salvation, redemption, freedom, liberty and deliverance, an agenda formed, worked out, and crafted in God's eternal infinite mind before time began. Jesus came to proclaim and declare the Jubilee, to demonstrate it and administer it, and to show that He is its very fulfilment, embodiment, and personification. He brings us exceeding and surpassing joy. He is the reason for us to jubilate and shout for joy, and to perpetually expect pleasures forevermore.

Jesus is the living reality of the 50-year Jubilee cycle recorded in the Old Testament. Put differently, the 50th year is now with us in the person of Jesus. However, we do not have to wait for each 50-year cycle to roll around to before we can celebrate the full benefits, rights and privileges of the Jubilee He brings.

His physical and literal arrival and entrance into the world, and His abiding presence in our hearts and lives, means that He is with us, every year, every month, every week, every day and every moment. He is now with us, and eternally in us and for us. That opens us up to the unceasing and eternal supplies of the Jubilee, and we can daily walk and enforce the freedoms that the Father has enacted, designed, and paved for us through the Son, Jesus.

It is important to note that, although the Jubilee was first introduced by God to the nation of Israel, it is not restricted to them alone. It is all encompassing, stretching beyond Israel, beyond time, and beyond history, reaching all peoples, tribes, nations, tongues and kindred.

This limitless mandate is fulfilled in Jesus Messiah, the lamb (ram) of God who takes away the sin of the *world* (John 1:29), and is a revelation of the loving nature and heart of God, and His plan for all of humanity.

Many are overwhelmed with the cares of life, oppressed by a foggy, cloudy or negative atmosphere, plagued with needs, wants, pain, uncertainties, struggles and spiritual battles. But this is the assurance that Jubilee brings - that, no matter what your background is or what your circumstances are, Jubilee is always standing right in front of you in the person of Jesus.

He came to declare and proclaim the Jubilee, which is a consolidation of good news to the poor, freedom from slavery to sin, healing, and deliverance from satanic and demonic oppression (Luke 4:16-21). He saves and reconciles us to God the Father. He transforms anyone who confesses Him as Savior and who surrenders his/her life totally to Him (Romans 10:8-10). He is the anointed one who breaks every fetter, removes every yoke, and lifts every burden. (Isaiah 10:27).

Indulge me for a moment and come along with me as I visualize and relish the Jubilee …

It is the assembly of all God's people on the intensely beautiful National Park of the kingdom of God. A glorious banquet, a feast for the senses, the likes of which has never been experienced before, has been set up by Jesus, the groom, for His bride, which is His Church. Jesus is the sacrificial ram (lamb) of God. He blows His shofar, the ram's horn. He announces the Jubilee to all to join His kingdom. He lets out the piercing victory cry, and His people break into songs of deliverance and shouts of joy, for indeed, He is their hiding place.

At the sound of the trumpet, He beckons His people to the banqueting table to capture the reality of the banner of His love (Song of Solomon 2:4), to enjoy the feast prepared for them in the presence of their enemies (Psalm 23:5), to revel in Him as He rejoices over them and serenades them (His bride Israel and the Church) with His singing (Zephaniah 3:17), and they all rejoice for the testimonies of the past, present and future.

# Chapter 2

## JUBILEE AND THE LORD'S SABBATHS

The Holy Sabbath of Jehovah God is the pivot that undergirds and maintains the balance of events leading to the year of Jubilee. It is the central theme running through all the Hebrew festivals and feasts. Understanding God's Holy Sabbath is therefore an important key to opening and operating the reality, effect and power of the Jubilee.

There has been ongoing debate for generations amongst Jews and Christians about the Sabbath compliance. The debate revolves around issues such as what time and day of the week it should be celebrated, the basis for the adherence to its edicts, and what its relevance is to salvation.

It is widely acknowledged that the Hebrew Sabbath falls on Friday evening to Saturday evening, Saturday being the seventh day of the week on the secular calendar. The New Testament does not give specific regulations or instructions to the New Creation believer regarding the keeping of the Sabbath on Saturdays; neither does it specifically state which day Christians are to worship. The early Christians did worship on the Sabbath. However, historical records indicate that, around 366 A.D., the Council of Laodicea designated Sunday as the day of worship. The Bishop of Rome also made Sunday the day of worship.

With respect to precursors requiring the people of Israel to adhere to the Sabbath, it appears that such laws were proclaimed under the leadership of Moses, through whom the Law was given.

Notwithstanding, it is very important to note that the Sabbath did not originate with the Law. It was actually first enjoyed and expressed by God and instituted right after creation by Him. After six days of creation, He rested on the seventh, thus observing the Sabbath. This was before the Law. Thus, the Sabbath is not limited to the observance of the Law of Moses. However, its progression and development show that it became an integral part of the Law and of Jehovah's ordained feasts of Israel.

The Sabbath unlocks God's plans and purposes for creation, and the redemptive provisions for Israel and the Church. Sin triggered the redemptive program; the Law was the vehicle to enunciate that redemption and the schoolmaster to enforce it, but it was too weak to provide salvation. The Law was primarily conceived by God to lead His people to grace, salvation and rest through Jesus, the Messiah.

On a cautionary note, it is important to point out that, in view of the universalism of God and His provision, the Sabbath must not be stringently perceived as a denominational set of rituals that adherents are bound to, in order to invoke the Lord's favor. Rather, it must be conceived of and experienced as God's initiative to process His redemptive grace for humanity as a whole. God blessed and sanctified the Sabbath day, but worshipping Him is not limited to the Sabbath; He must be worshipped every day.

There are essentially four broad Sabbath observances ordained by God, falling on a graduated scale. These are:

- The Sabbath Rest
- The Sabbath of Sabbaths
- The Sabbatical Year
- The Jubilee

These Sabbath observances are punctuated by time, as they are expressed as a day of the week (the Sabbath Rest), as a week (the Sabbath of Sabbaths), as a year (the Sabbatical Year), and as an accumulation of years (the Jubilee). They all embody the progressive expression of God's intent for man and relay the corresponding outpouring of His blessings.

## 1. THE SABBATH REST

The first Sabbath observance is the "Sabbath Rest", which falls on the seventh day of a seven-day cycle. The Sabbath rest idea originates in the fact that God created all things, completing His work of framing the heavens and the earth and the hosts thereof in six days, and resting on the seventh. The Sabbath therefore marks the completeness, fullness and perfection of God's handiwork.

"Thus the heavens and the earth were finished, and all the host of them. And on the seventh day God ended his work which he had made; and he rested on the seventh day from all his work which he had made. And God blessed the seventh day, and sanctified it: because that in it he had rested from all his work which God created and made." Genesis 2:1-3

The first mention of the Sabbath in the book of Genesis, then, was in relation to God resting after creation. As such, this requires, first, that all things and beings created must acknowledge God as the holy and perfect creator.

Second, it is noteworthy that God blessed the seventh day, the Sabbath, and hallowed it, making it a sacred and holy day. He sanctified and separated it from the six other days of work and labor. This signified that this day was special and unique in the mind of God. This blessing of the Sabbath by God is the blessing that seals all the things He has created.

In fact, the blessing and consecration of the Sabbath was so important to God that He made it a huge part of the Ten Commandments. The Sabbath observance is the longest provision of those Commandments, pointing to the emphasis God laid on its relevance.

"Remember the sabbath day, to keep it holy. Six days thou shall labour, and do all thy work: But the seventh day is the sabbath of the Lord thy God: in it thou shalt not do any work, thou, nor thy son, nor thy daughter, thy manservant, nor thy maidservant, nor thy cattle, nor thy stranger that is within thy gates. For in six days the Lord made heaven and earth, the sea, and all that in them is, and rested the seventh day: wherefore the Lord blessed the seventh day, and hallowed it." Exodus 20:8-11

The Jewish people were to honor the Sabbath with their families, their workers and their lands. The significant point that ought not to be missed is God's divine intent. He wanted His people and all that they owned and did to be subject to His sabbatical laws and to be identified with Him by taking a rest from their labors on the Sabbath as He Himself did. By so doing, they would optimally position themselves to enjoy fellowship with

Him and come into the fullness of His grace, redemption and liberty.

The Sabbath was therefore a day set apart for God to be acknowledged as the creator and maker of all things, and for all created things to be subject to Him and give Him glory, praise, honor and worship. The whole Sabbath day was to be fully dedicated to the Lord in total surrender to His sovereignty, might, power and majesty.

## 2. THE SABBATH OF SABBATHS

The second Sabbath observance is the "Sabbath of Sabbaths", which is seven cycles of Sabbaths, beginning on the 49$^{th}$ day into the 50$^{th}$.

"And ye shall count unto you from the morrow after the sabbath, from the day that ye brought the sheaf of the wave offering; seven sabbaths shall be complete: Even unto the morrow after the seventh sabbath shall ye number fifty days; and ye shall offer a new meat offering unto the LORD." Leviticus 23:15-16

One such Sabbath of Sabbaths observance is the Day of Pentecost, which is 50 days after the Passover. Another high Sabbath observance is the Day of Atonement (Yom Kippur), the day which powerfully displays the two main tenets of the Sabbath, namely, people abstaining from work, and also, having a reverential and repentant-laden posture before God. The people of God would demonstrate repentance, afflict their souls, draw closer to God, and reconcile with Him.

"And the LORD spake unto Moses, saying, Also on the tenth day of this seventh month there shall be a day of atonement: it shall be an holy convocation unto you; and ye shall afflict your souls, and offer an offering made by fire unto the LORD. And ye shall do no work in that same day: for it is a day of atonement, to make an atonement for you before the LORD your God. For whatsoever soul it be that shall not be afflicted in that same day, he shall be cut off from among his people. And whatsoever soul it be that doeth any work in that same day, the same soul will I destroy from among his people. Ye shall do no manner of work: it shall be a statute for ever throughout your generations in all your dwellings. It shall be unto you a sabbath of rest, and ye shall afflict your souls: in the ninth day of the month at even, from even unto even, shall ye celebrate your sabbath." Leviticus 23:26-32

Stipulations about the Sabbath demanded total rest and abstinence from work, and any breaches were punishable by death. During the wandering days of the children of Israel in the wilderness, they once found a man gathering sticks on the Sabbath. He was brought to Moses and Aaron for breaking the law. God commanded that he should be put to death by stoning. (Numbers 15:32-36). The severity of this punishment shows that deeper sense of holiness, purity, obedience and perfection God attaches to the keeping of the Sabbath.

## 3. THE SABBATICAL YEAR

The third Sabbath experience is the "Sabbatical Year". This year, known as "Shmita" in Hebrew, was the last year or end of every seven-year cycle. God promised Moses that He would bring His people to the land of promise. He required, however, that the land they would inherit from Him should be subjected to the observance of the Lord's Sabbaths.

"And the Lord spake unto Moses in mount Sinai, saying, Speak unto the children of Israel, and say unto them, When ye come into the land which I give you, then shall the land keep a Sabbath unto the Lord. Six years thou shalt sow thy field, and six years thou shalt prune thy vineyard, and gather in the fruit thereof; But in the seventh year shall be a sabbath of rest unto the land, a sabbath for the Lord: thou shalt neither sow thy field, nor prune thy vineyard." Leviticus 25:1-4

This passage shows the institution of the Sabbatical year in every seven-year cycle by Jehovah in the land of inheritance He brought them into. Six solid years had to be devoted to working the land, but in the seventh year, the land was to be left to lie fallow. In the eyes of divine purpose, the Sabbath was tied in to the devolution of a divine inheritance to the people, wherein the land must rest, the people of God must rest; they must all enter into the rest of God.

## 4. THE JUBILEE

The final Sabbath configuration is the "Jubilee", the zenith of all the Sabbaths. The Jubilee took place at the end of seven Sabbatical year cycles, which was the $49^{th}$ year. According to the commandment of Jehovah, the priests were to sound the trumpet of freedom and liberty at the end of seven Sabbatical year cycles. The sound of the trumpet, the shofar, was heard on the Day of Atonement in the $49^{th}$ year, and it marked the beginning of Jubilee which would run into the $50^{th}$ year (Leviticus 25:1-12).

The Jubilee was a time when all men were set free from servitude, and their lands were returned to them. Debts were forgiven. There was liberty and emancipation. The Jubilee was proclaimed by Isaiah as "the acceptable year of the Lord" (Isaiah 61:2). It served as a reminder to the people of God that they would not be in perpetual servitude.

This freedom from bondage is what the Sabbaths were incrementally and progressively building up to. The Jubilee is the peak or highest point of all the Sabbaths and festivals of God. Seven sabbatical years bring us into the Jubilee year. In other words, the Jubilee is the Sabbath of Sabbath of Sabbath of Sabbath of Sabbath of Sabbath of Sabbath!

The Jubilee unleashes on God's people, seven times the provisions of the sabbatical year. It is packed with the ultimate provisions of Jehovah for salvation, redemption, restoration, grace, peace, healing and deliverance for God's people, and the explosion of joy amongst them.

# Chapter 3

## THE YEAR OF JUBILEE

Let us follow the chain of Sabbaths leading to the Jubilee. Understanding this chain and the importance God attached to the Sabbaths enables us to have a deeper communion with God and to receive the blessed benefits of Jubilee.

The year of Jubilee is the accumulation of Sabbaths. In terms of progression, and as already discussed in Chapter Two, there is, first, the weekly Sabbath. The second is the Sabbath of Sabbaths which is 49 days after the Sabbath. The third expression is the Sabbatical year which occurs within every seven-year cycle. The fourth, which is the peak of these Sabbaths, is seven sabbatical years, the 49$^{th}$ year of which is the year of Jubilee, which runs into the 50$^{th}$ year.

Through the various Sabbaths staggered through time, God was gradually and incrementally piecing together for the consumption of humanity, the mosaic of His pre-ordained purposes and destiny for humanity through Christ Jesus, and revealing the depths of His love, articulated through the vector of His Jubilee blessings. In terms of progression and impact:

- The first Sabbath experience profiles the elementary or fundamental rest of humanity from their labors.

- The Sabbath of Sabbaths, the second model, accumulates the blessing of rest, and adds the dimension of solemnity and repentance.

- The Sabbatical year, the third configuration, expresses the notion of rest, not only for humanity, but also for the land, and highlights the supernatural provision from God when His people rest.

- The Jubilee, the final Sabbath expression, is the Sabbath, the Sabbath of Sabbaths, and the Sabbatical year all phased in or rolled into one cohesive celebration. During the Jubilee, therefore, there is a divine optimization set in motion, and the accrual of all the benefits embedded in the first three celebrations. There is the release of the fullness of God's rest for humans and for their lands, as well as the release of an anointing to bring complete freedom, emancipation, redemption and restoration to all who trust and believe in Him. Thus, the Jubilee is, at every point, a value-added and ever-increasing experience of God's blessings.

The first three Sabbaths, then, are a picture-perfect backdrop to what is to come in the Jubilee. Put another way, the first three Sabbaths find their ultimate intent, purpose and fulfillment expressed in the year of Jubilee, and the relevance and blessings they release peak at that time.

The Jubilee year presents to the believer four times God's blessings, support, and supplies, and a deeper experience of His holiness, majesty and glory. The Lord's promises to save, redeem, forgive, heal, deliver, protect and prosper His people are quadrupled in the year of Jubilee.

God modelled His redemptive Jubilee plan through the nation of Israel, and the Sabbaths, Jubilees and feasts instituted by God are still celebrated and observed in modern times by some ardent devoted Jews. They have an understanding or revelation of the times and seasons Jehovah has set forth in His holy Sabbaths and festivals. Likewise, believers who discern the times and seasons, who seek God to know what is on His agenda, and who dare to walk in obedience, tap into His grace, protection, provision and blessing.

It is important to register the fact that, in His instructions about the Sabbaths, God was very specific about who, when, where, what and how they should play out. In other words, there was a very contextual and seasonal dimension to observing the Sabbaths.

Accordingly, it should not be overlooked that there is always a seasonal, time-sensitive or time-capsuled blessing for those who obey the word of God and act on the terms of His covenant. Conversely, there is seasonal judgement on all who contravene His word and break His covenant. The Christian Church needs to be alert and sensitive to this, and must have the spirit of the children of Issachar who had an understanding of the times and knew what Israel ought to do and when. (1 Chronicles 12:32). Speaking about the Jubilee, God instructed Moses, saying:

"And thou shalt number seven sabbaths of years unto thee, seven times seven years; and the space of the seven sabbaths shall be unto thee forty and nine years. Then shalt thou cause the trumpet of the jubile to sound on the tenth day of the seventh month, in the day of atonement shall ye make the trumpet sound throughout all your land. And ye shall hallow the fiftieth year, and proclaim liberty throughout all the land unto all the inhabitants thereof: it shall be a jubilee unto you; and ye shall return every man unto his possession, and ye shall return every man unto his family. A jubile shall that fiftieth year be unto you: ye shall not sow, neither reap that which groweth of itself in it, nor gather the grapes in it of thy vine undressed. For it is the jubile; it shall be holy unto you: ye shall eat the increase thereof out of the field." Leviticus 25:8-12

Key aspects of the Jubilee, as delineated in the passage above, are discussed below.

- ## **THE SOUND OF THE TRUMPET**

In the Bible, the trumpet is a powerful instrument used by God to get the attention of His people. The sound of the trumpet does various things in the lives of the people. It may be:

- A Call for a Solemn Assembly and Repentance (Joel 2:15-19, Isaiah 58:1)
- A Signal for War or Danger (Judges 6:34; 7:16, I Corinthians 14:8-9)
- To Praise God (Psalm 98:5-6, Psalm 150:3)
- To Anoint Kings (I Kings 1:33-35)
- For Temple Dedications (2 Chronicles 5:12-14)
- For Releasing God's Presence (Psalm 47:6, 2 Samuel 6:15, 1 Chronicles 15:28)
- To Signal the Return of Jesus (1 Thessalonians 4:16-17, 1 Corinthians 15:51-53)

During the Jubilee, the priests sounded the shofar, the ram's horn, on the tenth day of the seventh month in the 49th year, which is the Day of Atonement (Yom Kippur). The trumpet of the Jubilee emitted a high sounding blast that persisted for long hours on that day, announcing the Jubilee, and signifying freedom throughout all the land, and peace and joy for God's people.

The shofar is the horn of a ram. As will be seen in the discussion on the feasts of Israel, Jehovah provided a ram as a substitute for Abraham's sacrifice of Isaac. The ram was a type of the Messiah, Jehovah's provision for redemptive Jubilee, making the shofar representative of His might, power, and His call to His people.

Jesus Messiah is alive forevermore. The sounding of the shofar is a living, redemptive reality during the Jubilee year. It is the persistent and unrelenting emancipation proclamation by Jesus Messiah that all who come to Him and believe in Him are free from sin, Satan, hell and judgment, and are ushered into the glorious liberty of God's kingdom.

- **DAY OF ATONEMENT**

Jehovah God is the master designer, and He skillfully constructed the pathway to Jubilee. It starts on the most holy day of the year, the Day Atonement. This day falls within the feast of Atonement, which is a period of awe and repentance, and is the most hallowed, holy season of the year on the Hebrew calendar; it is the way of holiness.

On the Day of Atonement, the High Priest would offer sacrifices for the sins of himself and the people. He would then go into the holy place in the Temple to pour the blood of lambs on the mercy seat to obtain forgiveness of sins. The sins of the people were thus atoned for, paid for, or redeemed. It was a time for the renewal of the blood covenant between God and the people, for reconciliation, and for getting right with God in sweet fellowship.

The backdrop to all of this is that man was created in the image and likeness of God to reflect God's purity, holiness, personality and glory. He was holy, as God is holy, until he fell into sin in the Garden of Eden.

At the fall of man, God set in motion the process of redemption to restore him to holy fellowship with Himself. It is important to grasp this fundamental truth, reality and revelation that, in order to relate to God, there has to be the total removal of sin, iniquity and transgression. That is the only way for anyone, any group, or any nation to experience the embrace of His person, His goodness and His mighty delivering power.

Therefore, His redemptive process had to begin with putting sin away. His plan to save, redeem, and restore all the original attributes that He had originally invested in man, and to bring humanity to righteousness and holiness before Him, could only be initiated, molded, perfected and consummated by He Himself.

As part of His divine design, Israel was chosen to model this agenda through the templates of His holy Sabbaths, the feasts of Israel, and the declaration of the year of Jubilee.

The awesome allocations of the Jubilee were never released without atonement and repentance. Atonement was the vehicle to start this work of God. The atoning work that was accomplished through the blood of animals meant that God covered the sins of the people. Everyone forgave their neighbor for any wrong done to them. Liberty was proclaimed throughout all the land and amongst its inhabitants, and there was great rejoicing.

Jubilee, then, is always preceded by repentance, that is, the confession of sin, the turning away from sin and iniquity, and obtaining grace, mercy and forgiveness from the Almighty God.

"Behold, the Lord's hand is not shortened, that it cannot save; neither his ear heavy, that it cannot hear: But your iniquities have separated between you and your God, and your sins have hid his face from you, that he will not hear." Isaiah 59:1-2

"He that covereth his sins shall not prosper: but whoso confesseth and forsaketh them shall have mercy." Proverbs 28:13

"If I regard iniquity in my heart, the Lord will not hear me: But verily God hath heard me; he hath attended to the voice of my prayer. Blessed be God, which hath not turned away my prayer, nor his mercy from me." Psalm 66:18-20

"If we say we have no sin, we deceive ourselves, and the truth is not in us. If we confess our sins, he is faithful and just to forgive us our sins, and to cleanse us from all unrighteousness. If we say we have not sinned, we make him a liar, and his word is not in us." 1 John 1:8-10

"If my people, which are called by my name, shall humble themselves, and pray, and seek my face, and turned from their wicked ways; then will I hear from heaven, and will forgive their sin, and will heal their land." 2 Chronicles 7:14

During the reign of King Joash (from 835 to 796 B.C.), Judah slipped into moral degradation, falling into the sin of drunkenness and showing abject disregard for the House of God. They did not present themselves in the House of God to offer unto Him, the prescribed meat and drink offerings, and served idols (2 Chronicles 24:14-27).

Going into the presence of God and offering sacrifices symbolized their act of continual consecration and devotion to God, and this is similarly illustrated in the life of the believer who is urged to continually present himself or herself as a living sacrifice, holy and acceptable to God, in daily worship and service (Romans 12:1-2).

The people's refusal to offer service and worship to God therefore meant a break in fellowship between them and Jehovah, and that disconnect exposed them to a plague of locusts which devastated the land and ate up the crops and vegetation. The land was hit with drought, and the people mourned.

The Lord spoke to Joel to declare to the people, the way to fix the problems that they faced and to reverse the judgement of Jehovah. God instructed the leaders of Judah to blow the trumpet in Zion and come together in a solemn assembly for prayer, fasting and repentance.

He made it clear that, if the people of Judah came before Him in repentance, He would forgive their sin, work great things amongst them, and restore all that they had lost as a result of the destructive work of the locusts, the cankerworm, the caterpillar and the palmerworm.

He promised to heal the land and take away their reproach. He would bring the rain, the former and the latter rain together in first month, the double blessing of harvest. Afterward, He promised, He would pour out His Spirit on all flesh, and the sons and daughters would prophesy, old men would dream dreams, and young men would see visions (Joel 2:12-30). That was Jubilee!

God is faithful to forgive confessed and repented sins. Those whose sins are forgiven are blessed because they are set free and are no longer under condemnation or servitude. The exit of sin makes way for the entrance of God's blessing, and reconciling with God opens the door for His active work of deliverance, favor and provision. The yoke and burden of sin and the oppression of the enemy are broken, and there is access into God's presence where there is fullness of joy.

"Blessed is he whose transgression is forgiven, whose sin is covered. Blessed is the man unto whom the Lord imputeth not iniquity, and in whose spirit there is no guile." Psalm 32:1-2

God does not bless sin. He rather brings His people out of sin, iniquity and transgression with the light of His holy Word.
Once repentance takes place and atonement is made, Israel is back in deep communion with God, and the stage is set for Jubilee, the peak of His activities in the redemptive processes of freedom and liberty.

The other side of the coin of repentance is holiness, which is also a central tenet and foundation of the Jubilee. God is a holy God.

He commanded that the year of Jubilee, the 50th year, be hallowed, that is, consecrated, set apart, sanctified, and regarded as holy.

His intent was to bring His people into the sanctified state of redemptive-jubilee, which is a season of walking in purity of heart and conscience before God and man. He expected His people to step into a deeper dimension of holiness in the Jubilee year because of His intent to visit them with a greater weight of glory. He commands His people to be holy because He is holy (1 Peter 1:16).

"Follow peace with all men, and holiness, without which no man shall see the Lord." Hebrew 12:14

"Having therefore these promises, dearly beloved, let us cleanse ourselves from all filthiness of the flesh and spirit, perfecting holiness in the fear of God." 2 Corinthians 7:1

We are not able to have communion with God without a conscious acknowledgement of His holiness and the radiance of His perfection of beauty on our hearts. Indeed, a continual relationship and fellowship between Him and His people is based on His word and a life of holiness. The pursuit of spiritual maturity and a deeper, closer encounter with Him may be futile without walking in holiness in the fear of the Lord.

In all of this, provision is already made for the believer to enable him to walk in holiness and sanctification (Ephesians 1:4). As articulated by the apostle Paul, God has dynamically fashioned out a way through Christ Jesus.

"But of him are ye in Christ Jesus, who of God is made unto us wisdom, and righteousness, and sanctification, and redemption." 1 Corinthians 1:30

God, through Jesus, has imparted to the New Creation, wisdom (through His word) and righteousness. Thus, the New Creation has received the nature and character of God. He has been sanctified and made holy, and He has right standing with God and has audience before Him. He is redeemed, bought back from sin and the dominion of darkness through the work of God in Christ Jesus.

Jesus is the atonement. He is the lamb of God that takes away the sin of the world. He is the pure light of God's word which consecrates and leads the people of God. He is our redemptive-Jubilee.

- **FREEDOM FOR BONDSERVANTS**

At Jubilee, freedom was to be granted to bondservants, the poor who had signed up to work for others/masters in order to repay their debts.

It is important to distinguish between bondservants and slaves. These bondservants were not slaves in the sense of slavery as recorded in history. Historically, as is well documented, some slaves were bought or kidnapped from Africa and other continents against their will, put in chains and stocks, and transported by ships bound for America or the New World. Most of these slaves had no rights, and were treated inhumanely and with utmost cruelty. The atrocities of the slave masters, and their abuse of the slaves' human rights, over time, came under strong criticism and opposition. Men like Granville Sharp and

William Wilberforce revolted against the Slave Trade and called for its abolition.

This dark part of history parallels the slavery and bondage the Israelites suffered in Egypt for over 400 years. They became slaves in Egypt, were accorded no rights, and suffered great oppression and persecution under the heavy-handed taskmasters of Pharaohs for hundreds of years. God raised Moses, His servant, to bring deliverance-Jubilee to His people with a mighty hand and great signs and wonders.

There are some who assert that the Bible endorses slavery which subjugates or binds men against their will. This is false. God does not sanction the abuse of human rights or slavery that brings oppression in any form.

In fact, the events amplified in the world historical records are not reflective of the contract between bondservants or slaves and their masters in the history of Israel. In Israel, they were indentured servants who had rights and privileges, and exploitation under indentured servitude was forbidden.

Such servants were protected from being subjects of abuse, affliction and suffering. Exodus 21:1-11, for instance, lays out the rights and privileges of indentured servitude. Several other passages dictate how they should be treated. Bondservants or indentured slaves were:

- Full members of the community. (Genesis 17:12)
- To receive holidays. (Exodus 23:12, Deuteronomy 5:14-15; 12:12)

- To receive humane treatment. (Exodus 21:1-11; 26-27)
- To serve for six years and set free in the seventh. (Exodus 21:2)
- Eligible for immediate release when they suffered cruelty. (Exodus 21:26-27)

During the year of Jubilee, the bondservants were released and returned to their families, and their debts were cancelled. They would go back to their families, debt-free.

Surely, then, Jubilee is good news to the poor. Through it, God breaks the back of bondage and debt, and releases His people. He does not intend for any of His people to be in bonds forever. No matter what precipitated their servanthood, be it need, poverty, deception or any form of enticement, at Jubilee, they were set free. All of God's people who dare to tap into the Jubilee's favor are sure to experience the miracle of freedom from bondage, lack, want, poverty and insufficiency.

- **DEBT CANCELLATION**

Poverty is the main reason why some people became bondservants in Israel. They suffered lack and insufficiency. As they became impoverished, they lost money and property. Some fell on bad times as a result of bad choices, wrong investments, natural disasters, or through the attacks of the enemy.

The merciful God laid out His plan to release all who were poor and in bonds during the Sabbatical year, in the seven-year cycle.

"And if thy brother, an Hebrew man, or an Hebrew woman, be sold unto thee, and serve thee six years; then in the seventh year thou shalt let him go free from thee. And when thou sendest him out free from thee, thou shalt not let him go empty: Thou shalt furnish him liberally out of thy flock, and out of thy floor, and out of thine winepress: of that wherewith the Lord thy God hath blessed thee thou shalt give unto him. And thou shalt remember that thou wast a bondman in the land of Egypt, and the Lord thy God redeemed thee: therefore I command thee this thing today." Deuteronomy 15:12-15

The Sabbatical year was the blessed period where debts were cancelled, and people were relieved of their servitude. The Hebrew man who was serving as a bondservant was freed after serving for six years. All of his debt was cancelled. In the seventh year, also, he was sent away by his master, not only as a free person, but as one who was inundated with great provision from his master. The master was to generously furnish him with supplies out of his flocks, out of his grounds, and out of his winepresses. This activity was the command of Jehovah to Israel, reminding them of how He redeemed them from the bondage of Egypt.

It was a Jubilee year when God delivered His people from the oppression of Egypt. They came out with great wealth and substance, with silver and gold. The Egyptians did not only let God's people go, but sent them forth with supplies and great provision. As the Bible records:

"He brought them forth also with silver and gold: and there was not one feeble person among their tribes." Psalm 105:37

God painted this picture of the great deliverance of Israel from Egypt and what that practically means for posterity. Just as He favored the people of Israel, such that they were sent away with bounty, He expected them to do the same, sending out their servants into freedom with material blessings.

This was designed by God to seamlessly and, in a magnified way, feed into, or transition into, the Jubilee. The year of Jubilee is itself a Sabbatical year as well, a super year of great freedom from bonds and debt cancellation. God has programmed the Jubilee year as His reservoir inherently packed with His supernatural provision, and has ordained it to be the supernatural channel for the breakout of spiritual, financial, and economic liberty. He commands profuse provision to minister to every need.

Walking in financial dominion and freedom has always been God's intent for His people. It is His way and His will for His people to experience abundant life, a life of joy, of surplus and excess, and freedom from any form of need (John 10:10).

- **SET FREE FROM PRISON**

In the Old Testament, people were only put in the prison when they were in debt and could not pay. At Jubilee, when debts were cancelled, they were set free from prison. Jubilee sets the prisoners of financial bondage free. May these blessings flow toward you now. Praise God!

- **POSSESSIONS RESTORED**

When Joshua, the successor of Moses, brought the people of Israel into Canaan, the land of promise, he divided the land among the tribes of Israel. Every tribe and family was allotted a portion of the land. It was their possession and inheritance forever, and was highly treasured and esteemed.

Thus, when King Ahab pressured Naboth to relinquish to him his vineyard, his ancestral inheritance, Naboth firmly declined:

"And it came to pass after these things, that Naboth the Jezreelite had a vineyard, which was in Jezreel, hard by the palace of Ahab king of Samaria. And Ahab spake unto Naboth, saying, Give me thy vineyard, that I may have it for a garden of herbs, because it is near unto my house: and I will give thee for it a better vineyard than it; or, if it seem good to thee, I will give thee the worth of it in money. And Naboth said to Ahab, The LORD forbid it me, that I should give the inheritance of my fathers unto thee. And Ahab came into his house heavy and displeased because of the word which Naboth the Jezreelite had spoken to him: for he had said, I will not give thee the inheritance of my fathers. And he laid him down upon his bed, and turned away his face, and would eat no bread." 1 Kings 21:1-4

For standing his ground, Naboth lost his life at the hands of Jezebel, the unscrupulous wife of Ahab. But Naboth's unflinching and uncompromising position reflected his understanding of the value attached to his inheritance, namely that it was so precious, cherished and priceless, and could not be traded for temporal desires.

In the process of time, however, some families in Israel fell on hard times and either sold their lands, or had them taken, confiscated, or inveigled from them. Jehovah commanded that, in the year of Jubilee, lost lands and possessions were to be returned to their original owners. That communicated His ordination that no family amongst His people was supposed to be without an inheritance perpetually. Jubilee was a time of restoration of all that His people had lost.

His ultimate intent was to have every family blessed with an inheritance. A people deprived, a people that were poor, a people subject to lack and want, or stricken with poverty, was never part of God's agenda for humanity. He is all about restoring, to His people, all they have lost when they step up in faith and trust Him. He declares:

"And I will restore to you the years that the locust hath eaten, the canker worm, and the caterpillar, and the palmerworm, my great army which I sent among you. And ye shall eat in plenty, and be satisfied, and praise the name of the Lord your God, that hath dealt wondrously with you: and my people shall never be ashamed. And ye shall know that I am in the midst of Israel, and that I am the Lord your God, and none else: and my people shall never be ashamed." Joel 2:25-27

"The thief cometh not, but for to steal, and to kill, and to destroy: I am come that they might have life, and that they might have it more abundantly." John 10:10

Our God is both a restorer and a rewarder of those who diligently seek Him. He restores lost years, lost money, lost health, lost relationships. He is always present to supply every need, to rain down His blessings, and to bring His people to the place of satisfaction, serenity, and abundance.

All said and done, Jesus Messiah is that inheritance that His people waited for, that thing of priceless value which was returned to them in the year of Jubilee. David understood this full well, saying:

"The LORD is the portion of mine inheritance and of my cup: thou maintainest my lot. The lines are fallen unto me in pleasant places; yea, I have a goodly heritage." Psalm 16:5-6

"Whom have I in heaven but thee? and there is none upon earth that I desire beside thee. My flesh and my heart faileth: but God is the strength of my heart, and my portion for ever." Psalm 73:25-26

Through Jesus' death and resurrection, God has brought us into an inheritance that can never perish, spoil or fade, kept in heaven for us. Amen.

- ## REST FOR THE LAND AND REST FOR THE PEOPLE

The people of Israel were to rest from their labors during the Jubilee. God granted them time off from working the land. They were not to till, sow, or reap the land. The land was also to rest, to lie fallow during the period. Essentially, it was a kind of vacation, an extended leisure time. It was also a sacred time, a time of fellowship with God, when they could enjoy His mercies and grace. In addition, they would enjoy one another, and none was to maltreat their neighbor or defraud them in any way.

The million-dollar question is - how were they supposed to be fed if they were not to sow or reap? The answer to that question is simply mind-blowing. Jehovah commanded a supernatural blessing of provision that was to last for three whole years after the Jubilee year! He said to them:

"And if ye shall say, What shall we eat the seventh year? behold, we shall not sow nor gather in our increase: Then I will command my blessing upon you in the sixth year, and it shall bring forth fruit for three years. And ye shall sow the eight year and eat yet of old fruit until the ninth year; until her fruits come in ye shall eat of the old store." Leviticus 25:20-22

God promised to command a blessing during the Jubilee season for three years. His people, who were precluded from working, simply had to live in expectation that their barns would be full for that entire period, and they would eat in plenty and dwell in safety. Obviously, then, the blessing Jehovah commands in the sixth year breaks forth in such bounty, and brings forth such a supernatural increase in the harvest, enough to supply the needs of the people for the next three years.

In this promise, God reveals Himself as the faithful One with the ability to do the impossible. He is the miracle-working God, the God of wonders, and He relates to His people through the avenue of faith that brings about the miraculous. This, fundamentally, translates into a call to His people to come closer and to implicitly trust Him during the time of rest.

The Jubilee and all its blessings are quickened and accessed by faith. Thus, the people must have faith in God. Faith releases His presence and His power, and produces unstoppable miracles. Believing what God has said and acting on it produces faith, and all things are possible to them that believe.

"But without faith it is impossible to please him: for he that cometh to God must believe that he is, and that he is a rewarder of them that diligently seek him." Hebrews 11:6

Faith is the crux of a deeper relationship with God. Our relationship with Him is initiated by faith at salvation. It is by grace that we are saved through faith; thus, our salvation is propelled by faith. We have peace with God by faith. We stand by faith. We live by faith. We also walk by faith, not by sight, and our faith will be consummated at the second coming of the Lord Jesus. In that realm of faith, then, God's covenant with His people is kept alive, and He is set loose to work His wonders in their lives.

All who would enjoy the Jubilee, access its wonders, and maintain its miraculous facilities, must believe that He that promised is faithful, and He would do it. He is not a man so as to be susceptible to lies; neither is He the son of man that He should change His mind regarding what He has promised. He has the ability, capability and the integrity of character to keep His word and make His word good.

Jesus has come as our Jubilee, not just for every $50^{th}$ year, but always as our Savior, redeemer, provider and deliverer. The beauty of this is that the amenities of this Jubilee, in Christ, reach beyond three years, and by faith, we are able to tap into them at any time. Jesus is our permanent Jubilee. We can enjoy perpetually, the commandment of supernatural blessings and resources of Jehovah that are riveted into, and ingrained in, the Jubilee.

The Lord God also promised rest for His people. In the year of Jubilee, they were to rest from their labors, struggles, financial concerns, anxieties, burdens about their lost properties, and bonded servitude. They were to come into the rest of God, that place of deep communion, fellowship and intimacy with Him, expecting His power to move on their behalf.

The Sabbath rest, the Sabbath of Sabbaths rest, the Sabbatical rest, and the Jubilee rest were deliberately configured by God as blueprints to show man the way of freedom and liberty. They were signposts along the avenue of life to celebrate the true joy of life through an awesome God who takes care of every minute detail of the lives of His people.

Coming into the rest of God is a command, and not an option. It is the design and plan from the loving heart of the Father God. He wanted His people to be free from burdens of the spirit, soul and body, free from any situation that would steal their joy, or that would war or battle against their inheritance in Him. He ordained that man would triumph over adversity and not be crushed with burdens, and that he would live in the peace of God and peaceably with his neighbor.

The depth of God's rest is inexhaustible. He does not only give an outward rest; He also brings a cessation from inner wrestles and wars within the soul of man. Jesus specializes in ministering salvation and deliverance to the whole man, spirit, soul, and body. That is His ministry. It is the reason He left heaven to come down to earth to announce the Jubilee, and to demonstrate its effects and power to all nations.

This is the revelation – that inner rest and peace is a person. His name is Jesus. To us who believe, He is the Prince of Peace, our Sabbath, our Jubilee, and our Rest.

"Let us therefore fear, lest a promise being left us of entering into his rest, any of you should seem to come short of it. For unto us was the gospel preached, as well as unto them: but the word preached did not profit them, not being mixed with faith in them that heard it. For we which have believed do enter into rest, as he said, As I have sworn in my wrath, if they shall enter into my rest: although the works were finished from the foundation of the world." Hebrews 4:1-3

We see here that the rest is promised; it is assured; it is a done deal. But it must be believed and mixed with faith in order to achieve or attain the desired peace and joy that come with it. The good news of the gospel was preached to many, but it was not beneficial to some because they did not accept, acknowledge or settle, in their hearts, the reality of the promise.

It is an unfortunate reality that so many fail to enter that divinely constructed rest promised by the loving God. They refuse to accept that there are issues of life which cannot be solved by human wisdom, might or power; rather, they seek solutions either through themselves and their resourcefulness, or from others. They look for answers in false gods or lying spiritual mediums, and fail to relinquish their problems into the able hands of Jehovah. However, rest cannot be found in material things, religions, situations or people.

The ways and works of God are locked in the realm of faith. We cannot find Him, see Him, or experience His power and glory, without faith. Thus, the promise of God must fill our hearts and be settled and entrenched in us. It must be sown on the good ground of our hearts to produce appreciable results. Our inner being must be the home and residence for the word of the living God.

"Let the word of Christ dwell in you richly in all wisdom." Colossians 3:16

"If you abide in me and my word abides (takes residence) in you, you shall ask what ye will and it shall be done." John 15:7

It is true that "life happens", and that there are so many struggles that man, even at his best, may not be able to handle or navigate through, not by his intelligence, abilities, or even endurance. At national and global levels, emergent crises such as pandemics and natural disasters highlight the limitations of governmental policy, political will, and capability.

But the solution is so simple. Humanity must place every need in the hands of God who is able to do exceeding abundantly above all any believer could ever ask or think, according to the sheer magnitude of His power that is at work in His saints. (Ephesians 3:20-21). The whole world must respond to the invitation of Jesus Messiah:

"Come unto me, all ye that labour and are heavy laden, and I will give you rest. Take my yoke upon you, and learn of me; for I am meek and lowly in heart: and ye shall find rest for your souls. For my yoke is easy, and my burden is light." Matthew 11:28-30

God's people have a glorious niche carved out for them. It is that place in Him where one ceases from his works and from his own efforts to please God, and is free from the sorrows and afflictions of this world. Access to that place is guaranteed when one steps out of unbelief and throws himself in the sovereign hands of the mighty Jehovah God.

"There remaineth therefore a rest to the people of God. For he that is entered into his rest, he also hath ceased from his own works, as God did from his. Let us labour therefore to enter that rest, lest any man fall after the same example of unbelief. For the word of God is quick, and powerful, and sharper than any two-edged sword, piercing even to the dividing asunder of soul and spirit, and of the joints and marrow, and is a discerner of the thoughts and intents of the heart." Hebrews 4:9-12

So why should you entertain the fear, doubt, helplessness and hopelessness the enemy has created for you? Why are you in the shackles of despair? Why must the spirit of falsehood, cults, occults, clairvoyance, psychic phenomenon, witchcraft and idol worship have you bound?

No matter what your situation is or what your personal circumstances are, it is God's promise to give you rest. That is His arena, His area of expertise, His safe zone, and it is a home for you where you can come and be renewed, refreshed, and empowered to celebrate God and the blissful life He has ordained for you.

The rest of God is not a place of sorrow or a place to pine, whine, murmur, complain, or lick wounds from life's battles. It is a place of renewed hope, strength, faith, praise, worship, leaping, dancing, and shouting with joy because God has given you the victory.

The rest of God is also not a place of chance, of uncertainty and lack of direction, not knowing what the future holds. It is the place where God unfurls His omniscience and majestic power to give His people wisdom, a fresh start, a clear plan, and the skills, strategies, giftings and anointings for His next move of great power, to put them in charge of His purposes for them and all that is theirs. Do not be crushed or bound by the issues of life that you cannot control. Take Jesus at His word. Cast your burdens and every load of care upon Him, and take on His yoke which is easy and light. He is the burden-bearer, our substitute for sin. Embrace and assimilate His ways. Thus will you find rest for your soul, for He will give you rest.

As your eyes connect with this message and you receive it into your heart, may Jesus, the Sabbath rest, make Himself known to you. It is Jubilee! Rise up and celebrate freedom. Lift up praise to God and watch every chain and fetter in your life break, for there is a mighty spiritual earthquake breaking the stocks and opening the prison doors.

Rest is yours now! Victory is yours now!

# Chapter 4

## JESUS OUR JUBILEE – HE IS THE LORD OF THE SABBATH

It is important to understand that all the Sabbath observances were a shadow of things to come, and were designed to be, or articulated as, a sign to reveal Jesus, the promised Messiah.

The Jubilee itself is a Sabbath; in fact, it is multiple Sabbaths rolled into one cohesive package, and Jesus is the Jubilee in person. He came to announce that He is the Jubilee, to demonstrate the power, glories and victories of the Jubilee, and to declare the Jubilee or proclaim the acceptable year of the Lord.

Jesus heralded Himself as the Lord of the Sabbath, and the Sabbath itself (Matthew 12:8). No one else ever dared to make such a bold pronouncement! He is indeed the Sabbath rest, and all who truly come to Him find rest for their souls (Matthew 11:28-30, Hebrews 4:10, Psalm 23).

The Biblical portrait of Jesus actually shows and justifies why He is the Sabbath, the Jubilee. The Holy Word of God unfolds His pre-existence, His creative power, the fact that He is the center of all existence, and that He took on flesh to consummate the purposes of the eternal God, and worked inexplicable miracles, signs and wonders. These show that He is the only one indisputably and eminently qualified to be the Sabbath/Jubilee.

He is that Sabbath, not as one who competed or qualified for it, but one who was chosen to be the Jubilee in person, to announce it and to reveal it to the world. This was engineered and manufactured in God the Father's foreknowledge and predestined purposes and plans.

## 1. THE PRE-EXISTENCE OF JESUS AS GOD

That Jesus is the Sabbath is displayed most forcefully and spectacularly in His pre-existence as God. Jesus is God. It is as simple as that. He is an integral part of the Godhead of Father, the Word (Jesus), and the Holy Spirit. Just like the two other personalities in the Godhead, Father and Holy Spirit, He shows up in the very first line of the Holy Bible.

"In the beginning God created the heaven and the earth." Genesis 1:1

The Hebrew word for "God", as used in Genesis 1:1, is "Elohim", a plural rendition of the word. Elohim is a reference to the Godhead or the Trinity - the Father, the Word and the Holy Spirit. Thus, the literal translation of the word "God" as used in the passage above would have been "Gods" in the English manuscripts. Making plain the dynamic interconnection between Jesus and the Godhead, the apostle John very crisply explains:

"In the beginning was the Word, and the Word was with God, and the Word was God. The same was in the beginning with God"

"And the Word was made flesh, and dwelt among us, (and we beheld his glory, the glory as of the only begotten of the Father,) full of grace and truth." John 1:1-2, 14

These passages affirm that Jesus pre-existed or existed before the beginning of time in the form of God, that He was in the class of Elohim, the Godhead, and was in the realm of God. He existed before there was anything called history.

Jesus is eternal, with no beginning and no end. He is Alpha and Omega. He was before all things, and it pleased the Father that the fullness of the Godhead should dwell bodily in Him. Being eternal, and being God, only He can make sense of the kaleidoscope of our lives, of our entry into, and exit out of, this world, against the backdrop of eternity.

## 2. JESUS, THE CREATOR

The second argument is that Jesus is the creator of all things (2 Corinthians 4:4, Genesis 1:26). Without Him was nothing made that is made. He created us in His image and likeness, and knows our frame. He is the reason we even exist, and in Him, all things hold together.

In the book of Genesis, the dramatic, majestic unveiling of the creative power of the Triune God takes place, and we see Jesus right in the center of creation. Speaking about the Lord of all creation, the Word, the apostle John states:

"All things were made by him; and without him was not anything made that was made." John 1:3

Jesus, the eternal Word, collaborated with the Father and the Holy Spirit to bring forth or into being, all things created or made.

That there would be no existence without Jesus is beyond contention. He is the God of creation. He is the living, creative Word that sustains all things, and without Him, all of existence and creation would be in disarray and would fall apart. The apostle Paul observes about Jesus:

"Who is the image of the image of the invisible God, the firstborn of every creature: For by him were all things created, that are in heaven, and that are in earth, visible and invisible, whether they be thrones, or dominions, or principalities, or powers: all things were created by him, and for him: And he is before all things, and by him all things consist." Colossians 1:15-17

Because He made all things, all must respond to His glory, excellence and sovereignty with their full attention, focus and consecrated hearts of worship and adoration, and acknowledge Him as the Sabbath.

The believer lives and moves and has his being in Jesus (John 15:5, Acts 17:28). Surely, if He created us, then He alone knows and can provide for us, what we need for our existence. And with such a resume depicting Him as the image of the invisible God who created for Himself all things, visible or invisible, there is no one other than Himself who would know the way to freedom, Jubilee, eternal life and reconciliation to the Father God.

Following that theme, the Bible records that the creator perfected all His works on the sixth day, and rested on the seventh.

The Sabbath is thus all about Jesus completing creation, resting, and inviting His people to come along in fellowship with Him to celebrate the Sabbath by ceasing from their labors to acknowledge and enjoy the greatness, wonder, craftsmanship and majesty of the creator.

## 3. JESUS, THE PROMISED MESSIAH AND SAVIOR

Thirdly, Jesus is the Lord of the Sabbath because He is the One who was sent by the Father to bring the permanent solution of salvation to humanity. He is the promised Messiah declared by the prophets over the ages. "Messiah", in the Hebrew, means savior, liberator or deliverer.

When God created the world, He created Adam and Eve in His image and likeness, and gave them dominion over the whole earth. He placed them in the Garden of Eden to enjoy everything therein, with only one exception – they were precluded from eating the fruit of the tree in midst of the garden.

Through the deception and enticement of the devil, however, they did eat the forbidden fruit, and the seed of sin - the disobedience to God's word or commandment - was sown in the heart and spirit of man. Through Adam's disobedience, he wittingly or unwittingly submitted his spirit, soul, body and will to Satan, and transferred the authority and dominion God gave him to Satan.

Sin originated from the devil. The devil, according to the Bible, sins from the beginning (1 John 3:8). Because of his rebellion at the beginning in heaven, God cast him down and prepared for him the lake of fire and eternal damnation. Because he is so evil and retaliatory, the devil works tirelessly to get everyone else to participate in this horrendous verdict and judgement (Revelation 20:11-15; 21:8).

The genesis of the whole problem of man was the entrance of sin. Sin meant spiritual death in the heart of man, a disconnection, separation and alienation from God, and judgement and eternal damnation for mankind (Genesis 3).

Adam's sin had dire, life-altering consequences for all of humanity. It was transmitted to the entire human race, and sin became a universal problem. As the apostle Paul explains, sin entered the world and death by sin through the sin of one man, and through that, death passed unto all men. Thus, all have sinned and fallen short of the glory of God (Romans 3:23, 5:12). On the flip side, owing to sin, man came into close proximity, fellowship and communion with Satan, was thrown into darkness, and was now at the mercy of Satan's wickedness, destruction and manipulation.

As bad as things were, however, we must always hold in our spirits the immutable fact that God is eternal. He has no beginning and no end, and He knows the end from the beginning. He is not held or locked up in time, and His knowledge is not partial or limited by time. Every event, plan and purpose is laid bare before Him at a go, before time, within time, and after time. He is the all-knowing, omniscient God who does not miss anything.

Hence, He knew, before the beginning of time, before He made anything, and before He created man, that man would sin; that he would be deceived, ensnared, and trapped by the devil, and that he would need the Messiah.

And this is where we see the real nature of God in full bloom. He is love. Love is His innate nature. The love of God is the "agape" kind of love. It fills every step He takes, and animates every one of His initiatives or lines of action. Creation was born out of His love and filled with His love. All men were formed and brought into being out of His everlasting and unchanging love.

He therefore could not countenance humanity, His precious creation and prized possession, being trapped forever in the chains of sin, eternal damnation, depravity, death, hell and the grave. That was simply out of the question.

Accordingly, before the foundation of the world, He devised the eternal plan, out of the depths and riches of His love and mercy, whereby He predestined Jesus Messiah to be the Savior of the world, and to bring true rest to as many as would believe on Him. Jesus was to be the expected King and deliverer, for the Jews first, and then for the Gentiles (Romans 1:16-17).

"According as he hath chosen us in him before the foundation of the world, that we should be holy and without blame before him in love." Ephesians 1:4

In the fullness of time, that plan of God was perfected in the incarnation of Jesus. He took the form of human flesh and was made in the likeness of men (Philippians 2:5-7), made of the seed of the woman (Galatians 4:4). He broke out into this natural world by being planted into the womb of the Virgin Mary, who went through the natural process of childbirth to bring Him forth in Bethlehem of Judea.

"And she shall bring forth a son, and thou shalt call his name JESUS: for he shall save his people from their sins." Matthew 1:21

"For unto you is born this day in the city of David a Savior, which is Christ the Lord." Luke 2:11

"And the Word was made flesh and dwelt among us, (and we beheld his glory, the glory as the only begotten of the father), full of grace and truth." John 1:14

Most people view the historical Jesus as the One who was born on Christmas day, and One who just popped up in the New Testament recitals. However, Jesus is much greater than anyone known in history, and at every step of His journey, God's indelible stamp of approval was upon Him.

"And Jesus, when he was baptized, went up straightway out of the water: and, lo, the heavens were opened unto him, and he saw the Spirit of God descending like a dove, and lighting upon him: And lo a voice from heaven, saying, This is my beloved Son, in whom I am well pleased." Matthew 3:16-17

The Father God had therefore worked out His eternal purpose before time even became a concept, and chose Jesus to be the Savior and redeemer to all who would believe in Him. (John 3:16). He sent Him out as the anointed and appointed one, anointed by the Holy Spirit to perform this mandate.

"And we have seen and do testify that the Father sent the Son to be the Saviour of the world. Whosoever shall confess that Jesus is the Son of God, God dwelleth in him, and he in God." 1 John 4:14-15

"This is a faithful saying, and worthy of all acceptation, that Christ Jesus came into this world to save sinners; of whom I am chief." 1 Timothy 1:15

"Neither is there salvation in any other: for there is none other name under heaven given among men, whereby we must be saved." Acts 4:12

Jesus died on the cross in our place. By His sacrifice on the cross, He conquered sin, erased eternal damnation, consumed the sting of death, hell and the grave, and rose triumphantly, disarming every principality and power and making a public show of them (Colossians 2:15). He fully paid the price for our sin.

"For the wages of sin is death; but the gift of God is eternal life through Jesus Christ our Lord." Romans 6:23

Any person who chooses to believe in the sacrifice of Jesus and the price He paid for our salvation, and who confesses that He died, and that God raised Him from the dead, shall be saved from sin and eternal condemnation.

"But what saith it? The word is nigh thee, even in thy mouth, and in thy heart: that is, the word of faith, which we preach; That if thou shalt confess with thy mouth the Lord Jesus, and shalt believe in thine heart that God hath raised him from the dead, thou shalt be saved. For with the heart man believeth unto righteousness; and with the mouth confession is made unto salvation." Romans 10:8-10

When the heart of man believes, it is qualitatively connected to the sacrificial work of Jesus on the cross, His death and His resurrection, and then the gospel then becomes the transforming power of God to break the power of sin, death, hell and the grave. A new heart and a new spirit is imparted to the believing one. He becomes a New Creation, totally free from sin (2 Corinthians 5:17; Ezekiel 36:25-27).

The Apostle Paul declared that he is not ashamed of the gospel of Christ, for it is the power of God that brings salvation to everyone that believes, to the Jew first and also to the Greek (Romans 1:16).

The gospel only becomes the very power of God when it is believed with the heart. Faith in the heart of the believing one invokes the power of the sacrificial act of Jesus on the cross to put sin away from the heart and snap the hold of eternal death, condemnation into hell and the lake of fire. As Jesus Himself stated, whoever hears His word and believes the One who sent Him shall not come into condemnation but is passed from death unto life (John 5:24).

Through Jesus, therefore, God ignited and set ablaze the greatest action plan, His redemptive process for humanity by dealing, once and for all, with the sin problem of mankind. That plan was to bring salvation from sin through our Lord Jesus Christ, the Messiah, and thus set in motion blessing, freedom and Jubilee.

Retracing history, though, it is absolutely fascinating that, before Jesus' physical entry into the world two thousand years ago, God, delineating His sovereign and eternal purposes, gave us glimpses of Him in types, shadows and exemplars throughout the Old Testament narratives. He used Israel, His covenant people, as His redemptive prototype for salvation to the whole of humanity.

Jesus revealed Himself to several people in "theophanic" encounters in the Old Testament records way before His arrival in flesh and blood in Bethlehem of Judea. "Theophany" means the manifestation or revelation of God in tangible ways to humanity, and Bible scholars agree that some of the angelic and supernatural appearances to personalities in the Old Testament were actually appearances of Jesus; they were the revelation of Jesus to man. A few Biblical records of theophany encounters include the following:

- God revealed Himself to Abraham. (Genesis 12:7-9; 14:18-20; 17:1; 18:1)
- God revealed Himself to Isaac. (Genesis 26:2)
- God revealed Himself to Jacob. (Genesis 32:24-30, 35:9)
- God revealed Himself to Moses. (Exodus 3:1-6; 33:11; 34:5-7)
- God revealed Himself to Joshua. (Joshua 5:14)
- God revealed Himself to Gideon. (Judges 6)
- God revealed Himself to Meshach, Shadrach and Abednego. (Daniel 3:19-25)

These Biblical references show how God tangibly encountered people and spoke to them. The Biblical records seem to present a paradoxical view of some of these visits. Sometimes, the divine beings were described as angels appearing to men, and yet, at the same time, God's name was invoked in these interactions, and the people bowed to the divine beings and worshipped.

The bottom line is that true angels do not accept worship (Revelation 19:10; 22:8-90). However, in those encounters, the supernatural beings did not refuse the worship of men. Therefore, if these angelic beings or representatives of God accepted worship, then they should be God Himself making Himself known.

Building on that theme, these theophany encounters had to be Jesus, and that extrapolation emerges deductively from the fact that no one can see God and live (Exodus 33:20). Jesus reiterated this, declaring that He is the only way to the Father, and that it is He alone, the only begotten Son, who is in the bosom of the Father, who has seen the Father and who has declared Him.

"No man has ever seen God, but the one and only Son, who is himself God and is in closest relationship with the Father, has made him known." John 1:18 NIV

If so, then it should be clear that the "Voice of the Lord" that came walking in the Garden of Eden, and the God that Abraham, Jacob, Moses and the rest saw in their theophany experiences, could only have been Jesus, who is the Word, the Son, and who was ordained by God the Father to be at the center of the redemptive process for Israel and the whole world.

This buttresses the pre-existence of Jesus as God, and shows Him making Himself known to the key players of the Old Testament. He existed before them and before time began. He has not changed. He is the same yesterday, today and forever (Hebrews 13:8). He showed Himself alive by many infallible proofs in Biblical times, and still reveals Himself in contemporary times (Acts 1:1-3, John 14:21).

A note of caution is necessary here. The devil is always at work, and his desire is, and always has been, to be like God and to be worshipped because he covets that position which belongs only to God. When he tempted Jesus in the wilderness, he was craving that worship, and promised to handsomely reward Him if He would fall down and worship him. Of course he was unsuccessful with that bait, but he inspires and authorizes false deities, false gods, false angels and demons to fake experiences of theophany, appearing to people and requiring their worship.

The Church must be very careful not to fall for anything that appears to be God or from God. The spirit of discernment is a necessary tool for the people of God to properly distinguish between the true and the false in any spiritual engagement or rendezvous.

Sadly, there have been instances throughout history down to contemporary times where false angels and demons who looked like they were from God engaged true men and women of God in spiritual encounters and gave them false direction or revelation. Some of these experiences led to the propagation of false doctrines, divisions in the Church, the formation of dangerous cults, and even mass suicides and murders.

This should be the takeaway for the people of God – when you think you have some kind of spiritual revelation from any kind of god or deity, the wise thing to do is to refrain from formulating doctrines or commandments, or starting groups or sects. Rather, test every spirit to see if it is from God (1 John 4:1-3).

You must also check to determine if those encounters line up with the principles of the Word of God given to us in the true translations of the Holy Bible. Also seek counsel from other mature, credible and knowledgeable Christian leaders to either affirm or judge your experience. The Bible urges, let the prophets speak by twos or threes, and let the other judge (1 Corinthians 14:29).

In sum, Jesus, as the Messiah, made His abode with humanity, revealing His glory, His personality, and His authority as the only begotten of the Father, to bring God's freedom to humanity. He is Immanuel, God (Jubilee) with us always. He was obedient and fulfilled His ministry, even to death on the cross; therefore, God also highly exalted Him and gave Him a name that is above every name, at the mention of which every knee shall bow in heaven, earth and under the earth (Philippians 2). Paul reveals:

"In whom we have redemption through his blood, even the forgiveness of sins…"

"For it pleased the Father that in him should all fullness dwell; And, having made peace through the blood of his cross, by him to reconcile all things unto himself; by him, I say, whether they be things in earth, or things in heaven. And you, that were sometime alienated and enemies in your mind by wicked works, yet now hath he reconciled. In the body of his flesh through death, to present you holy and unblameable and unreproveable in his sight." Colossians 1:14, 19-22

Jesus came from heaven, so He is the only One who can lead us back there. He declared that He is the way, the truth, and the life, and that no one comes to the Father except by Him (John 14:6).

He is also the only One with the record of victory over sin, death, hell and the grave. He is the only One who conquered Satan and all his cohorts. He is the One who has given the victory of His conquests to His people, and has endowed them with power to tread over snakes and scorpions and to overcome all the power of the enemy. He alone could therefore be the Messiah.

Foreordained and predestined before the foundation of the world to be the Savior, He was, is and will forever be, the expected Messiah, King and deliverer who brings the Sabbath rest, for the Jews first, and then for the Gentiles, for as many as would believe in Him (Romans 1:16-17).

## 4. JESUS' MIRACULOUS LIFE

A fourth indicator that Jesus is the Sabbath is His incredible supernatural ministry and incomparable miraculous life that brings rest into every situation.

God is a miracle-working God. A miracle is His supernatural intervention in the ordinary and natural course of nature. He does not move from a natural standpoint, or from the realm of reasoning or logic. He works from the realm of the spirit, in the realm of the unseen, and brings about the manifest, tangible, touchable experience of His operations in the visible realm of man.

Jesus is that miraculous God in person and in reality, and He moves in miraculous ways to perform His wonders. Centuries before His birth, Isaiah prophesied that His name would be called "Wonderful" (Isaiah 9:6). And, indeed, nothing about the revelation, life and ministry of Jesus was ordinary. Everything was extraordinary, miraculous, supernatural, a wonder. He was, is, and will forever be, a wonder and full of wonders.

It is a miracle that, although He emerged in time, He pre-existed before time. He is God the Word, the second person in the Trinity. He is the One who initiated time, who would be the end of time, and who will live forever beyond time with all who believe in Him. It is He who crafted the Sabbath as an expression of time, namely, as a day, a week, a year, and a Jubilee, but who, in fulfilling the Sabbath, is timeless. He is Alpha and Omega, the First and the Last, the One who was, and is, and is to come, the Almighty God (Revelation 1:8).

He is also the living creative Word. He called existence into being, calling forth that which did not exist. Through Him, the wonder of creation came to be, the universe, the heavens and the earth, the great mountains and vales, the oceans, rivers, planets, comets, stars, and the discovered and undiscovered bodies and creatures. They were all created by the mighty word of His power.

The birth of Jesus was a miracle. He was transported from heaven by the Holy Spirit into the womb of a virgin and was born as a man, defying the laws of nature and procreation. God made Him the seed of the woman at the fullness of time (Galatians 4:4).

It is important to recognize that, in the first advent of Jesus Messiah, He was fashioned as a man and functioned as a man in order to reveal and to demonstrate the amazing dominion, authority and power that the Godhead deposited in the first Adam (Genesis 1:26-28).

Jesus, according to the Bible, is the last Adam (1 Corinthians 15:45). Thus, His humanity did not exceed that of the first Adam. If His humanity had been greater than Adam's, He would not have been the perfect substitute to pay the price for our redemption.

In the likeness of Adam on the outside, He operated in dominion, authority and miraculous power. However, on the inside, He was the container of divinity, the carrier of the sum total of the powers of the Godhead in living reality, endued, empowered and anointed by the Holy Spirit (Colossians 1:19; 2:9-10. Luke 4:18-21). In His second appearance, He will come as the King of all kings, and the Lord of Lords, the Alpha and Omega, the righteous judge.

In His humanity, and with the authority and dominion of deity, divinity and the power of the Godhead residing in Him, Jesus superseded and overrode the laws of nature, and performed inexplicable miracles.

His first recorded miracle was at the wedding in Cana of Galilee where the supplies of wine ran out. He altered the chemical composition of water and turned it into wine, and brought great joy to all the wedding guests (John 2:1-11). Many more miracles followed. Jesus healed all kinds of sicknesses and diseases, and cast out devils that tormented people.

"And Jesus went about all Galilee, teaching in their synagogues, and preaching the gospel of the kingdom, and healing all manner of sickness and all manner of disease among the people. And his fame went throughout all Syria: and they brought unto him all sick people that were taken with divers diseases and torments, and those which were possessed with devils, and those which were lunatick, and those that had the palsy; and he healed them. And there followed him great multitudes of people from Galilee, and from Decapolis, and from Jerusalem, and from Judaea, and from beyond Jordan." Matthew 4:23-25

On one occasion, Peter had lent his boat to Jesus who sat on it on Lake Genesaret and preached to the crowds. Jesus then instructed Peter to cast his net into the deep for a catch during the day. Meanwhile, Peter and his crew of fishermen had gone fishing all night in the lake, had toiled and toiled, but had caught nothing.

Practically, the nighttime was the best time to fish in those crystal clear waters because the fish could see and evade predators during the day, and Peter knew that the daytime was the worst time to fish. So the instruction he received from Jesus did not make much sense.

He however obeyed the word of the Lord, and the results were astounding. He caught so much fish that his net began to break. His boat was also so full that it began to sink, and his other friends and colleagues had to come along with their boats to help load the excess catch (Luke 5:3-10). We see here that, in Peter's difficult season, Jesus showed up, worked a miracle, and brought about the biggest catch.

Miracles flow through Jesus into the lives of those who believe in Him, and who connect with the work of ministry. This miracle is a reminder to us that, when we support the work of God as Peter did, He will surely cause our barns to overflow with an overwhelming harvest of His blessings.

Jesus also countermanded the laws of nature. He was sleeping in the hinder part of a ship which was passing over to the other side. A great storm arose, and the winds and the waves beat upon the ship until it was full of water; the boat was well on its way to sinking and destroying lives. In fear, the disciples woke Jesus up. He rose and rebuked the storm, declaring "Peace! Be still." The winds and the storm obeyed His voice, and there was a great calm (Mark 4:35-41).

Jesus calms the raging seas. His power rules over the elements. He is still proclaiming peace to the whiplash of life, to any storm and wave beating you literally, financially, spiritually, emotionally or physically. In every area or arena of life, hear His voice rebuking the storm and saying "Peace! Be still." Respond with faith in your heart and rest in the Lord of the Sabbath, expecting many miracles.

Four thousand men (besides the women and children) from far and near gathered in the wilderness to hear the teachings of Jesus. He taught them for about three days, and it was evident that they were hungry. He did not want to send them back on empty stomachs, and so inquired of His disciples how much they had in the camp by way of supplies.

Their inventory was miniscule - there were only seven loaves and a few pieces of fish left. That was certainly not enough to feed the great multitude. Jesus however had the people sit down, and He took the loaves and fish, gave thanks to God, and turned them over to the disciples to distribute amongst the people. Miraculously, the food multiplied, and everyone was fed. There was excess, and seven baskets were left over (Matthew 15:32-39). Jesus' provision is a huge part of His Sabbath platform. There is no record that He ran a business or had investments, bank accounts, stocks, bonds, income property, etc. He did not need to because of who He was and where He came from. He made all things and owns all things.

He came from heaven to enforce the supernatural will of God's kingdom in the earth, and He meets the needs of His people through His compassion and love. He is the access door to pasture and provision, and supplies all needs according to the barometer of His riches in glory (Philippians 4:19).

In Capernaum, a tax collector queried Peter on whether Jesus, His Master, paid tribute. Jesus gave Peter a life lesson on the fact that the children of the kingdom were not required to pay tribute. Notwithstanding the fact that all things rightfully belonged to Him, Jesus still instructed Peter to go to the sea and cast his the hook to catch some fish, and that he would find a piece of money in the mouth of the first fish he caught. With that money, he was to go and pay the tribute for them both, to avoid any offence (Matthew 17:24-27).

Miracles were released when Jesus spoke words of faith. Finding a fig tree which had no fruit on it, He cursed it, saying that no one would eat of its fruit again. The next day, Peter observed that the fig tree which Jesus cursed had withered away. Jesus took the opportunity to teach His disciples that there is creative and accomplishing power in words spoken in faith and without doubt.

May we rise up to speak the promises of God, and release faith-filled words to see every challenge, test, trial, sickness, disease, poverty wither away into thin air. The anointing of Jubilee-freedom abides in us, and we need to release that through the spoken word, in the authority of Jesus' name (Mark 11:12-14; 20-25).

The death of Jesus was a wonder and a miracle. Through His death, He overcame the entire satanic corps and destroyed the sting and power of death. His resurrection from the dead was a miracle, demonstrating the exceeding greatness of God's mighty power. He laid down His life and picked it up again. The grave could not hold Him.

Events after His resurrection were miraculous. He showed Himself alive to His disciples by many infallible proofs, preaching the things that pertain to the kingdom. He showed His nail-scarred hands to doubting Thomas, walked through closed doors, and disappeared and reappeared at will. His ascension was an awesome miraculous event. He was caught into heaven in the clouds of glory as though the law of gravity was non-existent (Acts 1:1-11).

Jesus was all about bringing relief and joy to humanity. His ministry was characterized by the teaching and preaching the gospel of the Kingdom, healing the sick, delivering those possessed with devils, and casting out devils. He worked more wonders than could ever be recorded in any book.

Oh, the wonder, glorious power, of our majestic Savior and Messiah! We thank you, and honor, praise, worship and adore you now and forevermore for who you are and what you have done for mankind.

## 5. JESUS, THE EXECUTOR OF A NEW AND BETTER COVENANT

Fifthly, that Jesus is the Lord of the Sabbath is predicated on the fact that He has established a New and Better Covenant between God and His people.

The Old Covenant between God and man was represented by an earthly Sanctuary, the Tabernacle, in which the priests ministered, offering sacrifices to God on the Sabbaths and Jubilees. The first Tabernacle or Sanctuary was partitioned. There was the outer court, after which was a second veil, beyond which was the Holiest of all (the Holy of Holies).

Only the High Priest went into the Holiest of all, once every year, to offer sacrifices for himself and for the priesthood, and also on behalf of the people. The blood sacrifices of animals were offered for the purpose of atonement for sin, and to bring thanksgiving, praises and worship to God.

There was a limitation, however, in that the ministry of the priests in offering sacrifices was only temporal, and the efficacy of the sacrifices also could not reach beyond the senses to set the spirit and conscience of man free. The rituals had to be repeated year after year. In other words, a consistent, direct dialogue between God and man was not perfected or established under the Old Covenant (Hebrews 9:1-10).

This changed fundamentally and eternally when God offered Jesus as the sacrificial lamb on the cross. Jesus shed His own blood, and He presented that blood to the Father in the heavenly Sanctuary to atone for the sin of humanity. Through that sacrifice, the old Covenant was perfected; a New Covenant was initiated, one that is no longer represented by an earthly Sanctuary, but by a heavenly one.

Jesus Christ Himself is the Minister and High Priest of this heavenly Sanctuary. The services He rendered in this Sanctuary, the real, permanent heavenly Holiest of all, were not through the blood of animals but by His own blood. He also entered the Holy Place once, as the High Priest in the order of Melchizedek, to obtain eternal redemption for us.

This act of God, by which He consummated and brought forth a better Covenant, not only assures the believer of salvation and reconciliation to Jehovah, but also serves as an affirmation of even better things and better promises.

"He that spared not his own Son, but delivered him up for us all, how shall he not with him also freely give us all things?." Romans 8:32

God did not withhold His only Son but gave Him up as a ransom for all who believe. For this cause, we should be fully persuaded that He will freely supply and provide all our needs according to His riches in glory by Christ Jesus (Philippians 4:19). This assurance should elevate and activate the faith of God's people to expect God to address their every need and come through for them in every area of test or trial.

This New and Better Covenant is infinitely, inherently and intrinsically more superior and perfect, in that Christ offered His own sinless and perfect blood, and by token of that blood, He entered the heavens, the real Sanctuary, as the Lord of the Sabbath to rekindle, revive, reopen and forever establish the lines of sweet fellowship between God and man (Hebrews 8:1-6; 9:11-14).

## 6. JESUS, THE TEMPLE OF GOD

The sixth pointer to Jesus being the Lord of the Sabbath lies in His connection with the Temple. The earthly Temple was God's holy ground, a place where He would meet with His people and commune with them. It was also the place where His people brought to Him, various meat and animal sacrifices, thanksgiving, praise and worship. His presence filled the Temple, and they were empowered by His Spirit.

There are several layers symbolizing Jesus' integration and connection with the Temple. When the Jews asked for a sign after Jesus had driven the money changers and those selling animals out of the Temple, Jesus challenged them saying: "Destroy this temple, and in three days I will raise it up" (John 2:19).

The Jews could not comprehend how it was possible to tear down and rebuild a Temple which had taken forty-six years to construct, but the Bible shows that Jesus was speaking of the Temple of His body (John 2:21). He was symbolically speaking about His death and resurrection, through which the earthly Temple would find full expression and fulfilment in the real spiritual Temple.

He knew that He would offer the ultimate sacrifice, not the sacrifices of the blood of goats and calves, but the sacrifice of His own blood on the cross, once and for all. He actually did so, and entered into the real Temple in heaven in the holiest of holies and obtained eternal redemption for us (Hebrews 9:12).

In essence, Jesus is the real representation of the Temple in Heaven and on the earth.

Another prism through which Jesus' connection to the Temple is seen lies in the fact that people go the Temple on the Sabbath to seek the Father and to worship Him. Without a doubt, Jesus is the perfect representation and embodiment of the Father God, and thus, it is He they go to worship, and, indeed, all must worship Him. It is Jesus who reveals the Father. He boldly declared: "He that hath seen me hath seen the Father" (John 14:9). He stated: "I am the way, the truth, and the life. No one comes to the Father except by me (John 14:6). Isaiah declared that Jesus, the Son, *is* the everlasting Father (Isaiah 9:6).

Jesus is also that glory that fills the Temple. His shekinah glory and presence provided guidance, direction and protection for Israel from Egypt to the promised land. His presence filled King Solomon's Temple. He declared that, where two or three are gathered in His name, He is right there in the midst of them (Matthew 18:20). He told the people: "Come unto me, all that labour and are heavy laden, and I will give you rest." The Lord administers rest, joy, healing, deliverance and liberty through His presence.

The Temple connection is most evident in the fact that God also created man to be His dwelling place. He predestined that His person and presence would permanently reside in, and be upon, man (1 Corinthians 6:16-20; 1 John 4:4; Luke 24:49). For that to happen, though, Jesus had to clean man up with His blood so that God's Spirit could dwell in him. The Church, which is the body of Christ, was cleansed, and is the Temple of God. Jesus is the Head of the body, even the Church. Clearly, the Temple or Tabernacle of God was a key part of the Sabbath; it was the place where the people of God converged or gathered in order to bring their sacrifices to God and to worship Him. It was the place of strong communion and fellowship with Him. Jesus came to establish the eternal Temple, which is the Church and His body, of which He is the Head. In other words, the Temple, all its Sabbath activities, and all that it stood for, were totally fulfilled in Christ Jesus who is the Temple or Tabernacle of God who came to dwell among us.

## 7. JESUS, THE FULFILMENT OF THE LAW AND THE PROPHETS

Jesus' eminent position as the Lord of the Sabbath did not go unchallenged by men. The Pharisees stringently upheld the notion that the Jews were to strictly obey the laws and regulations regarding the Sabbath. Thus, they took issue with the fact that Jesus healed the man at the pool of Bethesda, who had been impotent and infirm for thirty-eight years, on the Sabbath (John 5:1-16). They also accused Jesus' disciples of violating the law when they plucked ears of corn from a field and ate them on the Sabbath day.

The reaction of Jesus to these allegations is insightful. He likened the situation to how David and his men went to the Temple when they were hungry and ate the shew bread, which was only for the priests. He also reminded them of the records in the Law about how some priests in the Temple profane the Sabbath and are blameless. Jesus declared that He is greater than the Temple, and that He is Lord even of the Sabbath day (Matthew 12:1-8).

Some have interpreted Jesus' response as meaning that, in times of desperate human need, the Law of God can be set aside. That is a wrong interpretation, for the Law of God must always be upheld and properly applied.

Actually, when viewed through the lenses of the Law, what the disciples of Jesus did on the Sabbath, namely, plucking the ears of corn, was actually permissible under the Law because they did not use a sickle, that is, a harvesting instrument, to get the corn (Deuteronomy 23:25). However, the Pharisees simply sought occasion to accuse them by relying on the Oral Tradition of the Elders of Israel and thus misinterpreting the Law.

The Oral Tradition was a set of rules utilized in the interpretation of the Law of God. By the second century, these were written down by the Rabbis and were called the Talmud. Jesus warned the people about such Traditions of the Elders, observing that they make the word of God of none effect (Mark 7:5-13).

Worth noting is that the Sabbath, the Law, and the Temple were all a shadow of the reality of things to come. They were all God's designs to guide and admonish His people, to bring them into His presence, and to commune and have fellowship with them.

Jesus' response to the Pharisees clearly indicated that His coming, in person, is the full expression or the living reality of the Sabbath, the Law, and the Temple. He is the Sabbath, and brought the Sabbath-rest to man not only from their external works, but also rest in their hearts and souls. As He declared, "For the Son of man is Lord even of the Sabbath day" (Matthew 12:8). He is also the Temple to which people came to worship.

Therefore, when David and his men were tired and hungry and went into the Temple to eat the shew bread, they went into Jesus' very presence, and they entered into His rest, the Sabbath rest that only He could give. They received from Him, the shew bread, the bread of life, even Himself, the Word. Through Jesus, we have also become a holy and royal priesthood, no longer disqualified from going into His presence and eating of the bread of life (Hebrews 4:16, 1 Peter 2:5,9).

Moreover, Jesus came to fulfill the Law and the Prophets. The Law, which embodied all the commandments, rules, edicts and directions of God, was inscribed and delivered to God's people by the holy prophets who were moved and inspired by the Spirit of the living God (2 Peter 1:19-21, 2 Timothy 3:16-17). Thus, the recording of the Scriptures was not subject to people's private interpretations or to their subjective wills and preferences.

Every part of the Scriptures is God-breathed, inherent with the life, power and person of God Himself, for the Word (Jesus) is God (John 1:1-3). This reality infuses all the numerous laws, commandments, regulations and instructions that make up the entirety of the Bible, making it imperative for God's people to comprehensively obey the totality of word of God, the manual that shows humankind the way of life. As Jesus explained:

"For verily I say unto you, Till heaven and earth pass, one jot or one tittle shall in no wise pass from the law, till all be fulfilled. Whosoever therefore shall break one of these least commandments, and shall teach men so, he shall be called the least in the kingdom of heaven: but whosoever shall do and teach them, the same shall be called great in the kingdom of heaven. For I say unto you, That except your righteousness shall exceed the righteousness of the scribes and Pharisees, ye shall in no case enter into the kingdom of heaven." Matthew 5:18-20

Practically, however, it would be a daunting and, most likely, impossible task for anyone to memorize or know all the Law, and also to have the presence of mind to obey or apply every rule thereof every second of their lives.

Thus, the Law was weak in that it could not, and did not, produce the righteousness required by God, that is, the strict adherence to every aspect of the Law. In other words, the power of sin (the transgression to the word of God) could not be broken by the works of the Law (Galatians 2:16-21).

The Law therefore pointed to Christ who knew no sin but whom God made sin, so that we might be made the righteousness of God through Christ (2 Corinthians 5:21).

As Paul revealed, Jesus is the end of the Law - "For Christ is the end of the law for righteousness for every one that believeth" (Romans 10:4). Righteousness is a gift imparted to us by God through Jesus Christ (Romans 5:17). He is our righteousness, and through Him, our righteousness no longer depends on our performance, as far as the Law is concerned.

Jesus is also the Word made flesh. He is the inspired "Law and the Prophets" in person. He came to fulfill the Law and the Prophets completely and thoroughly. He said: "Think not that I am come to destroy the law, or the prophets: I am not come to destroy, but to fulfil" (Matthew 5:17).

Even so, He still brought to the people of God a dynamic revelation that, once they are redeemed, there remains, for them, a residual action that they must take, a part they must play, to also fulfill the Law and the Prophets. He opened up the manual from God in one statement:

"Therefore all things whatsoever ye would that men should do to you, do ye even so to them: for this is the law and the prophets." Matthew 7:12

This important principle that Jesus taught simplifies things dramatically for the people of God, in terms of their fidelity to, and them fulfilling, the Law. Essentially, we must do unto others what we want them to do to us. This principle is one that governs all aspects of human life – the spiritual, the material, the physical and the social. It communicates the truth that we can shape or determine what happens in our lives through how we relate with others.

Our attitudes and reactions towards others set this divine law in motion, triggering a corresponding reaction back to us. Directly or indirectly, we impact others, and they, correspondingly, impact us. Therefore, our input into others is rationally linked to what we receive. Other permutations embedded in this key principle of life are sowing and reaping, and giving and receiving.

The seeds we sow eventually yield a harvest and return back to us. When we respond to people in love, mercy, forgiveness and kindness, which are the fruit of a regenerate heart, we create a spiritual environment around us which opens up the blessings of God, causing others to favor us and to react to us in like manner. When we love our neighbors as ourselves, an atmosphere of God's goodness and the goodness of men will not elude us.

Conversely, when attitudes toward others are bad, a toxic environment is created in which the devil thrives, causing animosity, disfavor and contention around us. That kind of atmosphere breeds a lack of freedom or a lack of progress and advancement in our lives. We open ourselves up for demons to have a field day, blocking our joy and liberty.

Jesus fulfilled the Law and the Prophets to bring us Jubilee. To hold fast to the fullness of the Jubilee blessing, we must guard our souls and minds, and create the right, optimal spiritual environment through what we do to others, which would move others to treat us well and favor us also.

In sum, Jesus is the Temple or Tabernacle of God who came to dwell among us. He is also the Word of God, the Law and the Prophets fulfilled. In the same vein, this Jesus, the Christ, is the Lord of the Sabbath. He is the rest of God, the Jubilee, through whom people can experience the restoration of glory and the glorious liberty of the Father God.

## 8. JESUS, THE SABBATH FULFILLED

Clearly discernible in the Sabbath and in all of its expressions is the progression of the dealings of God with His people, how He brings His grace and blessings to them as they reach out and enter into His rest. Fellowship and communion with God become deeper from the Sabbath to the Sabbath of Sabbaths; the Sabbatical year is even better, more special and more holy with the greater outpouring of blessings of God in the lives of his people; and the Jubilee is the epitome of God's Sabbath engagements with His people.

By keeping the Sabbath, God's people unequivocally declare that He is the creator and maker of all things, and that man did not make himself, nor did he evolve out of the cell of an animal; God created man in His own image and likeness (Genesis 1:26-28).

They also acknowledge that He is the almighty and omnipotent One who holds all things by the word of His power.

An offshoot of that is the realistic appraisal of their human limitations and their insufficiency – that, in all their labors, they cannot attain fullness and fulfilment without God, and that they are the created and God is the creator.

The Sabbath was also given by God to be a sign of sanctification between He and them. In other words, through the Sabbath, God was pledging to His people and giving them the assurance that He would cleanse and sanctify them. As God explains:

"Moreover also I gave them my sabbaths, to be a sign between me and them, that they might know that I am the Lord that sanctify them." Ezekiel 20:12

Observers of the Sabbath therefore reach out to God to totally surrender their lives, will, hearts and minds on God's holy altar of sanctification, consecration and devotion.

The Sabbath is also purpose-driven and value-laden. The inner depths and relevance of keeping it lies in separating, and consecrating one's heart, life and day, to worship God. These are spiritual activities to connect to God, who is a Spirit, and who must be worshipped in spirit and in truth.

This means that, when people abstain from keeping the Sabbath, their lives become void of spiritual reality, and they lack the impact of God's presence, guidance and power in their lives. This translates into spiritual dryness and death, and a disconnection from communion and fellowship with God. When the Sabbath is observed, however, the opposite is true, and people experience life and sanctification as they tap into the special blessing God imputed to, and invoked on, the Sabbath day.

The Sabbath has always maintained its original connotations of rest for the people of God from their labours. In the process of time, however, its import was extended, and it became synonymous also with the rehearsal of the miraculous mighty hand of God that brought His people out of bondage to the land of promise. It was marked, by God, to be celebrated as a remembrance of the salvation and deliverance of God's people from Egypt, from slavery, and from the house of bondage (Deuteronomy 5:12-15).

In that wise, the Sabbath unveils a faithful God who saves His people from any kind of bondage and brings them into freedom, liberty and abundance. Man, in his own efforts and works, cannot save himself from slavery to sin, hell and the judgment of God. Indeed, the struggles of man to attain right standing with God are futile. As Isaiah declares, all our righteousness are like filthy rags before God (Isaiah 64:6).

The Sabbath of the Lord is therefore a type of His invitation to man to cease from his battles with sin, the flesh, Satan, and the issues of this life, so he can enter the rest of God and be identified with God's provisions of salvation and deliverance (Hebrews 4:10).

Again, the observance of the holy Sabbath demonstrates the believer's total reliance on God's unfailing promises of supplying our every need according to His riches in glory (Philippians 4:19). God spreads a table of His supplies before us in the presence of our enemies (Psalms 23).

The Sabbath, then, holistically understood, is an overview of God's excellent greatness, the beauty of His craftsmanship and handiwork. The observance of the holy Sabbath and its regulations also signifies that the believer comes into complete rest in God. As well, it is a time that the Lord has set apart to enjoy fellowship with His people, and for Him to impart wisdom, strength and empowerment to them. In essence, the Sabbath is when God's people spend quality time with Him.

All of these converge into the one irrevocable fact - that the Sabbath is Jesus revealed. Jesus is the very expression and embodiment of the Sabbath, and is that One whom we spend quality time with. He is the One who created the Sabbath, He is that faithful God who designed and brings rest to His people. He is the One to whom all creation brings worship in the Sanctuary. He is the mediator of the New Covenant, and He breaks the bands of hell and darkness. He is, in every conceivable sense, the Lord of the Sabbath.

# Chapter 5

## JESUS OUR JUBILEE – THE FEASTS OF ISRAEL (THE LORD'S FEASTS)

The feasts of Israel are those times when Israel celebrates God's goodness and His great acts of deliverance and redemption in their lives. They come before God to acknowledge His faithfulness to His promises, and to worship Him in His perfection, majesty, beauty and holiness. Every feast is God's call to bring His people closer to Himself to effect deep change in them, and to impact them with His word, presence and power.

The feasts unveil the blueprint, intent and purpose of God to bring liberty, freedom and Jubilee to His people. Year after year, every feast provides an incremental experiential level of freedom and liberty, until God brings His people to the crescendo or highest point during the year of Jubilee. Jubilee is a celebration of joy, freedom and liberty from any form of bondage, indebtedness, stress, suppression and oppression, and it takes the presence, Spirit and anointing of God to bring this freedom.

There are four main spring feasts of Israel, each unveiling God's eternal purposes for His people, and pointing to the Messiah. The spring feasts are:

- The Passover
- The Feast of Unleavened Bread

- The Feast of the First Fruits
- The Feast of Pentecost

There are also three main fall feasts of Israel, although these are not exhaustive of the feasts celebrated. There are other feasts which emerged over time and gained prominence on the Hebrew calendar. Just as with the spring feasts of Israel, the fall feasts typify the distinct counsel of God and embody His divine purposes for His people, and are unmistakeable signposts pointing to Jesus, the Messiah. The fall feasts are:

- The Feast of Trumpets
- The Feast of Atonement
- The Feast of Tabernacles
- Other Feasts of Israel (Purim, Hannukah)

There are several important aspects of the feasts of Israel that are worth noting. Firstly, the feasts of Israel are really the feasts of God; they are His appointed times (moadim of Adonai) to meet with His people.

"And the Lord spake unto Moses saying, Speak unto the children of Israel, and say unto them, Concerning the feasts of the Lord, which ye shall proclaim to be holy convocations, even these are my feasts." Leviticus 23:1-2

The feasts are thus not the design of man but, rather, are the statutes and ordinances of God crafted by Him to bring His people into His presence. God clearly takes ownership of the feasts.

Secondly, the feasts are corporate, not private, events, addressed to, and requiring the participation of, all of Israel. The feasts are conceived of as "convocations". A convocation is the calling together of people for a large formal assembly, or the gathering of a large group of people in an orderly fashion. All the people of Israel are expected to participate in, and enjoy, the feasts.

Thirdly, the convocations of God are proclaimed to be "holy" convocations. This vests them with the important quality of being hallowed, set apart, and reverential. This means that the feasts are God's holy and sanctified call to His people. They are God's call to obedience, sacrifice and fellowship with Him.

Fourthly, the feasts define and identify the Jewish people as God's people, as a unique race that is shepherded, guided and taught by God Almighty, and that is not supposed to live as the heathen. During the celebration of the feasts, the instructions and knowledge of Jehovah, which communicate a structured, guided, godly lifestyle to the Jewish people and which are embedded in the Jewish culture, are passed down to generations and are to be celebrated indefinitely.

Fifthly, through the feasts, the Jews respond to God as their King, leader, keeper, provider, saviour, deliverer, and their all in all. The feasts are therefore commemorative. They commemorate the interventions of God from the past and the present. Essentially, the feasts serve as a platform for enriching the relationship between God and His people.

Sixthly, the feasts are predictive and prophetic. They provide God's calendar and agenda for His people around the year. They demonstrate and articulate what God would do in every season, and how His people are to respond to Him. This reality is embedded in the Hebrew word for feasts, "moad", which means a rehearsal of actual or real events to take place in the future. As Paul admonished:

"Let no man judge you in meat, or in drink, or respect of an holyday, or of the new moon, or of the sabbath days: Which are a shadow of things to come; but the body is of Christ." Colossians 2:16-17

In other words, the feasts are types, shadows and images of the reality of that which is to come. It is also very interesting that the feasts, at various points, merge with the Sabbaths ordained by God. In other words, the different feasts, as they play out, show an integration, interplay and overlap with the Sabbath, the Sabbath of Sabbaths, the Sabbatical year, and culminating in the Jubilee. This is not coincidental. God was articulating the comprehensiveness and cohesiveness of His counsel and intent for the people of Israel.

Seventh, the most momentous and decisive prophetic event portrayed or painted by all the feasts is the first and second coming of the Messiah, His life and ministry on earth, His suffering and His passion, and His power to destroy sin, death, hell and the grave to bring salvation and redemption to humanity.

The revelation of the person of the Messiah and His redemptive work is thus the central theme of the feasts of Israel. He is revealed in every part of the feasts and at each level. He is peace personified, and the proclaimer of peace, liberty, reconciliation and Jubilee to all who come to God through Him. Jesus is the First Fruits, the Passover Lamb, the Unleavened Bread, the

Atonement, the Trumpet and Horn of our Salvation, and the Sabbath Rest.

Finally, the feasts of Israel demonstrate, not only the singular path to salvation, but also, the boundless or universal nature of its spectrum of coverage. The people of Israel were God's chosen vehicle to rehearse, through the feasts, His plans and purposes which would be fulfilled in Christ, but they were not destined to be the only recipients of that wondrous event.

There was, in fact, a global intent of God implicit therein, in that the Christ would make the counsel of God's salvation available to the entire world, Jews and Gentiles alike.

"For ye are all children of God by faith in Christ Jesus. For as many of you as have been baptized into Christ have put on Christ. There is neither Jew nor Greek, there is neither bond nor free, there is neither male nor female: for ye are all one in Christ Jesus. And if ye be Christ's, then are ye Abraham's seed, and heirs according to the promise." Galatians 3:26-29

"For I am not ashamed of the gospel of Christ: for it is the power of God unto salvation to every one that believeth; to the Jew first, and also to the Greek." Romans 1:16

The Jews were the first and original recipients of the gospel and oracles of God, and their feasts painted images of Jesus Messiah and His purchased possession, the Church. What they received from God was however channelled, through Christ, to the entire world. Jesus shed His blood for all, whether Jew or Gentile. Through Christ Jesus, therefore, the non-Jewish believer comes into a covenant relationship with God and, for that matter, the

Jew as well. In Christ Jesus, the barrier between Jew and Gentile is broken, and they become one new man, the body of Christ.

In Ephesians 2:11-20, Paul reinforces Christ's work of redemption in bringing Jews and Gentiles together as one body, stating that, in Christ Jesus, we all have become fellow citizens with the saints, and of the household of God. The Church is built by God and founded on the apostles and prophets, with Jesus Christ Himself being the chief cornerstone. The body of Christ, of which He is the head, is made up of every nation, tribe, tongue and kindred, and is erected as a holy habitation, and the dwelling place of God through the Spirit.

As such, it would certainly enrich the understanding, faith and spiritual experience of New Testament believers if they grasp the intent and purpose of God's appointed feasts. There would be a further progression of the revelation of the person of Jesus, the glory of His presence, and His authority and dominion over all that is, and ever would be.

However, it is important to be mindful of the apostle Paul's caution that the New Testament believer is not required to observe or go through the ceremonies and motions of the Jewish feasts in order to attain salvation (Colossians 2:16-17). Notwithstanding, a closer look at the feasts does enrich and empower the believer's understanding of Jesus Messiah.

The feasts also represent an invitation to the non-Jewish believer to participate in the origins of their faith. The Messiah is Jewish; for this reason, all believers are engrafted into the Jewish family (Romans 11:1). Thus, understanding the feasts supplies a deeper understanding and revelation of God's heart and mind for His people.

In conclusion, it is evident that the New Testament Church is indelibly connected to the prophetic wonder of the wealth and riches of God's futuristic timelines for the ages, as they are unveiled in the feasts of Israel. The appointed feasts unveil the blueprint, intent and purpose of God to bring liberty, freedom and Jubilee every step of the way.

# Chapter 6

## JESUS OUR JUBILEE - UNVEILED IN THE SPRING FEASTS OF ISRAEL

The four main spring feasts of Israel signify the birth of new things and fresh initiatives by God Almighty, and the unfolding of His redemption plan for His people. They reveal the emergence of Jesus, the Messiah, in the eternal plan of God. The spring feasts are:

- The Passover
- The Feast of Unleavened Bread
- The Feast of the First Fruits
- The Feast of Pentecost

### 1. THE PASSOVER

The Passover celebrates the deliverance of Israel from Egyptian tyranny, slavery and bondage. The Israelites were in Egypt for over four hundred years. What had started for them as a great breakthrough, and a relief and reunion mission, soon turned to oppression, repression, suppression and hard labour.

Their advent to the land of Egypt was precipitated by a worldwide famine which led them to Egypt, where they could access and purchase supplies. Jacob's sons encountered Joseph, their long lost brother, who had been used by God to interpret the dream of the then incumbent Pharaoh, and through whom plans and strategies were put in place that would save the world from famine. Once Joseph finally revealed himself to his brethren, he migrated the entire family to Egypt where they would enjoy sustenance.

Israel grew in strength and in number in Egypt. With the passage of time however, there arose a new Pharaoh who "knew not Joseph", in other words, who was not apprised of the significant and revered place Joseph had in Egypt. Thus, the leadership of Egypt hated the Israelites, totally eliminated the privileges and courtesies formerly accorded to them, and over-burdened them with hard labour and slave tasks.

The cry of God's people for deliverance ascended before Jehovah's throne, and He raised Moses, the prophet, to deliver God's unequivocal word to Pharaoh. The message to Pharaoh was - "Let my people go, that they may serve me." Pharaoh's heart, however, was hardened, and he refused to let Israel go. Accordingly, God, by the hand of Moses, inflicted terrible punishments on Egypt by sending nine plagues on Egypt.

Despite the devastation caused, Pharaoh was still unbending, and so God ordered the tenth judgement to fall on Egypt - an angel of death would go through the land and slay every first born of Egypt. This was highly significant as every firstborn of Egypt was a god, and firstborns were the chief of the gods of Egypt. As the Bible recounts: "He smote also all the firstborn in their land the chief of all their strength." (Psalm 105:36).

When the angel of death walked through the land, every firstborn was to die. It was ordained by God that the only ones that would escape the judgement were households whose doorposts and lintels were painted with the blood of a lamb without blemish. Those households would experience redemption. He instructed Moses to tell the people of Israel:

"And they shall take of the blood, and strike it on the two side posts and on the upper door post of the houses, wherein they shall eat it…"

"For I will pass through the land of Egypt this night, and will smite all the firstborn in the land of Egypt, both man and beast; and against all the gods of Egypt I will execute judgment: I am the Lord. And the blood shall be to you for a token upon the houses where ye are: and when I see the blood, I will pass over you, and the plague shall not be upon you to destroy you, when I smite the land of Egypt." Exodus 12:7, 12-13

The people of Israel did just as God instructed. They applied the blood of the lamb to the doorposts and lintels at the entrance of their homes, and then entered their homes to celebrate the Passover feast, the menu for which was the roasted unblemished lamb, unleavened bread, and bitter herbs.

As promised by God, salvation, protection and redemption became the portion of all who dwelt in those houses. Their firstborns were saved from destruction. However, all the firstborns of Egypt were slain, and the painful cry of the people in the land finally turned Pharaoh's hardened heart to let God's people go. Over three million of God's people walked into their freedom, liberty, and jubilee by the use and application of the blood of the lamb at Passover.

The people of Israel, after applying the blood on the doorposts and lintels, "passed over" that blood to enter the safety and security of their houses. The Hebrew term for Passover is "Pesach." Pesach means to come under protection of deity by crossing over, leaping over, stepping over, or jumping over, something at the threshold. When the spirit of death and destruction saw that blood, it could not enter to destroy, and therefore "passed over" those houses.

This Passover was, as it were, the last straw that broke the camel's back. Through it, God punished Pharaoh, crushed the powers of his gods, and redeemed the people of Israel. Its celebration brought Israel out of Egypt and delivered them from the terrible rule of Pharaoh. Thus, God instituted the feast of the Passover to be celebrated on the fourteenth day of the first month (Nisan) on the Hebrew calendar (Leviticus 23:5).

After the Temple was built, the people of Israel would come every year with their lambs to the Temple to celebrate the Passover, with praise, worship, great joy, and the singing of the Psalms of David. They would dance before the Lord Jehovah, celebrating the victories of the past when He delivered them with a mighty hand. They would honor their maker with the testimonies of the present, and look into the future with faith and expectancy, holding the assurance that, if He had wrought such mighty works for them, He was sure to do it again.

Not surprisingly, there has been, and continues to be, a counterfeit expression of the essence of the Passover. Ancient cultures went through the ritual of slaughtering animals, collecting their blood, pouring it over the entrance of their homes, and leaping over the blood to get into their homes. Through this process, altars were set up to invoke and connect with their gods who would come into their homes and also stand at their doors to protect them or to provide for them. In other words, the adherents to such practices would come into blood covenants with their gods.

Indeed, so many people in the world, in the name of culture, tradition and ancestral worship, and also through their own consummate choices, are entangled in evil blood covenants and serve idols. They invoke demons from the spirit realm as they worship stones, trees, animals, graven images and other objects, and connect with the demonic under water, rivers and seas. They invoke demons as they participate in cults and in the occult. They invoke demons also as they comingle with agents of the devil, such as fetish priests, psychics, palm readers, spiritualists, magicians and necromancers (those calling the spirits of the dead), to name a few.

These are altogether demonic and ungodly practices and, without argument, Satan is the author of false gods and religions. He subverts, inverts, and perverts the truth of God's word to deceive and hold people under his rule to destroy them.

Serving idols is an abomination to the one true Jehovah God, and means a separation from Him, the maker and creator of all things. Idol worship of any form incurs His wrath and judgment. He says:

"Thou shalt have no other gods before me. Thou shalt not make unto thee any graven image, or any likeness of anything that is in the heaven above, or that is in the earth beneath, or that is in the water under the earth: Thou shalt not bow down thyself to them, nor serve them: for I the Lord thy God am a jealous God, visiting the iniquity of the fathers upon the children unto the third and fourth generation of them that hate me; And shewing mercy unto thousands of them that love me, and keep my commandments." Exodus 20:3-6

"But the fearful, and unbelieving, and the abominable, and murderers, and whoremongers, and sorcerers, and idolaters, and all liars, shall have their part in the lake which burneth with fire and brimstone: which is the second death." Revelation 21:8

It is obvious, then, that the human race needs salvation from Satan, sin, hell and eternal damnation. Every person needs to be saved, reconciled and restored to God, the maker and creator of all things, and to pass over from darkness to light, from bondage to liberty, and from condemnation to absolution.

This is the power of the Passover – that Jesus is the reality of the Passover. The feast of the Passover was a clear image of what was to come through Christ Jesus. God, in His eternal wisdom and predestined purpose, prepared Jesus, from the foundation of the world, as the reality of the Passover lamb that was to be slain, not only for the deliverance of Israel, but for the salvation, redemption and jubilee of all mankind from sin and bondage to the devil. Expounding on this, the apostle Paul stated:

"Purge out therefore the old leaven, that ye may be a new lump, as ye are unleavened. For even Christ our Passover is sacrificed for us." 1 Corinthians 5:7

As the Passover lamb, Jesus has presented to every living soul, the only pathway to salvation, which is through Him. The apostle Paul stated there is one God and one mediator between God and man, the man Christ Jesus (1 Timothy 2:5). Jesus Himself unambiguously repudiated and discounted the idea espoused in world cultures, traditions and religions that there are multiple routes to salvation, declaring:

"...I am the way, the truth and the life; no man cometh unto the Father, but by me." John 14:6

The significant portions of the Passover sacrifice and meal were the unblemished lamb that was killed and roasted, the unleavened bread, and bitter herbs. Unpacking these, we see, in every emblem, Jesus revealed:

- **The Unblemished Lamb**

Jesus was the unblemished lamb of the Passover. He was without sin and knew no sin. He was examined by Pilate who found no fault whatsoever in Him. In every sense, therefore, He was the lamb of God without spot or blemish, and He laid down His life to take away the sins of the world. He was, and is, and will forever be, the sacrificial lamb (John 1:29).

- **The Blood of the Lamb**

The people of Israel were in unimaginable bondage in Egypt. The spotless lamb was killed at Passover, and its blood was collected and applied to the doorposts and lintels of their houses. It was the blood that redeemed the people of Israel from bondage.

This is a picture of the human state. Adam, the first man, disobeyed God by eating the forbidden fruit in the Garden of Eden. That disobedience was disastrous for humanity as it resulted in a total sell-out of all of humanity into Satan's horrific claws of bondage (Romans 3:23; 5:12). Mankind was sold to Satan, sin, and slavery to the power of darkness.

However, Jesus, the lamb of God who was slain before the foundation of the world, offered Himself and His blood as the price to redeem or buy back from the power of Satan, sin, spiritual death, power of darkness and eternal judgement, all who would believe in Him and accept His sacrifice.

For all persons who believe on Jesus and His sacrifice on the cross, there is unlimited power in the blood of Jesus. It is the spiritual weapon within the faith and testimony of the saints to overcome the devil and all his cohorts (Revelation 12:7-11). It has the power to set the captives free, power to provide liberty, power to bring jubilee to people in their spirits, souls, and bodies. The blood has the power to bring forgiveness, and is the remedy for sin and bondage to sin, and it cleanses the believing one from all unrighteousness (1 John 1:7-9).

"In whom we have redemption through his blood, the forgiveness of sins, according to the riches of his grace." Ephesians 1:7

"Who hath delivered us from the power of darkness, and hath translated us into the kingdom of his dear Son: In whom we have redemption through his blood, even the forgiveness of sins." Colossians 1:13-14

Believers ought to constantly make bold declarations as the blood-bought redeemed of God, and unpack the victories that belong to them in the blood of Jesus.

- **The Unleavened Bread**

Jesus is the bread of life (John 6:35). He is also the giver of life, and the supplier of every need (John 6:51). He is the unleavened bread, sinless, pure and uncontaminated.

- **The Bitter Herbs**

The bitter herbs represent Jesus' sufferings and the travail of His soul. He was beaten beyond recognition. He received the stripes in His back. His body was broken. He went through crucifixion and death, all to heal and redeem mankind.

In conclusion, the Passover celebration was, in every sense, a rehearsal of the true redemption that was to be made available to all who would accept the sacrificial act of Christ Jesus on the cross of Calvary. At Calvary, Jesus shed His blood for all mankind, and whoever applies that blood to their hearts and souls would be set free from sin and the wages of sin, which is eternal death, alienation and separation from God. Hallelujah!

## 2. THE FEAST OF UNLEAVENED BREAD

The feast of Unleavened Bread takes place the next day after the Passover. This falls on the fifteenth day of the month of Nisan, and is celebrated for seven days. The people of Israel were required by God to eat unleavened bread throughout this period (Leviticus 23:6-8).

Unleavened bread is bread made without yeast. Israel was commanded, during this period, to remove all yeast from their household as yeast was reckoned as a type of sin. They were required to thoroughly clean their clothes, cooking utensils, cabinets and anything in their houses that may have been contaminated.

There are several significant insights about the feast of Unleavened Bread, all of which typify and point to the cleansing and sanctification that God brings to His people through Jesus.

First, this feast was an expression of the intrinsic reality that Jesus is the bread of heaven. Therefore, it is He alone who can give life and sustenance to the world.

"Then Jesus said unto them, Verily, verily, I say unto you, Moses gave you not that bread from heaven; but my Father giveth you the true bread from heaven. For the bread of God is he which cometh down from heaven, and giveth life unto the world." John 6:32-33

Jesus, the bread of heaven, is the provider of all our material, physical, spiritual and emotional needs (John 6:35). As the Bible explains, God supplies every need according to His riches in glory by Christ Jesus (Philippians 4:19). Jesus is also the great shepherd of the sheep; accordingly, the sheep would not want for anything (Psalm 23). He provides healing to His people, as healing is the children's bread (Mark 7:27). He is also the door, and anyone who goes in and out of that door will find pasture and experience life even more abundantly (John 10:9-10).

As the bread of heaven also, Jesus is the source of life and eternal life. Bread sustains and feeds people, and perpetuates life only after it has gone through the rigorous process of being kneaded, formed, baked at intense temperatures, broken, and eaten. All these steps are evident in Jesus' body which was the bread of life that had to be broken and eaten by the world, in order that they would have healing and life. That necessitated His death. He said:

"I am the living bread which came down from heaven: if any man eat of this bread, he shall live forever: and the bread that I will give is my flesh, which I will give for the life of the world." John 6:51

"And as they were eating, Jesus took bread, and blessed it, and brake it, and gave it to the disciples, and said, Take, eat; this is my body." Matthew 26:26

Jesus died during the feast of Unleavened Bread so that all who would believe in Him would have everlasting life. He had power to lay down His life, and had the power to pick it up again. He was crucified, and He died for all humanity as the perfect sinless bread of heaven that could be eaten by all so as to receive life.

A second important feature of the feast lies in the nature or character of the bread. The bread for the celebration was unleavened, with no yeast or leaven in its preparation. As has already been established, Jesus was, and is, the unleavened bread. In other words, He was sinless and pure, altogether perfect, and was thus in every respect, the spotless unblemished sacrifice for all of humanity. In His incarnation, He experienced the whole gamut of the temptations of humanity, and yet maintained His purity and was not tainted by sin. There was no leaven in Him.

"For we have not an high priest which cannot be touched with the feeling of our infirmities; but was in all points tempted like as we are, yet without sin." Hebrews 4:15

Thirdly, the feast of Unleavened Bread is a demonstration of the purity and righteousness of God. It reveals God as the righteous and just God who sent Jesus, the Son, in human form and in all His purity and perfection, to overcome sin at every point as a man, and ultimately to be made or fashioned as sin for humanity. The intent of God was that Jesus would lay down His life for all, that His righteousness would be imparted to the believing one. The Bible states:

"For he hath made him to be sin for us, who knew no sin; that we might be made the righteousness of God in him." 2 Corinthians 5:21

"All we like sheep have gone astray; we have turned every one to his own way; and the LORD hath laid on him the iniquity of us all." Isaiah 53:6

It pleased the Lord, and was entirely by His design, to lay upon Jesus the sin, transgression and iniquity of the world, and to make Him an offering for sin (Isaiah 53:8-11). Thus, Jesus, as the unleavened bread, took the place of fallen man by becoming sin.

His "unleavened" nature became innately corrupted, defiled and tainted with the scourge and yeast of sin. He did this to bring to humanity the prized gift of righteousness, and the result was the transmission or dispersion of His righteousness to all those who believed. In other words, through that process of divine exchange, those who believed also became "unleavened." The Bible says:

"Purge out therefore the old leaven, that ye may be a new lump, as ye are unleavened. For even Christ our passover is sacrificed for us." 1 Corinthians 5:7

Righteousness is an attribute of God, and presents the purity, nature and character of God. He is Jehovah Tsidkenu, the Lord Our Righteousness (Jeremiah 23:5-6). He wants His people to share His attributes, and righteousness is His gift to humanity through the inner workings of salvation. It is received and appropriated by faith as no one can work out his/her own righteousness and attain the excellent nature and character of God; all of man's righteousness are as filthy rags in God's sight (Isaiah 64:6). Man is only reconciled to God by receiving the gift of righteousness that brings him back in union and fellowship with God (Romans 5:17). Jesus, who alone is the unleavened bread, makes this happen.

Finally, and related to the above, the feast of Unleavened Bread unveils the power and reality of the "New Creation" that Christ made possible. That New Creation is a new species of being that never existed before, one that is pure, holy and righteous. The Bible declares that, if anyone is in Christ, he is a New Creation, and that the old nature has passed away, and all things become new (2 Corinthians 5:17). That signifies the putting off or total eradication of the old sin nature, and heralds the arrival of the new nature of righteousness.

Human beings have long grappled with the old self and nature of sin, pride, worldliness, ungodly and lustful desires. The believer is not immune from these human frailties, and they must be removed to enable the child of God to walk in righteousness and true holiness (Ephesians 4:22, Galatians 5:19-21).

To be clear, though, the believer's sin or desire to sin does not come from his inner, recreated human spirit because the recreated spirit has no sin nature, only the character and purity of God's righteousness. Rather, that desire to sin comes from areas within the believer's soul or mind, and the outward man (the flesh). The soul or mind and the flesh must therefore unlearn and put off the sinful activities of the past, so that God can be glorified in spirit, soul and body (Romans 12:1-2, 1Corinthians 6:17-20).

The force of righteousness in the New Creation is the enabling power of God within him to obey the word of God and to walk in the good paths of righteousness that God has foreordained that he should walk in (Ephesians 2:8-10). The pure word of God is likened to unleavened bread. As bread, the word of God is spiritual food. Jesus made this clear:

"But He answered and said, It is written, Man shall not live by bread alone, but by every word that proceedeth out of the mouth of God." Matthew 4:4

The feast of Unleavened Bread therefore reinforces the unassailable truth that spiritual growth and strength cannot be attained without the Word, even Jesus. Through prayer and meditation and fidelity to God's Word, the indwelling Holy Spirit enacts a life changing process in the believer that brings him into a victorious life of true holiness.

## 3. FIRSTFRUITS

Firstfruits are the first and best part of an entire harvest. The Lord instructed the people of Israel to bring to Him, once they possessed the promised land, the firstfruits of their harvest.

"And the Lord spake unto Moses, saying, Speak unto the children of Israel, and say to them, When ye be come into the land which I give unto you, and shall reap the harvest thereof, then ye shall bring a sheaf of the firstfruits of your harvest unto the priest: And he shall wave the sheaf before the Lord, to be accepted for you: on the morrow after the sabbath the priest shall wave it." Leviticus 23:9-11

Notice that God's instruction was for the people to present the firstfruits to the priest. In other words, they could not go into God's presence themselves, but had to channel their offerings through the priest, and the priest was to wave the sheaf of firstfruits before the Lord. That act was required so that the people would be accepted by God, or granted audience before the Holy God.

Having anointed leaders in the Church pray over our offerings is God's design, and He stamps His governance through the authority of spiritual leadership. The Lord accepts the offering, anoints it with His Spirit, and unlocks the unlimited flow of His provision.

This act of presenting our choicest offerings to the set leadership is an act of obedience and is vital to the supernatural release of a blessed and uninhibited increase in our harvests. It constitutes an act of faith, worship, submission and surrender to the Lord. The entire process of the feast of Firstfruits was actually a prophetic representation of Jesus who has become our High Priest, the Mediator between God and man, and it is to Him that we present our offerings and our worship, and He releases the blessing on us (Hebrews 9).

The feast of Firstfruits was also a time for the people of Israel to honor God as the provider and the source of every blessing, and to acknowledge Him as the source of their total supply. It is unmistakeably God who gave them the land flowing with milk and honey, who gave them the strength to work the land, and who caused the land to yield its harvest.

Observing the Firstfruits also sets in motion, the law of giving to God, characterized by the continual, uncontrollable flow of His blessings and power to prosper His people. God brings to His people, freedom and Jubilee as He meets their needs with abundant provision. As He urged:

"Honour the Lord with thy substance, and with the firstfruits of all thine increase: So shall thy barns be filled with plenty, and thy presses shall burst out with new wine." Proverbs 3:9-10

These firstfruits also showcase the pre-eminence of God, and demonstrate to His people that He comes first in all things, and must be accorded first place in their lives. He is the first and the last, Alpha and Omega. No one or nothing comes before Him or after Him.

God is honoured by His people when they put Him first and recognize that every good and perfect gift comes down from Him. Bringing their offering of firstfruits is an act of faith, and He empowers them and sets them up to succeed. He fills their barns with plenty, and causes their vine presses to profusely overflow with new wine. In other words, God releases to them, a consistent supply of bounty during their harvest season.

New wine refers to the freshness of the move of the Holy Spirit, and the message there is that, the people who put God first in everything would never lack the fresh oil of the Spirit, and the vitality and power to get wealth (Deuteronomy 8:18). May we develop the habit of putting God first in our giving whenever we receive a harvest, an income, or any increase from Him.

The firstfruits offering was also an acknowledgment that God Almighty is the Lord of the Harvest (Luke 10:2). It was symbolic and representative of the entire harvest and all that harvest represents to man. Once the firstfruits were offered to God, it meant that the remainder of the harvest was also consecrated by, and dedicated to, God, and His blessing would thus come upon the entire produce.

It was also symbolic of the fact that the people of God were to be fruitful in every aspect of their existence and in every good work (Colossians 1:10). Furthermore, it spoke of the spiritual harvest, the harvest of souls that was to come to the entire world (Matthew 9:37-38).

The focal point of the feast of Firstfruits is that it was prophetically pointing to Jesus, the Son of God, who took on human form and came to earth as a sacrifice offered by the Father God (Philippians 2:6-8). That feast was fulfilled in Him. There are inexhaustible "firsts" in Jesus, amongst which are the following:

- He was the firstfruits in the merger of divinity/deity and humanity. He, as the Word/God, became flesh, so that man could be reconciled to God. (John 1:1,14). The apostle Paul explains:

"Forasmuch then as the children are partakers of flesh and blood, he also himself likewise took part of the same; that through death he might destroy him that had the power of death, that is the devil; And deliver them who through fear of death were all their lifetime subject to bondage. For verily he took not on him the nature of angels; but he took on him the seed of Abraham." Hebrews 2:14-16

- Jesus is the exact living image or representation of the invisible God. He boldly declared that anyone who has seen Him has seen the Father (John 14:9). The fullness of the Godhead dwells bodily in Him.

- He is the firstborn of all creation. He existed, and is, before all things, and by Him all things consist or hold together (Colossians 1:15-17).

- Jesus also laid down His life by His death on the cross to become a ransom for all who believe. He made peace through the blood of His cross.

- Jesus was the first to conquer death and to rise from the dead. Through His resurrection from the dead, and he became the firstfruits of those who would rise from the dead.

"If in this life only we have hope in Christ, we are of all men most miserable. But now is Christ risen from the dead, and become the firstfruits of them that slept. For since by man came death, by man came also the resurrection of the dead. For as in Adam all die, even so also in Christ shall all be made alive." 1 Corinthians 15:19-22

"And he is the head of the body, the church: who is the beginning, the firstborn from the dead; that in all things He might have the preeminence." Colossians 1:18

- Jesus is eternally the head, the life-source and the leader, of His body, the Church (Colossians 1:18).

- Jesus is our High Priest in the order of Melchizedek, and He offered Himself as a sacrifice once and for all to God, on our behalf (Hebrews 7:22-27, Hebrews 9).

In essence, Jesus is the fulfillment of the feast of Firstfruits. The reality of the human state desperately required His advent into the world and His intervention in the affairs of man. Through sin, man was enslaved and made a prisoner of the devil. Sin transmitted spiritual eternal death to man as the wages of sin is death.

Jesus paid the price of death by dying for the world. He declared that He had power to lay down His life and the power to lift it up again, and surely, He did just that. He laid down His life, rose, and is the first begotten from the dead (John 20:17, Matthew 27:52-53).

Jesus' resurrection signifies that the dead in Christ shall also rise at the sound of the trumpet at the rapture, because He made the way for their resurrection by breaking the power of the devil and the sting of sin and death, and being the first to rise in newness of life without sin (1Thessalonians 4:15-18, 1Corinthians 15:51-58, Romans 6:1-4).

Through His resurrection, therefore, He became the firstfruits from the dead, and He brought that same comprehensive victory-jubilee in every aspect of life to all those who were subject to the bondage of death and who believed.

And then He sent the Holy Spirit, releasing the outpouring of the new wine, the fresh move of the Spirit, and the outburst of the greater glory of God upon His people.

Jesus Messiah, the firstfruits, is the author of salvation, and salvation comes to every person who believes, confesses, proclaims and affirms His death and resurrection (Romans 10:8-10). He is the Lord of the Harvest, and the harvest of souls is His heartbeat for humanity.

## 4. THE FEAST OF PENTECOST

On the instructions of God, the feast of Pentecost was to be celebrated on the sixth day of the Hebrew month of Sivan, the third month, during the wheat harvest. This would place the celebration between May to June on the secular calendar. Pentecost was observed fifty days after the feast of Firstfruits, and the people of Israel were to bring a thanksgiving offering of two loaves of bread made of fine flour and baked with leaven.

"And ye shall count unto you from the morrow after the sabbath, from the day that ye brought the sheaf of the wave offering; seven sabbaths shall be complete: Even unto the morrow after the seventh sabbath shall ye number fifty days; and ye shall offer a new meat offering unto the LORD. Ye shall bring out of your habitations two wave loaves of two tenth deals; they shall be of fine flour; they shall be baken with leaven; they are the firstfruits unto the LORD. And ye shall offer with the bread seven lambs without blemish of the first year, and one young bullock, and two rams: they shall be for a burnt offering unto the LORD, with their meat offering, and their drink offerings, even an offering made by fire, of sweet savour unto the LORD. Then ye shall sacrifice one kid of the goats for a sin offering, and two lambs of the first year for a sacrifice of peace offerings. And the priest shall wave them with the bread of the firstfruits for a wave offering before the LORD, with the two lambs: they shall be holy to the LORD for the priest. And ye shall proclaim on the selfsame day, that it may be an holy convocation unto you: ye shall do no servile work therein: it shall be a statute for ever in all your dwellings throughout your generations." Leviticus 23:15-21

The two loaves of leaven bread represented the limitations of human strength, and illustrated and acknowledged that God was to be totally depended on for the harvest. Although man is equipped with the ability to work hard, prepare the land, and plant the seeds, only God can bring the growth and create the harvest. Consequently, He deserves to be worshipped, honored and glorified with thank offerings from the harvest.

The thanksgiving offerings showed the submission of Israel to God, and their faith and reliance on Him to supply them with the harvest. Worshipping God with our offerings is thus paramount in our relationship with Him.

The two wave loaves also embedded a profound prophetic declaration of how two streams of humanity would be integrated and engrafted into "one new man." They pointed to the future access to, and outpouring of, the Holy Spirit without discrimination on both Jews and Gentiles. Speaking about the ultimate convergence in His mission to the world, Jesus Himself declared:

"As the Father knoweth me, even so know I the Father: and I lay down my life for the sheep. And other sheep I have, which are not of this fold: them also I must bring, and they shall hear my voice; and there shall be one fold, and one shepherd." John 10:15-16

The apostle Paul further explained about Jesus:

"For He is our peace, who hath made both one, and hath broken down the middle wall of partition between us; Having abolished in His flesh the enmity, even the law of commandments contained in ordinances; for to make in himself of twain one new man, so making peace; And that He might reconcile both unto God in one body by the cross, having slain the enmity thereby: And came and preached peace to you which were afar off, and to them that were nigh. For through him we both have access by one Spirit unto the Father." Ephesians 2:14-18

The prophet Joel declared that the Lord would pour out His Spirit on all flesh in the last days, irrespective of race, color, ethnic group or gender (Joel 2:28-29). How awesome is our God! The two loaves of bread at Pentecost also signified two major and momentous events in history, namely, the giving of the Law and the advent of the Holy Spirit.

Some Jewish Scholars are adherents to the traditional belief that God gave the Torah (the Law) to Moses on Mount Sinai at the time of the feast of Pentecost. Moses and the people of Israel arrived at their camp destination on the third day of Sivan, and three days later, on the sixth day of Sivan, God came down on Mount Sinai and gave the Law to Moses (Exodus 19:1-11).

Contrary to popular belief, then, the first Pentecost did not take place in Zion in Jerusalem after the death and ascension of Jesus, but on Mount Sinai. The first Pentecost was characterized and accompanied by the giving of Law, the Word of the living God, to Moses.

That event was altogether glorious. The Scriptures record a terrifying dramatic, but majestic, occurrence during this process of Jehovah bringing His Word to His people. It was a fearful but holy experience which would forever be inscribed in the memory of Israel.

"And it came to pass on the third day in the morning, that there were thunders and lightnings, and a thick cloud upon the mount, and the voice of the trumpet exceeding loud; so that all the people that was in the camp trembled. And Moses brought forth the people out of the camp to meet with God; and they stood at the nether part of the mount. And mount Sinai was altogether on a smoke, because the Lord descended upon it in fire: and the smoke thereof ascended as the smoke of a furnace, and the whole mount quaked greatly. And when the voice of the trumpet sounded long, and waxed louder and louder, Moses spake, and God answered him by a voice." Exodus 19:16-19

God brought His Word to His people in the manifestation of His glory in thunders, fire and smoke. The awe, power and majesty of this encounter with His people in the delivery of the Law contained a clear message from God – that He is in His Law (the Word), that His Word is who He is, and that the Word is of utmost importance.

God's glory, fire and presence indwelt His voice which declared, communicated or gave His Word and His Law. His Word is holy and sacred, and inherent in it is His eternal power. It is forever settled in the heavens. God will not compromise his Law, and His Word must be approached with reverential fear and awe!

The feast of Pentecost is, in effect, Israel's embrace of God's holy Law and commandments. It demonstrates Israel's submission to the Law which is the "schoolmaster" that instills discipline and provides oversight, and that throws light on their paths, guiding and leading them to the Messiah. The Jews celebrated this occasion during the diaspora as a memorial to the giving of the Law.

The resurgence of the experience of Pentecost in the New Testament unfolds an event just as awesome and inspiring as the first Pentecost, and the narrative relays the descent of the Holy Spirit, which was in fulfilment of the promise made by Jesus that He would send another Comforter after His ascension into heaven.

"And when the day of Pentecost was fully come, they were all with one accord in one place. And suddenly there came a sound from heaven as of a mighty rushing wind, and it filled all the house where they were sitting. And there appeared unto them cloven tongues like as of fire, and it sat on each of them. And they were all filled with the Holy Ghost, and began to speak with other tongues, as the Spirit gave them utterance." Acts 2:1-4

This outpouring of the Holy Spirit, which was prophesied by Samuel, Isaiah, Joel and all the prophets. and affirmed by Jesus Messiah, took place on the day of Pentecost. It was another eventful, dramatic and glorious manifestation of the power and majesty of the Holy God.

The occasion was characterized by the sound of a mighty rushing wind, the descent of tongues as of fire on the disciples, and the supernatural enablement to speak in different languages they had not learned.

The Pentecost experience speaks to the fact that the Holy Spirit has arrived, and it is He who equips, empowers, and enables God's people to worship Him in purity, holiness and righteousness, to declare, under the anointing of the Spirit, the gospel to all nations, and to demonstrate the power of God in miracles, signs, wonders and gifts of the Spirit (Luke 24:49, John 14:1-21, Acts 1:1-10, Hebrews 2:1-4, Romans 15:19-20, Acts 2:1-8).

The Pentecost experience also signifies the empowerment of God's people to overcome bondage to sin, Satan and the powers of darkness, and their induction into the liberty and freedom of God, for God is that Spirit, and where the Spirit of the Lord is, there is liberty (2 Corinthians 3:17).

The amazing reality is that, with the advent of the Holy Spirit, the feast of Pentecost has become a relevant, every day affair in the heart and life of the New Testament believer, and this Holy Ghost baptism is available to both Jew and Gentile and to them that are afar off (Acts 2, Acts 10).

And the wonderful news is that, in every conception and expression of the Pentecost in the Old and New Testament, we see Jesus Christ revealed. In the Old Testament, He was the "Voice of the Lord" that came walking in the Garden of Eden. He was the living Word given to Moses in the form of the Law on Mount Sinai, with the manifestations of Holy Ghost power in the thundering, smoke and fire, and the shaking of the mountain and earth.

The Voice of God, bringing forth His Word, was so petrifying, and it resounded exponentially and with such great force that it impacted nature and the elements. This is emblematic of how the Spirit of God anoints the Word of God, creating supernatural waves, and manifesting the wonder of God's glorious majesty.

Jesus was, and is, that Word, and He was anointed with the Holy Ghost and with power (dunamis, explosive power) during His ministry on earth. Under that anointing, He went about doing good and healing all who were oppressed of the devil, for God was with him (John 1:1, Acts 10:38). Jesus declared that the Spirit of the Lord was upon Him to preach the good news to humanity, to heal the broken-hearted, to preach deliverance to the captives, to bring recovery of sight to the blind, to bring liberty to the oppressed, and to proclaim the Jubilee, the acceptable year of the Lord (Luke 4:18-21, Isaiah 61:1).

In the New Testament, He baptized the saints with the Holy Spirit, the Comforter. There was a sound from heaven as of a rushing mighty wind, which filled the Upper Room, and cloves as of fire settled upon all those gathered there, and they were filled with the Holy Ghost. They began to speak with other tongues as the Spirit gave them utterance.

Pentecost was celebrated fifty days after the feast of Firstfruits. The number fifty speaks to freedom, liberty and Jubilee. The feast of Pentecost was thus a prelude to the eternal emancipation that Jehovah was to bring to His people, both Jew and Gentile, who would confess and believe in Jesus Messiah.

# Chapter 7

## JESUS OUR JUBILEE – UNVEILED IN THE FALL FEASTS OF ISRAEL

This Chapter discusses three main fall feasts of Israel, as well as some of the minor feasts. The fall feasts paint the portrait of God's end-time agenda and the consummation of His plans for His people, all converging in the revelation of Jesus, the Messiah. The fall feasts are:

- The Feast of Trumpets
- The Feast of Atonement
- The Feast of Tabernacles
- Other Feasts of Israel (Purim, Hannukah)

### 1. THE FEAST OF TRUMPETS

The Feast of Trumpets fell on the first day of the seventh and last month of the Jewish religious calendar, the month of Tishri. The month of Tishri also happens to be the first month on the Jewish civil calendar.

The people of Israel welcomed the birth of each new month with the blowing of trumpets. However, more trumpets were blown and sustained for longer periods at the feast of Trumpets.

"And the LORD spake unto Moses, saying, Speak unto the children of Israel, saying, In the seventh month, in the first day of the month, shall ye have a sabbath, a memorial of blowing of trumpets, an holy convocation. Ye shall do no servile work therein: but ye shall offer an offering made by fire unto the LORD." Leviticus 23:23-25

The blowing of the trumpets did not only hail the advent of the new month and the new year, but also announced the Day of Atonement, which fell on the tenth day of the same month.

The type of trumpet that was blown is significant. It was the shofar, the ram's horn. This horn was used during the feast of Trumpets as a memorial to the faith that Abraham, the father of the nation of Israel, exhibited or displayed in his obedience to God's call to sacrifice his only son, Isaac.

Although inconceivable and even morally reprehensible to some that God would ask him to offer Isaac as a sacrifice, Abraham did not waver, second-guess or rationalize God's instruction; he was poised to do exactly what God required of him. He was persuaded by the promise God had made to him, and firmly believed that, even if Isaac died, God would raise him from the dead. His obedience and faith moved the hand of God to save Isaac and to provide a ram for the sacrifice.

"And Abraham lifted up his eyes, and looked, and behold behind him a ram caught in a thicket by his horns: and Abraham went and took the ram, and offered him up for a burnt offering in the stead of his son. And Abraham called the name of that place Jehovahjireh: as it is said to this day, In the mount of the LORD it shall be seen." Genesis 22:13-14

God provided a ram for the sacrifice miraculously. This reinforces the faithfulness of God and His supernatural provision in the lives of His people. He revealed himself to Abraham as Jehovah Jireh, the Lord our Provider. The feast of Trumpets is therefore a unique season where Jehovah reminds His people that He is their provider, and He moves to provide for them in supernatural ways.

God has not lowered His standards regarding faith for miracles in contemporary times. All things are possible to Him, and also to them that believe. He wants us to trust fully in Him. We can reach out to Him in boldness and with confidence and make our requests or petitions known to Him. He is faithful to honour His promises and to meet our needs exceedingly and abundantly above all that we ask or think (Ephesians 3:20).

The horn of the ram (the shofar or trumpet) represents strength, dominion and power, and the sound of the shofar, the ram's horn, is symbolic of the sound of the voice of the God of all might and all power. It represents the potency and supremacy of God's voice and His Word. During the blowing of Trumpets, Jehovah visits His people and demonstrates His glorious power.

The feast of Trumpets also serves as a prophetic image of how God would, in the fullness of time, provide Jesus, His only begotten Son, Jesus, as the lamb of God who would take away the sin of the world and bring salvation and righteousness to all (John 1:29). Abraham's faith immensely touched the heart of God, and it was credited or imputed to him as righteousness, giving him right standing with God (Romans 4:1-5). This relayed the message that, in time, those of like faith, whether Jew or Gentile, would also receive God's gift of righteousness by faith in Christ Jesus.

Moreover, this feast is a call-out, a shout, or an invitation to all to seek Jehovah; they would be saved, redeemed and set free from the captivity of the devil. Provision is made for the stranger in this monumental event (Leviticus 23:22). This symbolizes the embrace and engrafting of the Gentile world, the Christian Church, into the blessings and covenants of the Most High God.

Abraham's experience also established the incontrovertible truth that salvation has always been, is, and will forever be, the initiative of God. It is not dependent on man's actions, ability, or efforts to reach God in his own strength or self-directed endeavours. Rather, salvation originates with God, and the provision of His own sacrificial lamb, Jesus, to atone for sin and to provide redemption to the world, is entirely His idea.

Jesus is the feast of Trumpets personified. He is the horn of our salvation, the voice proclaiming our salvation, and the Saviour who rescues the world from sin and eternal damnation. He fulfilled the feast of Trumpets by coming to proclaim good news, and to deliver the world from the power of darkness and to translate us into the kingdom of God (Colossians 1:13). Jesus, as the Warrior King, defeated Satan and his cohorts, broke their dominion over humanity, and gave the victory to His Church (Colossians 2:15). He raised the Church as His army to engage in spiritual warfare to enforce the triumphs and victories of Christ (2 Corinthians 10:1-5).

Jesus is still blowing the Trumpet of Jubilee through the proclamation of the gospel, and all who hear it and respond in faith shall be saved and delivered. He fulfils the Jubilee by bringing freedom and liberty from enemy spirits, and healing for all who are oppressed of the devil. He also brings rest to His people and supplies their needs in inexplicable ways according to His riches in glory (Philippians 4:19).

## 2. THE FEAST OF ATONEMENT

The feast of Atonement began on the tenth day of the month of Tishri, the seventh month on the Hebrew calendar, and was observed for ten days. This period is also referred to as "Awesome Days" or "Days of Awe", or a time of repentance (Leviticus 23:26-32).

Atonement means to make amends or to make right what has been wrongfully done, a requital, or the reparation or expiation of sin through repentance. Conversely, it is also a time of judgement for the unrepented who have not been justified.

The feast of Atonement was the period when the people of God would express repentance for their sin by afflicting their souls, and when they sought to reconcile with God. The feast commenced on the Day of Atonement, which is the most holy day of the year.

On that day, all of Israel would come before the Lord God in repentance and godly sorrow, in consecrated fasting and repentant prayers, and they would confess their sins and shortcomings. They would humble themselves before the Most Holy, and would petition Him to forgive their sins, save them, deliver them from every evil, and heal their land.

Jehovah, the Most Holy God, is of such pure eyes that He cannot behold iniquity. He cannot look on sin, neither can He be reconciled with it. Thus, His way, His requirement, and His demand has always been that repentance, atonement and expiation should precede salvation, reconciliation, intervention, healing and deliverance. Consequently, any person seeking to reach God to be blessed and touched by Him must approach Him with humility, a surrendered heart, a submitted will, and a broken and contrite spirit, and must confess every sin, laying them bare before the Holy One.

"If my people, which are called by my name, shall humble themselves, and pray, and seek my face, and turn from their wicked ways; then will I hear from heaven, and will forgive their sin, and will heal their land." 2 Chronicles 7:14

Furthermore, for God to visit His people to bring liberty or freedom to them, there must, of necessity, be the shedding of blood to atone for, pacify, and administer expiation for, the sins of the people.

"And almost all things are by the law purged with blood; and without shedding of blood is no remission." Hebrews 9:22

On that basis, the people of Israel were required to bring their sacrifices and present them to the priests to make amends for their wrongs or to pacify God.

On the Day of Atonement, the High Priest laid aside his golden robes. This was very significant because it was these robes that distinguished him from the ordinary priests, who had linen robes. He washed himself with water, and then proceeded to put on linen garments, so as to be identified with, on the same level as, the other priests.

These actions of the High Priest were a clear painting of that which was to come, namely, how Jesus, the Messiah, would step out of the throne of heaven, put off His royal High Priestly garments, strip Himself of His divinity, and how He would be fashioned or made in the likeness of men. Isn't God amazing!

The High Priest offered to God, a ram as a burnt offering, and two goats for a sin offering. The fate of the goats was determined by lot. The sins of the people were confessed on one goat, which was released into the wilderness as the scapegoat. The other goat was slain; its blood was to make atonement for sin.

This, again, was a prefiguration of the substitutionary, atoning-redemptive work of Jesus on the cross. He who knew no sin, even Jesus, was made sin by God, so that we might be made the righteousness of God in Christ (2 Corinthians 5:21). In other words, He became the scapegoat, taking up our sins, and we were set free.

In adherence to the Law of God, the High Priest would then enter into the Holy of Holies in the Temple and sprinkle the blood from the animal sacrifices on the Mercy Seat to atone for, or cover, or make propitiation for, his own sins and the sins of the people, and to obtain God's forgiveness, remission of sin, grace, mercy and reconciliation with the Holy God. Notice that the Day of Atonement was the only day in the year that the High Priest went into the Holy of Holies.

Upon appeasing God in this manner, the High Priest laid aside his linen clothes, washed himself again with water, put on his High Priestly golden garments, and resumed his sacred ministry. He pronounced blessings on the people, and thus finished his work on the Day of Atonement.

In the year of Jubilee, the trumpet-shofar of Jubilee was sounded after these holy ceremonies and rituals by the High Priest. The year of Jubilee was announced on the Day of Atonement. It was imperative for that trumpet sound to be heard throughout the land. It announced and proclaimed the good news of emancipation for all. It was the joyful sound of freedom, liberation, salvation, reconciliation with the Holy God, and deliverance from servitude in any form or shape. Debts were cancelled, bond servants were sets free, farm lands were to be left fallow, and all laborious assignments came to a complete halt!

This was the time that Jehovah God, who had been pacified through the repentance of the people and the blood sacrifices of the High Priest, released an anointing, the Spirit of refreshing, renewal, rest, peace and blessings to the people.

These rituals on the Day of Atonement were repeated year after year, and the need for the regurgitation of the process signified its inherently limited efficacy as a permanent solution. The blood of the animals, although it superficially and temporarily served the purpose of interim atonement, could not, and did not, put away the sin nature within the spirit, conscience and soul of man.

That necessitated a more enduring and thorough solution, and that solution came through Jesus. God, in His predestined purpose, made provision for the forgiveness, cleansing and sanctification of all who would confess their sin before Him and turn away from sin. He foreordained, before the foundation of the earth, that Jesus would be the sacrificial lamb to be slain to atone for the sins of humanity.

The feast of Atonement, then, was actually the rehearsal of the real deal that was to be unveiled in Jesus who shed His blood and died on the cross to remove and put away the sins of all who believe. He was manifested in the fullness of time to fulfill His eternal prophetic destiny on Calvary's cross (Revelation 13:8, 1 Peter 1:20, 1 John 1:7-9).

Jesus is our eternal High Priest in the order of Melchizedek, with no beginning and no end, and He ever lives to make intercession for us. He was without sin, and did not have to make any sacrifice of animals for Himself or the people. But He himself was the sacrifice, the perfect, sinless lamb of God, who takes away the sin of the world (John 1:29).

The High Priest in Israel had to go through the motions of offering the blood of calves and goats every year. Jesus, the fulfilment of all things and the eternal High Priest, did not need to make sacrifices annually on the Day of Atonement like the earthly High Priest. He put sin away once and for all by the sacrifice of Himself (Hebrews 9:24-26, Matthew 26:26-39). Consequently, the need for the repetitive offer of animals and other sacrifices was done away with.

The Old Testament High Priest ministered in the earthly Tabernacle in Jerusalem, which stood as a shadow of the real Tabernacle in the heavenly Jerusalem (Hebrews 9:20-27; 12:22-24). Jesus perfected this. He is the High Priest who passed into the heavens, appeared in real time in the real Tabernacle before God Almighty, presented His sinless, perfect blood and sprinkled it on the Mercy Seat to atone for the sin of man, and who made expiation for the sin of the believing one.

Thus, Jesus came to execute a better and eternally efficacious blood covenant by the sacrifice of Himself. He paid the price for the redemption of the New Testament Church to establish a more perfect Tabernacle. His blood, unlike the blood of bulls and goats, did not just cover the sins of the people but provided remission, eradication, purging and the total cleansing of sins. Therefore, anyone who acknowledges his sin and confesses that before God has the assurance that God is faithful and just to forgive him and to cleanse him from all unrighteousness (Romans 5:9-11, 1John1:7-9, Leviticus 16).

Moreover, Jesus, by His own blood, eternally put away sin, and that cleared the way for God to put a new spirit within mankind and to purge their conscience from dead works, so that they could, without fear of recrimination or any form of insecurity, serve the living God.

"But Christ being come an high priest of good things to come, by a greater and more perfect tabernacle, not made with hands, that is to say, not of this building; Neither by the blood of goats and calves, but by his own blood he entered in once into the holy place, having obtained eternal redemption for us. For if the blood of bulls and of goats, and the ashes of an heifer sprinkling the unclean, sanctifieth to the purifying of the flesh: How much more shall the blood of Christ, who through the eternal Spirit offered himself without spot to God, purge your conscience from dead works to serve the living God?." Hebrews 9:11-14

As such, the blood of Jesus avails for the vilest offender who comes to God by faith, and who accepts the sacrifice of Jesus on the cross at Calvary, His shed blood to make atonement for sin, and His death and resurrection.

An amazing result of all that Jesus did was to make accessible to us who believe, the throne room of God Almighty, the real Tabernacle of heaven. Whereas, in the Old Testament days, only the High Priest could enter the Holy of Holies once a year, Jesus, the eternal High Priest, has presented to the believer a new and living way into the very presence of God. He tore the veil, and opened up the most holy place to us all. The apostle Paul tells us:

"Seeing then that we have a great high priest, that is passed into the heavens, Jesus the Son of God, let us hold fast our profession. For we have not an high priest which cannot be touched with the feeling of our infirmities; but was in all points tempted like as we are, yet without sin. Let us therefore come boldly unto the throne of grace, that we may obtain mercy, and find grace to help in time of need." Hebrews 4:14-16

We are therefore urged to boldly come into God's presence. There is fullness of joy and eternal pleasure in His presence, and we can find all that we need in the challenging times of life. We are granted access to all the privileges that the loving Father has cooked and baked for us.

The Jubilee connection to the feast of Atonement must not be overlooked. The Jubilee year actually begins on the Day of Atonement, where blood sacrifices are made, and then prisoners are set free, properties are returned, and lands are given a break from work. That communicates an important truth that the Jubilee, which is a time of rejoicing, is predicated on the eradication of sin, and is packaged as a time of rejoicing for those who have appropriated the atonement and have had their sins forgiven. The blood of the sacrifices breaks the barrier of sin between man and God, and they come into union and fellowship. Then liberty, joy and freedom can flow from God to the redeemed. Jesus shed His blood for us so we can enter the presence of the Lord and experience the liberty He has for us.

## 3. THE FEAST OF TABERNACLES

The feast of Tabernacles, also known as the feast of Ingathering or the feast of Booths, is called 'Sukkot" in Hebrew. It was a time of celebrating the final agricultural harvest, and was a time of great rejoicing. It was the last of the seven main feasts of Israel, representing the consummation of the spiritual redemptive process in the lives of the people, and was designated a time of rest for them.

"And the LORD spake unto Moses, saying, Speak unto the children of Israel, saying, The fifteenth day of this seventh month shall be the feast of tabernacles for seven days unto the LORD. On the first day shall be an holy convocation: ye shall do no servile work therein. Seven days ye shall offer an offering made by fire unto the LORD: on the eighth day shall be an holy convocation unto you; and ye shall offer an offering made by fire unto the LORD: it is a solemn assembly; and ye shall do no servile work therein. These are the feasts of the LORD, which ye shall proclaim to be holy convocations, to offer an offering made by fire unto the LORD, a burnt offering, and a meat offering, a sacrifice, and drink offerings, every thing upon his day: Beside the sabbaths of the LORD, and beside your gifts, and beside all your vows, and beside all your freewill offerings, which ye give unto the LORD. Also in the fifteenth day of the seventh month, when ye have gathered in the fruit of the land, ye shall keep a feast unto the LORD seven days: on the first day shall be a sabbath, and on the eighth day shall be a sabbath. And ye shall take you on the first day the boughs of goodly trees, branches of palm trees, and the boughs of thick trees, and willows of the brook; and ye shall rejoice before the LORD your God seven days. And ye shall keep it a feast unto the LORD seven days in the year. It shall be a statute for ever in your generations: ye shall celebrate it in the seventh month. Ye shall dwell in booths seven days; all that are Israelites born shall dwell in booths: That your generations may know that I made the children of Israel to dwell in booths, when I brought them out of the land of Egypt: I am the LORD your God. And Moses declared unto the children of Israel the feasts of the LORD." **Leviticus 23:33-44**

This feast recounts and reveals the faithfulness of God to the people of Israel in the days when they traveled through the wilderness. In those forty years, they dwelt in booths, totally dependent on the gracious God who dwelt in the midst of them. He kept and preserved them, and ministered to their every need. He was their strength, provider, protector and the lifter of their heads. He saved them from the dangers posed by enemy forces and powers.

The Israelites marked this feast by giving thank offerings to God and praying to Him for bountiful rainfall. On the seventh day of Sukkot, "Hoshanah Rabbah" or "Day of Great Hosanah", which means "save us now" or "deliver us", they would implore God to come through for them. The faithful God, Jehovah, honoured their prayer for rain, granting them a bountiful harvest, and also saving them from hunger and from their enemies.

As part of the celebration of this feast, the High Priest would go with a golden vessel to the pool of Siloam which, within the boundaries of ancient Jerusalem, was the only source of fresh water. For seven days, he would draw water from the pool. Each day, he would take the water amidst shouts of joy to the Temple, and would pour it into the basin at the altar. That act was symbolic of the wells of salvation from which people could joyfully draw living water (Isaiah 12:1-6).

On the eighth and final day of the feast, the holy convocation, this ritual of drawing and pouring water was not repeated. On that day, the priests would go round the altar in the Temple seven times, reading the Scriptures and proclaiming the salvation and prosperity of God on the people.

"Save now, I beseech thee, O Lord: O Lord, I beseech thee, send now prosperity." Psalm 118:25

The priests also read from Zechariah 12 and Ezekiel 47. The High Priest then poured out the water collected during this event on the last day of the feast.

The feast of Tabernacles was also celebrated with the blowing of trumpets, the waving of palm branches, and singing to the Lord. Torches were lighted throughout the city.

The feast of Tabernacles highlights the presence of God amongst men. He came to tabernacle with us, or to dwell amongst us. Jesus fulfilled the feast to the letter when He came down from heaven as the living Word.

"And the Word was made flesh, and dwelt among us, (and we beheld his glory, the glory as of the only begotten of the Father,) full of grace and truth." John 1:14

Jesus literally put on humanity, and pitched His tent, made His booth, and tabernacled among men, in order to minister salvation to the lost and to the sinner, bring deliverance to the oppressed, provide healing to the sick, and to preach good news to the poor.

Here are some other parallels in the feast of Tabernacles that prophetically pointed to Jesus. The people prayed for rain during the feast, and God gave them rain and a bountiful harvest. But Jesus, who was the real deal, perfected this. He brought the outpouring of the rain of the Holy Spirit, and the glorious harvest of souls.

It is also no coincidence that, on the last day of the feast, the day when the ritual of drawing water from the pool and pouring it at the altar was not performed, Jesus stood up right when the High Priest was pouring out the collected water, and made some incredulous loud proclamations:

"In the last day, that great day of the feast, Jesus stood and cried, saying, If any man thirst, let him come after me and drink. He that believeth on me, as the scripture hath said, out of his belly shall flow rivers of living water. (But this spake he of the Spirit, which they that believe on him should receive: for the Holy Ghost was not yet given; because that Jesus was not yet glorified)." John 7:37-39

Jesus certainly did not win the popularity contest by interrupting such a sacred event of the High Priest pouring out the water! In terms of eternal significance, however, He was proclaiming that those who would come to Him would freely drink of the Holy Spirit, in essence, confirming that He is the fulfillment of the Scriptures the priests read on the last day of the feast.

The Jews referred to the Temple as the navel or the belly of the earth. When the High Priest poured out the water in the basin on the last day of the feast, he was dramatizing how the Spirit would pour out of the Temple. Jesus said rivers of living water would flow out of the belly of them that believed on Him. By that proclamation, Jesus was showing that He is the Temple in living reality and in person, and in Him was the overflowing reservoir of the Holy Spirit of the living God.

For those who are thirsty and hungry for spiritual reality, and who receive Him, they also become the Temple of the Holy Spirit, and therefore, out of their innermost being shall flow rivers of living water. This signified the baptism of the Holy Spirit in the believer's life.

The last day of the feast of Tabernacles was also reckoned to be "that great day" because that was when the priests released blessings from God, and they symbolically poured out water to demonstrate the prophecy of the outpouring of the Holy Spirit in the last days.

In essence, all the prophecies read by the priests, and all the ceremonies performed, as well as the Temple and the holy things it stood for, were strong prophetic symbols, images and indicators pointing to Christ.

He is here now in person to dish out the rivers of the Holy Spirit in which the believing ones can bathe and swim in freedom, power and great glory. If anyone thirsts, if anyone is craving for more of God, if anyone wants to see more of His glory and experience more of His presence, let him seek Jesus and drink of Him. O, taste and see that the Lord is good!

Obviously, it was Jesus alone who could bring the celebration of the feast of Tabernacles to its foreordained climax, its crescendo, and its glorious peak, and that is why He stood up on that great day, the last day of the feast, and invited the people to come to Him and drink of the Spirit. He brought the rain of the outpouring of the Holy Spirit, the renewal and refreshing from God's presence, and the ushering in of the harvest of souls by the preaching of the gospel (John 7:37-39, Acts 2:1-17, Acts 2:37-41). He brought to us the rivers of the Spirit and life pouring out of the Temple in the end-time move of God.

At the feast of Tabernacles also, the people rejoiced before God, waving palm branches and boughs of trees. Fast forward many years, and we see Jesus hailed as King, and the people shouting "Hosanna: Blessed is the King of Israel that comes in the name of the Lord", essentially saying to Him, "save us now" and "deliver us" (John 12:13, Matthew 21:9).

Recall also that the people of Israel lighted torches throughout the land during the feast, symbolizing that God is light and life. Fast forward many years, and we see Jesus boldly declaring that He is the light of the world (John 8:12, John 1:4-5).

In sum, Jesus' advent into the world, His incarnation, represents God's divine act of salvation, consummated in Him being united with man, meeting the needs of humanity, and bringing to His people abundant life, a great harvest, and peace.

Correspondingly, having received so much from God, all His people are expected to step into the blessing of His rest and enjoy His presence among them. Jesus has come to give to all life, and life more abundantly, both spiritually and materially.

We are in the days of the greatest outpouring of the Spirit of God in all of history. In Jesus' life and ministry, the multitudes saw the undeniable power of God. They rejoiced and marveled at the authority and unction with which He worked the works of God. But His cry on that last day of the feast was yet another revelatory prism of prophecy about His advent into the world.

He came to announce, preach and proclaim Jubilee mercies and grace, and to demonstrate the power of the kingdom by the anointing of the Holy Spirit. But He was now showing the world that the same Spirit and anointing is available to all who believe on him. He was introducing the Holy Spirit that would be poured out onto those who would believe on Him, people who would be endued with power to continue to declare the gospel of liberty and enforce His mandate of demonstrating the Jubilee and kingdom power.

## 4. OTHER JEWISH HOLIDAYS

The Jewish holidays of Purim and Hanukkah were not part of the seven main feasts of Israel recorded in Leviticus 23. However, they are important holidays celebrated by the Jews to commemorate the great victories God wrought in their lives to preserve them and to bring honour and glory to His name.

- ### THE FEAST OF PURIM

The feast of Purim commemorates the victory God gave to the Jews in Persia through Queen Esther and Mordecai, when Haman targeted and came against them. Israel went into prayer and fasting to break the power of Haman whose desire was to see the Jews totally wiped out by King Ahasuerus. However, God gave Queen Esther great favour before the King, he reversed the destruction of the Jews and rather brought judgement on Haman (Esther 9:20-28).

This feast is celebrated between February and March. "Pur" means to cast lots. It is a great time of joy, and it is characterized by the exchange of gifts. Non-Jews are invited to participate in this feast, a representation of how both Jew and Gentile would access the good things of God.

Esther is a type of the New Testament Church, redeemed by the blood of the lamb, glorious, majestic and beautiful, and clothed with the jubilee-favor which Jesus came to proclaim. Jesus assured the Church that He would build it, and the gates of hell would never prevail against it. God contends with those who contend with His people. He destroys them, and gives great victories to His people, His chosen and His anointed.

- ## THE FEAST OF HANUKKAH

Hanukkah is one of the special Jewish holidays. It is also referred to as the "Feast of Lights" or the "Feast of Dedication", and it is observed during the month of December. This celebration was not part of the original feasts of Israel, but was rather a period of celebration praising the God of Heaven for the great victory he gave the Jews over Antiochus Epiphanes in 164 B.C.

During the second century B.C., the Greeks conquered many nations, including the Jews, and their worldview and agenda was to impose their language, culture and religion upon all their subjects. The Greeks worshipped idols, and in consonance with their political strategy and religious ideology, their subjects were expected to do the same.

Antiochus sent his army to the Temple in Jerusalem, and they desecrated the altar by sacrificing a pig on it and pouring its blood on the Torah, the Jewish holy book. He mounted the statue of Zeus, the Greek god, in the Temple.

A small number of Jews under the leadership of Mattathias, named the Maccabees, boldly refused to offer sacrifices to the Greek idols. Mattathias killed an officer of Antiochus, as well as a Jew who wanted to do obeisance to the idol.

Mattathias died shortly thereafter, but his son, Judah Maccabee, and his brothers picked up the fight. Although, in the natural, they were no match for the Greek army, they successfully led a revolt, defeated the Greeks, and gained their religious freedom. Once free, the Jews went into the Temple, broke down the statue of Zeus, consecrated the Temple, and rededicated it to the worship of Almighty God.

Just as the defeat of Antiochus by a handful of Jews was a miracle, so was the rededication of the Temple. There was only one bottle of oil available to light the candles in the Temple for one day. Supernaturally and inexplicably, the oil lasted for eight days until new oil could be made according to the religious instructions. This period became known as the feast of Dedication, the festival of Lights, or Hanukkah.

It appears that Jesus, when He was on the earth, participated in the feast of Dedication. The apostle John records:

"And it was at Jerusalem the feast of the dedication, and it was winter. And Jesus walked in the temple in Solomon's porch." John 10:22-23

Jesus was obviously in the Temple during this feast of Lights and Dedication. More importantly, though, He was, and is, the fulfilment and reality of this feast.

Like the Jews in the time of Antiochus, humanity was sold out to the devil and to his kingdom of darkness, and was in desperate need of God's deliverance. Jesus is that invisible power that wrought the resounding victory over Satan and his squadrons when it was humanly impossible. He made a public show of them, triumphing over them in the grave and delivering His people from the clutches of hell, for He is the God to whom all things are possible.

Jesus is also that holy altar that was ravaged, desecrated and violated. All of our uncleanness, filth, sin and ungodliness was laid on Him. He became sin, who knew no sin, that we might become His righteousness, consecrated and rededicated to Him.

He is the oil, the anointing, the Spirit that miraculously kept the lights going when, by any metric of measurement, they should have been extinguished. He is also the light. He came into the world as the true light, not only as the light that shines in the Temple in Jerusalem, but as the light in the hearts of all men who acknowledge Him as Lord and Saviour, the Messiah, the Daystar. He is the light that dispels darkness and brings illumination, the light that destroys sin and the power of darkness, and the light that redeems humanity from bondage and translates them into the glorious jubilee and liberty of God's presence.

Praise God for His wonders! As you imbibe the truth of this message, may your life never lack the power of God and the oil of the Spirit, and may the light of Christ shine in your heart and upon your path as He leads you from grace to grace, and from victory to victory.

# Chapter 8

## JESUS OUR JUBILEE – UNVEILED IN THE SEVEN REDEMPTIVE NAMES OF GOD

What is in name? This is a question that many have asked through time. Well, to mention a few, a name identifies a person. It also describes the person and, over time, may acquire, or become associated with, a range of qualities. A name exudes and releases the authority of a person. A name carries the weight of a person's reputation and accomplishments. A name also dictates, or may impinge on, how others will relate to the bearer of the name. The better a person is known, the more he can be trusted.

To an even more magnified level, to an even greater extent, all of these are true of the various names of God. He identified Himself to Moses as "I am that I am", attesting to His everlasting and all-powerful existence. What only His name will do is also simply amazing, pointing to His exclusivity as Savior.

"Neither is there salvation in any other: for there is none other name under heaven given among men, whereby we must be saved." Acts 4:12

"The name of the LORD is a strong tower: the righteous runneth into it, and is safe." Proverbs 18:10

The Lord's name is filled with all authority, power, dignity, and accreditation, and extols His reputation and accomplishments.

"Wherefore God also hath highly exalted him, and given him a name which is above every name: That at the name of Jesus every knee should bow, of things in heaven, and things in earth, and things under the earth; And that every tongue should confess that Jesus Christ is Lord, to the glory of God the Father." Philippians 2:9-11

The Lord's name is altogether trustworthy, faithful, reliable and dependable, and opens manifold treasures to the believing one.

"And they that know thy name will put their trust in thee: for thou, LORD, hast not forsaken them that seek thee." Psalm 9:10

"And whatsoever ye shall ask in my name, that will I do, that the Father may be glorified in the Son. If ye shall ask any thing in my name, I will do it." John 14:13-14

This brings us to the crux of the matter – that Jubilee is all in a name. The whole Jubilee package of salvation, freedom and deliverance is assured in only one name, the name of Jesus. Jesus is our Jubilee. He came to fulfill the Father's predestined and foreordained Jubilee agenda, and it is He who opens us up to the eternal supplies of the Jubilee so we can walk and enforce the full benefits, rights and privileges of our redemption and the freedoms that the Father has enacted, designed, and paved for us through the Son.

As will be seen in the next few Chapters, Jesus was revealed as the Jubilee, not only in the Sabbaths and the feasts of Israel; He was also communicated as such through His dealings with key personalities in the Old Testament and the redemptive names that He revealed to them.

At every step of the life experiences of the people of Israel, through the prisms of life, they saw a facet of God, even Jesus, and His attributes and character. Clearly, then, a major channel He used to articulate and bring those Jubilee packages to His people was through His redemptive names.

There are seven major redemptive names of Jehovah revealed in the Old Testament to the people of Israel in diverse times. They present the perfect line of action mapped out by Jehovah God to bring the benefits and blessings of salvation to humankind through Jesus Christ, and spoke prophetically about His place in eternity as our Jubilee.

Salvation through Jesus releases seven major streams of experiential power in the redemptive process of man, and these are unveiled in the seven key redemptive names of Jehovah, which are:

- Jehovah Tsidkenu
- Jehovah Nissi
- Jehovah Shalom
- Jehovah Shammah
- Jehovah Rapha
- Jehovah Rohi / Jehovah Raah
- Jehovah Jireh

In the next few Chapters, we explore the names of God and how they intersect with and impact the Jubilee experience of God's people. We can join the Psalmist to say:

"O Lord, our Lord, how excellent is thy name in all the earth! who hast set thy glory above the heavens." Psalm 8:1

# Chapter 9

## JEHOVAH TSIDKENU – THE LORD OUR RIGHTEOUSNESS

When Moses asked God to show him His presence, God said He would proclaim His name to him. This shows how important God's names are to Him and to us:

"And he said, I will make all my goodness pass before thee, and I will proclaim the name of the LORD before thee." Exodus 33:19

"And the LORD descended in the cloud, and stood with him there, and proclaimed the name of the Lord. And the Lord passed by before him, and proclaimed, The Lord, The Lord God, merciful and gracious, longsuffering, and abundant in goodness and truth, Keeping mercy for thousands, forgiving iniquity and transgression and sin, and that will by no means clear the guilty; visiting the iniquity of the fathers upon the children, and upon the children's children, unto the third and to the fourth generation." Exodus 34:5-7

Jehovah is a righteous God, and righteousness is His nature and character. He is pristine, and He is pure and holy, and it is inherently impossible and inconceivable for Him to entertain, or function and operate within the context of, sin and unrighteousness. Neither can He clear the guilty because He is a just God.

God is also a God of covenant. Thus, for Him to commune or fellowship with humanity on the level of a covenant relationship, He had to bring mankind to the place of righteousness. The sin nature of man could not be overlooked; it had to be dealt with, and totally eradicated.

In His infinite and eternal love for the world, God made every provision available to rescue mankind from judgement. He did not hold back; He fully delivered, giving up His only begotten Son Jesus to pay the price of sin and to cleanse humanity from all unrighteousness.

Speaking prophetically about whom God would raise to bring judgement, justice and salvation to Israel, Jeremiah introduced Him as "The Lord our Righteousness."

"Behold, the days come, saith the Lord, that I will raise unto David a righteous Branch, and a King shall reign and prosper, and shall execute judgment and justice in the earth. In his days Judah shall be saved, and Israel shall dwell safely: and this is his name whereby he shall be called, THE LORD OUR RIGHTEOUSNESS." Jeremiah 23:5-6

This was pointing to Jesus, the Son of David, who is the righteous Branch that God raised up in the line of David, the King.

Jesus is the Lord our Righteousness. He is the exact picture, the explicit image, of the invisible God. He possesses the nature and characteristics of God. He is in the form of God and equal with God (Philippians 2:5-8). He declared that anyone who has seen Him has seen the Father. (John 14:9). He is the embodiment and personification of the righteousness of God.

He is Jehovah Tsidkenu because it is He that broke the power of sin and all its effects through the blood of His cross. Although He knew no sin, God made Him to be sin in order that all who believe might be made the righteousness of God in Christ (2 Corinthians 5:21).

Being made sin, Jesus offered Himself as the sacrificial lamb of God. Out of sheer love for us, He shed His blood to pay the price for the sin of humanity, and to flush out, eradicate, remove, wash, and put sin away (Revelation 1:5).

"For then must he often have suffered since the foundation of the world: but now once in the end of the world hath he appeared to put away sin by the sacrifice of himself." Hebrews 9:26

Through His sacrifice, we have received the atonement for sin (Romans 5:11). He also shed His blood for the remission of our sins (Mathew 26:28). Jesus thereby settled the age-old problem of sin, establishing irrefutably that He is the King that has dominion over sin, death, hell and the grave, and who rules over Satan and all his cohorts.

This is the result - the blood of Jesus washes and cleanses us from all unrighteousness, and through that, we are made righteous (1 John 1:7-9). Jesus imparts righteousness to all who believe.

Ordinarily, our righteous acts are like filthy rags before the righteous God. However, salvation in the name of Jesus alone is that which restores righteousness to man, and that reveals Jehovah Tsidkenu at work. Righteousness is the attribute of God that is imparted to the one who believes and receives the sacrifice of Jesus.

Righteousness does some key things in the life of a believer. It brings him into full fellowship and communion with Jehovah, and grants him right standing with God, free of condemnation, guilt, or any sense of inferiority. The righteous one also has unlimited and unrestricted access into God's presence. He is authorized to boldly enter the throne of grace to obtain mercy and find grace to help in time of need (Hebrews 4:16).

Righteousness through Christ Jesus also reinstates man to his kingly authority, reign and regime in this life which was lost through Adam's sin.

"For if by one man's offence death reigned by one; much more they which receive abundance of grace and the gift of righteousness shall reign in life by one, Jesus Christ." Romans 5:17

The impartation of righteousness, then, brings man back to the place of rulership, dominion and authority over all things (physical and spiritual) that God originally endowed him with; all things God made are brought back into subjection before man through Christ Jesus (Genesis 1:26-28, Psalm 8, Hebrews 2:5-15, Luke 10:17-19). Through righteousness, therefore, man has regained rule over creation and its elements, and he now has authority over sin, Satan, demons, sicknesses, diseases, poverty and premature death as well.

Jesus has done it all. The Lord our Righteousness. The demands of justice in the eternal courts of heaven have been met by Him on the behalf of the New Creation, and therefore, the New Creation has freely received God's righteousness.

In terms of positioning, therefore, the New Creation shares in the heavenly authority. He is made to sit together with Christ on the right-hand side of God the Father in heavenly places, far above every principality and power, throne or dominion (Ephesians 2:5-6). In terms of eternity, righteousness has worked out the future for the New Creation - he shall forever be with God (1 Corinthians 15).

The righteous one, using the name of Jesus, can access all the rights and privileges embedded in the redemption package - salvation, deliverance, protection and every spiritual blessing in heavenly places in Christ Jesus (Ephesians 1:3).

This is the liberating Jubilee message of the gospel – that the purification process is here. Sinners become righteous through Christ, and are free from the chains, fetters and horrors of sin. The Lord our Righteousness, Jehovah Tsidkenu, enforces the gains of Jubilee to humanity by setting them on a pedestal as a royal priesthood, a chosen generation, a peculiar people, a company of people who show forth God's praises, and who are thrust into the royal monarchy of God's kingdom (1 Peter 2:9).

# Chapter 10

## JEHOVAH NISSI – THE LORD OUR VICTORY / BANNER

Jehovah Nissi means "The Lord our Victory" or "The Lord our Banner." This name shows us the warrior side of God. Our God is the God of war, and His name is associated with warfare.

"The LORD is a man of war: the LORD is his name." Exodus 15:3

This aspect of God is potently evident in His relationship with humanity. God is in a covenant relationship with His people. Thus, the enemies of God's people are the enemies of God. This means that, if anyone or anything provokes God's people into battle or adversity, they would have to deal with Jehovah Nissi.

He said to Abraham, His covenant friend: "I will bless those who bless you and curse those who curse you" (Genesis 12:3). The Lord goes to war on the behalf of His people and fights their battles. He takes down their enemies and subdues them under their feet. This is the assurance that eternally rings:

"…Be not afraid nor dismayed by reason of this great multitude; for the battle is not yours, but God's." 2 Chronicles 20:15b

God, who owns and fights the battle, cannot fail and cannot be defeated, and so His people cannot fail or be defeated either. His name is a strong tower; the righteous runs into it and is safe (Proverbs 18:10). He revealed Himself to Joshua, the son of Nun, as the Captain of the Hosts, unconquerable and ever present to fight for His people (Joshua 5:13-15).

There is also an unchanging, written verdict against any struggle, pain, affliction, battle of any sort or kind that the people of God may face, even before they manifest. That verdict is VICTORY, given through none other than Jehovah Nissi, the Lord our Victory. It is impossible for God to lose any battle, and correspondingly, it is impossible for the devil to win any battle because he is an eternally defeated foe.

"The LORD shall go forth as a mighty man, he shall stir up jealousy as a man of war: he shall cry, yea, roar; he shall prevail against his enemies." Isaiah 42:13

Victory is written, decreed, designed and packaged for the child of God in the predestined purposes of God, inscribed in the mind of eternity even before the conception or start of any warfare.

In life, many resort to their own strengths, abilities, skills, intelligence, resources, endowments, and wisdom to navigate the pathways of life. There is a place for all that. However, when that reliance on oneself fails to acknowledge God as the source of life and every good thing, and where that self-confidence minimizes, diminishes or eliminates the supremacy and lordship of the Most High God, relegating Him to the background or failing to acknowledge Him altogether, then there is a big problem.

As the Bible cautions, we obtain victory in battle and warfare, not with status, titles, credentials or fame, but through the name of our God. It is the name of the God of Jacob that is our defense.

Biblical records affirm the presence and works of Jehovah Nissi. During the Israelites' journey to the promised land, they faced times of distress, disaster, opposition, and misadventure.

In their wanderings, Israel got to Rephidim where they came under attack by the Amalekites (Exodus 17:8-16). There were two parts to Israel's war strategy. Moses commanded Joshua to choose men who would go out to fight Amalek. For his part, the plan was for him to stand on the hill with the rod of God lifted in his hands while the men fought the battle.

This rod of God was originally Moses' shepherd staff, but it was transformed by the power of God into a supernatural weapon when God met Moses at the burning bush. It became the rod that he used to work mighty signs and wonders in the land of Egypt. This was the rod that turned into a snake before Pharaoh, and which also swallowed up the snakes of Pharaoh's magicians. This was the rod that turned the Nile and all the waters of Egypt into blood. It also parted the Red Sea and brought water out of the rock.

As the battle ensued, it became evident that the outcomes were dependent on how the rod of God was handled. As long as Moses held up his hands with the rod, the Israelites prevailed in the battle. When he let down his hands, the enemy prevailed. Therefore, Aaron and Hur joined to support his hands, and Israel won the battle.

This was a clear indication that the people of God won the battle, not by their own strength and skill, but by the power of God demonstrated through the rod of Moses. In gratitude and acknowledgement, Moses erected an altar of worship.

"And Joshua discomfited Amalek and his people with the edge of the sword. …..And Moses built an altar, and called the name of it Jehovah nissi." Exodus 17:13&15

The rod of Moses represented the redemptive name of God, Jehovah Nissi, the Lord our Victory, Banner and Deliverer. Some Bible historians believe that the rod of Moses had the letters YHWH inscribed on it, which was the hidden or unpronounced name of God (Yahweh). When Moses lifted the rod with his hands during the battle, that was symbolic of the fact that he was submitting himself and all of Israel under the name and authority of God. Therefore, they fought under the authority and power deposited in the name Yahweh, Jehovah Nissi, and thus, Israel prevailed over its enemies in the name of Yahweh.

The name Jesus is YHWH revealed. This rod is the name of Jesus, the name that is above all names. When the name of Jesus is lifted up, every knee shall bow, of things in heaven, earth, and under the earth (Philippians 2:7-10).

David, the King of Israel, experienced this firsthand, and relayed what he learned in simple terms:

"Some trust in chariots, and some in horses: but we will remember the name of the Lord our God." Psalm 20:7

David got that insight, that warfare, safety, defense and victory are vested in the name of the Lord. The Philistines, led by

Goliath, came against Israel with their skilled men of war and most sophisticated weapons of war.

Goliath came forth to challenge anyone from the camp of Israel to engage with him in single combat. He was thicker, taller, stronger, and more advanced in battle than anyone in either camp. He was well armed, had his armor bearer with him, and had the giants of the Philistine army with him and cheering him on.

The armies of Israel, on the other hand, were not so equipped. They were not as skilled, and did not have much by way of military arsenal; in fact, they had no commensurate artillery which could be used in the battle against the Philistine giants. Probably, the best they would have had in their garrison would have been gadgets suitable for non-warfare activities like hunting.

In the natural, then, there was no indication that anyone from the camp of Israel would be a match for the great general Goliath of the Philistine army. This caused serious consternation amongst the people of Israel, and they were gripped with fear.

After a long debate in Israel's camp of who could face Goliath, David showed up. He was a young lad with no weapons but a sling and five smooth stones from the brook. Everyone from both sides feared for him. Goliath considered his appearance to face him as a joke and insult.

"And the Philistine said unto David, Am I a dog, that thou comest to me with staves? And the Philistine cursed David by his gods." 1 Samuel 17:43

The giant disdained David, and invoked his gods to curse David. With arrogance, he proclaimed that David would be meat for the fowls of the air and beasts of the field. Obviously, he trusted in his greatness, weapons and gods.

What we should not miss is what was being orchestrated in the spirit realm. Behind the obvious scene of a battle set in full array in the field, the Philistine had invoked the satanic and demonic forces of his gods.

Very often, negative events that take place in the natural are cooked and baked in the spirit realm, such that what happens in the tangible realm of the seen are just manifestations of activities in the unseen. Thus, although there may be some effective ways to deal with adversity from the natural standpoint, we must understand that the root causes of many terrible issues in life must be addressed in the spirit.

David evidently understood and wielded this key. He did not face Goliath with his natural skills or weapons. Rather, he was totally dependent on the name and power of Jehovah Nissi, the Lord of Hosts.

"Then said David to the Philistine, Thou comest to me with sword, and with spear, and with shield: but I come to thee in the name of the Lord of hosts, the God of the armies of Israel whom thou hast defied. This day will the Lord deliver thee into my hand: and I will smite thee, and take thine head from thee; and I will give the carcases of the host of the Philistines this day unto the fowls of the air, and to the wild beasts of the earth; that all the earth may know that there is a God in Israel. And all this assembly shall know that the Lord saveth not with sword and spear: for the battle is the Lord's and he will give you into our hands." 1 Samuel 17:45-47

David's secret to triumph was not to trust in his skill, greatness or natural human strength. He knew that the enemy would not be defeated by human might or by human power, but by the Spirit and anointing released through Jehovah Nissi. David acknowledged that the battle is the Lord's.

All said and done, it was through the name of Jehovah Nissi that David slew Goliath and brought victory to Israel. The Bible tells us that God has conferred on Jesus the name that is above all names, at the mention of which every knee should bow in heaven, earth and under the earth (Philippians 2:8-10). Jesus existed before time, and this name, Jehovah Nissi, is wrapped up in His name, Jesus. We must therefore use, at all times, that name which is above all other names.

Some keys for victorious living that can be extrapolated from David's conquest are the following:

- First, that God fights for His people, not by natural weapons but by the supernatural.

- Second, that in any form of affliction, woe or heartache that we face, we are not alone. Jehovah Nissi is with us and fights for us. He cannot forsake us because of His covenant with us. One person, plus God, makes a majority.

- Third, David applied and used the name of the Lord of Hosts, releasing all the inherent virtue and power in that name.

- Fourth, he moved by faith and unleashed the power of the first stone right into the forehead of Goliath, causing the mighty giant to fall.

The cry of victory reverberated throughout the camp of Israel as the Philistines run helter skelter for their lives. In this encounter, not only were the Philistines defeated, but their gods and demons they worshipped were also decimated.

King Jehoshaphat also faced an incredibly fearsome situation. Multitudes of the combined armies of Moab, Ammon and others came up against him and the people of Judah.

Interestingly, the children of Ammon, Moab and Mount Seir, who were now on the offensive and had come to attack Judah, had been spared by God; He did not allow the people of Israel to destroy them (2 Chronicles 20:1-12). After they had been spared, they turned around to attack the very people who showed them favor and had mercy on them. Sadly, such unfortunate things happen in life. People, to whom we show goodness and kindness, often disparage what good has been done to them, and turn around to repay good with evil.

King Jehoshaphat conceded that this enemy was too much for him in number and in skill and prowess in battle, and he was sore afraid.

"It came to pass after this also, that the children of Moab, and the children of Ammon, and with them other beside the Ammonites, came against Jehoshaphat to battle. Then there came some that told Jehoshaphat, saying, There cometh a great multitude against thee from beyond the sea on this side Syria; and, behold, they be in Hazazontamar, which is Engedi. And Jehoshaphat feared, and set himself to seek the Lord, and proclaimed a fast throughout all Judah." 2 Chronicles 20:1-3

He could only place his hope in God, the One who is strong in battle, the mighty warrior, Jehovah Nissi. In the spirit of true, inspiring leadership, he called for national, corporate, united prayer and fasting, and he assembled the whole nation of Judah to seek the face of God, the only One who could give them the victory. The Spirit of God came upon Jahaziel, a Levite of the sons of Asaph, and he prophesied the word of the Lord:

"And he said, Hearken ye, all Judah, and ye inhabitants of Jerusalem, and thou king Jehoshaphat, Thus saith the Lord unto you, Be not afraid nor dismayed by reason of this great multitude; for the battle is not yours, but God's. To morrow go ye down against them: behold, they come up by the cliff of Ziz; and ye shall find them at the end of the brook, before the wilderness of Jeruel. Ye shall not need to fight in this battle: set yourselves, stand ye still, and see the salvation of the Lord with you, O Judah and Jerusalem: fear not, nor be dismayed; to morrow go out against them; for the Lord will be with you." 2 Chronicles 20:15-17

The king and all of Judah, upon hearing the prophecy, fell on their faces to worship the Lord. The next day, he appointed singers and musicians to sing before their army as they marched to war. Jehoshaphat stirred up the people to believe in the Lord

God to be established, and in His prophets to prosper (2 Chronicles 20:20).

The Lord delivered. He set ambushes against the enemy camp as Judah lifted praise and worship unto Him, and the enemies fought and killed each other.

Prayer, praise and worship moved the hand of God to destroy the adversaries, and Judah got the victory without having to fight in the battle, according to the word of the Lord. Remember, Saints of God, that though we walk in the flesh, we do not war after the flesh, and we must therefore use spiritually-honed combat skills. We have the name of Jehovah Nissi!

The Bible expounds on this, stating that the weapons of our warfare are not carnal, or are "not natural physical weapons." They are mighty, through God, to the pulling down of strong holds, casting down imaginations and every high thing that exalts itself above the knowledge of God, and bringing into captivity every thought to the obedience of Christ (2 Corinthians 10:3-5). Hallelujah!

Jehovah Nissi, rendered another way, is "the Lord our Banner." Banners have great significance in the lives and histories of people. The raising or setting of banners identifies a people, their proud history, and the leadership, direction and authority they operate under.

Usually, the banners would display colors and/or inscriptions that invoke the spirit and power behind the authority they submit to. The banners, in subtle or clearly discernible ways, portray the image of the deity the people worship, and represent their trust that that force or power will lead them to accomplish their spiritual, military, political and economic destinies.

The people of Israel proudly unfurled and set up their banners in battle in the name of the Lord, Jehovah Nissi, and the name of the Lord is what they blessed, praised and worshipped. In setting up their banners in the name of the Lord in warfare, they were invoking the Spirit of the living God to fight for them. They drew their strength, might and power from that name, and God never let them down. The Psalmist expressed it thus:

"We will rejoice in thy salvation, and in the name of our God we will set up our banners: The LORD fulfil all thy petitions. Now know I that the LORD saveth his anointed; he will hear him from his holy heaven with the saving strength of his right hand. Some trust in chariots and some in horses: but we will remember the name of the LORD our God." Psalm 20:5-7

In the name of Jehovah Nissi, their victory was certain and assured. Their salvation was in this name. It was their defense, and represented greater forces than that of chariots and horses. It was in the name of the Lord that they got their petitions fulfilled and prayers answered. They waged war and achieved great conquests in this name, Jehovah Nissi.

Everything Jehovah Nissi was and is to the people of Israel is true for the Church as well. The bride of Christ, the Church, is a mighty army, founded on Christ, the rock Himself. It is indomitable, and is anointed, equipped, deputized and authorized by God, in the name of Jesus, to advance against the gates of hell which can never prevail against it.

"Who is she that looketh forth as the morning, fair as the moon, clear as the sun, and terrible as an army with banners?." Song of Solomon 6:10

In the Song of Solomon, the fair bride that Solomon speaks about is a type of the Church. Like a Bride appears the first time, so breathtaking and ravishing, so does the Church break forth in elegance like the morning. It is as beautiful and glistening as the moon in the evening, and bright, clear and strong as the sun in the day. The empowering strength and grace of God radiates from the Church, and its intensity is as clear and piercing as the sunlight which swallows the gloom and horrors of the night, announcing the freshness of the morning and heightening its majestic aura at noonday.

It is a glorious Church which marches into battle as a "terrible army", a fearsome and formidable force. The Church engenders fear and dread in enemy forces, and this gives a clear picture of the power that the Church has to overcome all the power of the enemy. Jesus assured us that He will build His Church, and the gates of hell shall not prevail against it.

It is equipped with authority and power in the name of Jesus to heal the sick, cast out devils, preach the gospel, and to bring humanity to salvation and freedom. Its banners are set up in the name above all names. It holds the keys of the kingdom of heaven, and whatever she binds on earth shall be bound in heaven, and whatever she looses on earth shall be loosed in heaven (Matthew 16:18-19). God is always with the Church.

"The LORD thy God in the midst of thee is mighty: he will save he will rejoice over thee with joy; he will rest in his love, he will joy over thee with singing." Zephaniah 3:17

In life, there are times and seasons for battle and war, and times for peace (Ecclesiastics 3). In fact, the body of Christ is engaged in spiritual warfare. However, no child of God is destitute of the presence of God or void of the mighty hand of Jehovah Nissi to save, deliver, heal, restore and redeem. When we go to war in the name of the Lord, we place the battle in God's hands, and He is obligated and moved to go to war on our behalf. The battle is won!

The takeaway in all of this is that Jesus is that banner of victory, the battle axe for the Church. His name is become our salvation and song, our strength, shield and fortress. He fights for us. He goes to war on our behalf because He is Jehovah Nissi. He is seated on the right hand of the Father, far above every principality and power, and has in subjection under His feet, every evil force. He is able to save to the uttermost, all those that come to God by Him because He lives eternally to make intercession for them (Hebrews 7:25).

There is no better warrior than our God, no greater conqueror than our God, and no greater victor than Jesus, the Captain of our salvation. There is no battle that cannot be won, no victory that cannot be attained, and no conquest that cannot be wrought for those who establish their trust and faith in the name that is above all names, Jesus Christ, the King of kings and the Lord of lords. Saints, we are the begotten of God, born of God, and we are destined to overcome the world; and this is the victory that overcomes the world, even our faith!

# Chapter 11

## JEHOVAH SHAMMAH – THE LORD IS THERE

Jehovah Shammah means "The Lord is there." This speaks of God's abiding presence and communion with His people, and that reinforcement and reassurance by God was necessary because of the unfortunate detour that humanity took, and its impact on their destiny.

God's original intent was for man to be in constant fellowship and communion with Him, and it appears there was such a thick glory, the "shekinah" (Hebrew) on Adam and Eve that provided for both their spiritual and natural covering. When they walked in tandem with God, man was clothed with the glory of God.

However, Adam and Eve sinned by eating of the fruit of the tree of knowledge, which God had expressly withheld from them. Thus, when they heard the voice of the Lord God (the Word) walking in the garden in the cool of the day, they hid themselves from the presence of God because they felt naked.

The sin of Adam in the Garden of Eden altered the blueprint God had for humanity. Communion and fellowship with the holy God was severed. The spiritual covering, protection and position that He gave to man was lost because of sin. In essence, man fell short of the glory God that was wrapped around him round him from the beginning. That sin brought about

"Ichabod", a departure of the glory and presence of God that He had endowed man with from the beginning.

But God is a loving God, and He worked out redemption for man. The central theme of God's redemptive process was to bring man back to Himself and restore the position, glory, fellowship, presence and communion that He originally had with His creation. Through the ages, He incrementally made known His plans and purposes in shadows and types, until the grand unveiling of the Messiah.

God brought His people to the land of promise, and He commanded that the land should be divided among the tribes of Israel. Within the inheritance, a city was to be built with four walls, and with three gates on each wall. Those twelve gates were named after the tribes of Israel. The Lord proclaimed that the name of the city from that day should be called "The LORD is there."

"It was round about eighteen thousand measures: and the name of the city from that day shall be, The LORD is there." Ezekiel 48:35

That city represented the whole nation of Israel and was a revelation of Jehovah's restored position amongst His people, and His deposited, abiding presence in the city. We know Jerusalem is this beloved city of God. In revealing Himself as Jehovah Shammah, God covenanted with His people to be with them forever.

Covenant is God's way of forging unions with humanity. Jehovah God made a covenant with Abraham, the patriarch, and the unchanging promise that came with that pact became the major route carved by Jehovah to bring His presence back to mankind. The covenant promise was to Abraham and his seed, which is Christ; therefore, all those who belong to Christ are Abraham's seed and are heirs according to the promise (Galatians 3:28-29).

This means that God worked His way back to humanity through Christ, and access to the fullness of His grace was thus made available, not only to the Jews but to the Gentiles as well (Romans 1:16-17).

Jehovah Shammah has established His presence and name in the city of Jerusalem, which is the gateway for God's people forever. Every Christian is permanently and ineradicably connected to Mount Zion (Sion), and to the city of the living God, the heavenly Jerusalem (Hebrews 12.22).

The presence of Jehovah Shammah releases so much power, love, comfort and assurance to the people of God. To highlight a few, it means that God is united with us in covenant forever. We are His bride, and He celebrates His bride, Israel and the Church, with joy and singing (Zephaniah 3:17). He is perpetually with us, His bride, and He is for us. He is above all, and there is none other beside Him because we are in an exclusive relationship with Him. He gives us the victory in every way.

Again, when God is with His people, He removes fear from their hearts because His perfect love casts out fear. He dismisses all discouragement. He is their strength and present help, and He undergirds and upholds them with His right hand of righteousness. He silences and confounds the enemies of His people, and He brings their adversaries to nothing, to total decimation (Isaiah 40:10-11; 49:24-26, Joshua 1:5-6). Therefore,

God's people are bold, strong and courageous as He is their salvation, shield, security and defense, and He demonstrates His sovereign and mighty power in their midst.

As well, when God is amongst His people, He manifests Himself in miracles, signs and wonders and in diverse gifts of the Holy Ghost. This was made clear in Gideon's experience with the Lord. Israel was in dire straits at that time, under the tyranny of the Midianites. An angel appeared to Gideon and saluted him, saying: "The Lord is with thee, thou mighty man of valour."

Gideon could not hide his disbelief, and his unadulterated and instinctive first response reveals what the expectation of people is, when God is with them. He asked the angel: "If the Lord be with us, why then is all this befallen us? And where be all his miracles our fathers told us of?" In other words, miracles should be a staple and a given when God is with any person or group. The angel's response was just as eye-opening. He said to Gideon: "Go in this thy might, and you will save Israel from the hand of the Midianites. Have I not sent thee?"

Saints, you need to catch this: the truth the angel was conveying was that the might of Gideon lay in his expectation that miracles happen whenever God is amongst His people. Empowered by this word, Gideon smote the Midianites and brought victory to Israel because God was with him (Judges 6:11-16).

Nicodemus also had that same insight that, when God is with His people, miracles happen. He was keenly following the activities and works of Jesus, and he remarked to Jesus that no one could perform the kinds of miracles He wrought if God were not with them. Indeed, the Bible points out that God anointed Jesus of Nazareth with the Holy Ghost and with power, and He went about doing good and healing all who were oppressed of the devil, because God was with Him (John 3:2, Acts 10:38).

Another benefit of God's presence is that, in times of tests, trials and trauma, He promotes, prospers and elevates His followers. Joseph's brothers, filled with envy and disdain for him, ultimately sold him into slavery in Egypt. He suffered persecution and false accusations and was thrust into prison. But the Lord was with him and delivered him from his afflictions. God radically changed his fortunes and gave him favor and wisdom in the sight of Pharaoh, king of Egypt, who made him governor over Egypt and over all his house (Acts 7:9-10).

Furthermore, people receive divine direction and guidance from God when He is with them. Moses was reticent about taking up the assignment of leading Israel without the assurance of God's presence with him. He therefore sought God's leadership and presence to lead Israel. God heard him. He led His people by the pillar of cloud by day and by a pillar of fire by night. These pillars were the manifestation of God's presence among His people. He led, directed, and provided guidance for His people with His glorious presence (Exodus 13:21-22).

Jesus, in His time on earth, sent His disciples to go and preach the gospel, heal the sick, and cast out devils. The Lord was with them, confirming the word with signs following (Mark 16:15-20). God bore witness to the preaching of the disciples with signs, wonders, and diverse gifts of the Holy Ghost, according to His own will (Hebrews 2:3-4). So, clearly, the presence of God is the gateway to miracles.

Jesus is Jehovah Shammah. He is Immanuel, which is interpreted "God with us." He has come to dwell among us, and He has given us the assurance that He is with us always, unto the end of the world (Matthew 1:21, 28:20). He is the mediator of the New Covenant that is established on better promises, and has come to unite God with humanity (Matthew 1:21-23, Hebrews 8:1-10).

Therefore arise, O Church, for the Almighty God, the ultimate and sovereign One, is united with us. His presence separates us from the world. He is on our team, and we draw our strength, authority and power from Him. He said He will never leave nor forsake us (Hebrews 13:6). God, in our midst, brings to us a refreshing and renewal, and a rest like none other.

# Chapter 12

## JEHOVAH SHALOM – THE LORD OUR PEACE

The name Jehovah Shalom is a revelation of the God of Peace, the One who alone holds all things together in a perfect and beautiful balance, with no piece missing, no piece out place, and nothing broken. Everything in Him flows smoothly like a river and makes perfect sense.

"Shalom" means that all things are weighted and aligned, and in accord with God's purpose. It is synonymous with the Hebrew word "sozo", which means soundness, prosperity, preservation, protection and deliverance.

The peace of God is a very comprehensive and far-reaching package. It is that supernatural force and provision from Him which grants us calmness, stability, grace, and ability to overcome insurmountable circumstances. It is that energy of God that generates in His people an unshakeable, indomitable attitude even in perilous and dangerous times. It is His mighty hand revealed to rescue His people from the claws of the enemy to bring deliverance, and to eliminate fear, anxiety, worry, thoughts of tomorrow, and the cares of this life. It is also the grace and mercy of God unfolded and directed to His saints for their spiritual, emotional and physical wellbeing, to infuse healing into their spirit, soul and body.

Contrary to what many believe, peace does not always mean the absence of trouble. In some cases, it does. However, often, peace is rather the supply of the tools required to face opposition and problems, and the tenacity to endure hardship, leap over walls, run through troops, and still land beside still waters. Once those tools are applied according to the wisdom of God who supplies them, victory comes.

Witness the experience of Gideon, the one who would save Israel from the Midianites. All was not well with him and the people of Israel in the land of Midian. The Midianites were so much stronger than the people of Israel, and were oppressive, inflicting terror and poverty on them, and they were sore troubled. It was at this time of sheer desperation that an angel of the Lord appeared to Gideon, bringing a message that God was going to use him to deliver Israel from the Midianites.

Gideon had severe doubts that God was with them, and questioned the message that the angel brought, noting particularly, the marked absence of the awe-inspiring miracles by God that the older generations had fondly recounted to them. To add to that, he did not even feel qualified to lead an army to victory over Midian. He gave excuses, citing his family's known poverty in Manasseh, and the fact that he was the least in his father's house (Judges 6:15-16).

Nevertheless, it was against this same background of personal inadequacy and low self-esteem, and within the global milieu of starvation, deprivation, fear and vexation by the Midianites, a time when there was no reason to believe that any good thing would happen, that the message of peace, salvation and freedom from God came to Israel.

Gideon decided to be converted from his fears, and to move from unbelief into faith. He prepared cakes of unleavened bread, a kid and broth, and brought the meal to the angel. The angel received the offering by consuming it with fire from his staff. At that point, Gideon knew he had encountered God and was alarmed, but the Lord assured him of peace. He then built an altar acknowledging the God of peace, Jehovah Shalom.

"And when Gideon perceived that he was an angel of the Lord, Gideon said, Alas, O Lord God! For because I have seen an angel of the Lord face to face. And the Lord said unto him, Peace be unto thee; fear not: thou shalt not die. Then Gideon built an altar there unto the Lord, and called it Jehovah shalom: unto this day it is yet in Ophrah of the Abiezrites." Judges 6:22-24

Gideon acknowledged and accepted the peace of God in his heart when he had this supernatural encounter with the God of peace, Jehovah Shalom.

Note that nothing had changed yet in his circumstances, but the spiritual impact of God's peace settled deep in his spirit and soul, providing him with an inner strength and stability. With those resources deposited within him, he knew he could now lead God's people out of captivity, and that the God of peace, Jehovah Shalom, would bring them out of captivity into His freedom and peace that passes all understanding (Judges 6:22-24).

As should be evident from Gideon's experience also, God does not always bring peace or salvation by the hand of the mighty, the rich, the great, or people of great authority or influence. Sometimes, He does use such personalities, but that is not always His modus operandi.

As He taught Gideon, He is a God who saves, not by few or by many. In painful, distressful, poignant moments, He may even use the foolish things of this world to confound the wise, things that are disregarded to bring to naught things that are, so that none can boast in His presence. God is His own interpreter, and He is the sole selector of what keys, methods, principles and strategies He would use in a given situation to bring His people peace.

We must also understand that storms can arise for various reasons and under different circumstances in life. However, the authority and power to still the storms of life does not rest in our human skills, but in the power and might of God Almighty, who is the Prince of Peace (Isaiah 9:6). We ought to simply rest in the knowledge that He brings peace to every heart, to every situation, and to every need.

Jesus, the Prince of Peace, was comfortably asleep in a boat that was being beaten up by storms and waves. The water poured into the boat, and disciples were petrified, seeing that they faced destruction and apparent extinction. They woke Jesus up, and He spoke peace to the raging sea, saying "Peace, be still." The winds and the waves obeyed His voice, and the raging seas ceased, and there was a great calm (Mark 4:35-41).

In this episode, we see that the disciples had set out on that trip at the Lord's instruction. Expressed another way, they were being obedient, and were in the centre of God's perfect will. Storms can strike even where we are being good or obedient to God's purpose. Weird things sometimes happen when people seek to obey God. There could be resistance from the spiritual realm, from Satan and demons; there could be false accusations from people; there could be painful and heart-breaking life events occurring. The list is endless.

Many of those difficulties in life are engineered by the enemy, and are meant to derail, distract, break and demoralize people, and designed to shift their focus from God's agenda. Unfortunately, many who are battered by the storms of life lose focus, give up the fight and throw in the towel. Their peace is disturbed, and their foundations shaken.

But this is the message - do not be moved, and do not give up! The Prince of peace is in your boat. Jehovah Shalom arises in the midst of the storm and brings peace to the storm. He supplies strength for every weakness, grace for every challenge, healing for every sickness. There is no mountain that you cannot climb, no hurdle you cannot go over, no enemy you cannot conquer, with the presence of the God of Peace.

Jehovah Shalom always steps in and delivers big time when His people draw from, and depend wholly on, His strength in times of affliction.

"Thou wilt keep him in perfect peace, whose mind is stayed on thee: because he trusteth in thee." Isaiah 26:3

His glorious provision of peace and rest is activated when His people feed and constantly meditate on His Word and His promises, and call on Him with prevailing prayers, for the intense, effectual fervent prayers of the righteous man does accomplish so much, and will cut through any impossible situation.

"Great peace have they which love thy law; and nothing shall offend them." Psalm 119:165

"Be careful for nothing; but in every thing by prayer and supplication with thanksgiving let your requests be made known to God. And the peace of God, which passeth all understanding, shall keep your hearts and minds through Christ Jesus." Philippians 4:6-7

Jehovah Shalom, even Jesus, the Prince of Peace who makes us whole in every way, is always with us. Therefore, be whole from any brokenness. Be whole from a fragmented past and bad decisions in your life. Be whole from anxiety and fear, and from any kind of bondage. Develop the consciousness of His abiding presence in you and around you. Establish your heart and faith in His unfailing grace and faithfulness. Rest assured, and let not your heart be troubled, but trust Jehovah Shalom to fight for you.

Let His peace reign in your life as you prevail in fiery, empowering, victorious prayers. He rebrands every negative situation and says to you today and always: PEACE BE STILL!

"Peace I leave with you, my peace I give unto you: not as the world giveth, give I unto you. Let not your heart be troubled, neither let it be afraid." John 14:27

# Chapter 13

## JEHOVAH RAPHA / ROPHE – THE LORD OUR HEALER

Jehovah Rapha, also rendered Jehovah Rophe, is interpreted "God our Healer."

This name of God was revealed to the people of Israel during their wilderness wanderings. After they came out of the Red Sea, they travelled three days in the wilderness of Shur without finding water. They were worn and thirsty. And then, when it seemed that the breakthrough had come when they found water at the place they would call Marah (meaning "Bitter"), that water was so bitter, and was undrinkable.

Not surprisingly, the people became upset, agitated, disgruntled and discontented, and they murmured against Moses saying: "What shall we drink?" They blamed Moses for bringing them into such harsh conditions.

Moses cried out to the Lord, and the Lord showed him a tree. He cast that tree into the waters, and the waters were made sweet and drinkable. At Marah, God made a statute and an ordinance with Israel and proved them there, saying:

"And said, If thou wilt diligently hearken to the LORD thy God, and wilt do that which is right in his sight, and wilt give ear to his commandments, and keep all his statutes, I will put none of these diseases upon thee, which I have brought upon the Egyptians: for I am the LORD that healeth thee." Exodus 15:26

A statute or ordinance is a decree or law passed by a legislative body. In Biblical usage, it is typically a rule or binding proclamation issued by a sovereign, or by God Almighty. It was such a decree of binding force that was promulgated by God for His people at Marah after He turned the bitter waters into sweet, drinkable waters.

There are some lessons to be learned as we seek the Lord for healing. His command is for His people to keep His word and obey it, and to do that which is right in His sight, in order to access His healing. The Bible says that He sent His word and healed them and delivered them from their destructions. Further, God says:

"My son, attend to my words; incline thine ear unto my sayings. Let them not depart from thine eyes; keep them in the midst of thine heart. For they are life unto those that find them, and health to all their flesh." Proverbs 4:20-22

God assures His people that, if they keep His word, He will be to them, Jehovah Rapha, the Lord who heals. He promises them that, when they serve Him, He will bless their bread and their water, and will take sickness away from their midst, (Psalm 107:20; Exodus 23:25-26). Therefore, let us take God's word seriously and live by it as we invoke His miraculous hand to bring us healing.

As should be evident also, Moses came under attack and under a vote of no confidence, it seems, by the very people he had led out of Egypt, from under the yoke of slavery. Sadly, this is a phenomenon that cuts across the board – in our Churches, governments, communities, workplaces, schools, and even in our families.

The Church is often plagued by such human urges, and is not always sanctified in its actions, sentiments and responses. Spiritual leaders are subjected to intense criticism and come under attack by congregants, some of whom are chronic murmurers, disgruntled, divisive, immature, and who fail to grow up. Such elements complain, kick against authority, breed division in the camp, and blame every problem on their leaders. Even when things go well, they do not celebrate or acknowledge the leaders, neither do they give them any credit. The Bible has a lot to say about people who do these things:

"Do all things without murmurings and disputings. That ye may be blameless and harmless, the sons of God, without rebuke, in the midst of a crooked and perverse nation, among whom ye shine as lights in the world." Philipians 2:14-15

"These are murmurers, complainers, walking after their own lusts; and their mouth speaketh great swelling words, having men's persons in admiration because of advantage." Jude 1:16

"Neither murmur ye, as some of them also murmured, and were destroyed of the destroyer. Now all these things happened to them for examples: and they are written for our admonition, upon whom the ends of the world are come." 1 Corinthians 10:10-11

Understand this - that it is extremely tough for leaders when they go through such problems, especially when all they seek to do is to serve the flock of God. It is important for us all, the people of God, to be beyond reproach and to preserve and insulate ourselves from God's displeasure by eschewing those things that are unpleasing to Him. We must refrain from using our influence, advantage and clout in the House of God to engender division, unrest, murmuring and disrespect for the holy things of God.

And here is a caution to leaders as well - you need to live and walk right, in the integrity of your heart and in the sight of God, honorable in every way as the authority set by God, and honoring the God who called you to serve. You also absolutely need the wisdom and the power of God to function well in ministry. This is the key - Moses knew his God and walked in His ways, and as a result, he did not crumble under attack and pressure.

Moses was a humble person, a man of faith and prayer, and these are especially important qualities that mark out strong leaders. Godly leaders tap into the wonders of God through faith and prayer. They produce the miraculous signs and wonders of God because they are in tune with God, who provides supernatural direction to them. The Bible records that God brought His people out of Egypt with a mighty hand and with silver and gold, and there was no feeble person among them (Psalm 105:37). The people that know their God, the Bible says, shall be strong and do exploits.

This is the message of the Lord our Healer. Though there may be times in life where we face our "Marah" hour, those times where bitterness, pain and adversity overwhelm us and seem to block any hint of sweetness, Jehovah Rapha is ever-present. He will make His sweetness flow by the move of His Spirit, activated by the faith of His people. There is no sickness, disease, pain or affliction that can withstand His power or presence.

Jesus is the full manifestation of Jehovah Rapha. The bitter waters of Marah depict the human state with all its sin and pain. That tree which turned the waters of Marah into sweetness represents Jesus' humanity and the cross on which He died, that rugged cross.

It is believed that the tree was itself extremely bitter. Guess what – so was the cross a bitter cross, and it is that base thing that was used to accomplish the supernatural. When God showed Moses the tree, therefore, He was pointing him to the cross and the sacrifice of Jesus, and how, through the sacrifice of that cross, He would turn the bitterness of sin, death, hell and judgement, and the evil of infected lives, into extreme joy, pleasure, peace and liberty.

Jesus is also the Word of God that must be believed and adhered to. God has enacted a covenant to be the healer of His children when they believe His word and walk in His ways. In His body, also, Jesus received the scourge of thirty-nine lashes/stripes, and by those stripes we are/were healed. He is the bread of life that was broken for our healing. He gives the water that gives life and not the bitterness of death and sin. He is, and will forever be, Jehovah Rapha, the God that heals us.

# Chapter 14

## JEHOVAH ROHI / JEHOVAH RAAH – THE LORD OUR SHEPHERD

God shows Himself as Jehovah Raah or Jehovah Rohi, "the Lord our Shepherd." The two renditions convey the same meaning. In Psalm 23, David paints the clear picture of the Lord our Shepherd, and His role in our lives. He says:

"The Lord is my shepherd; I shall not want. He maketh me to lie beside green pastures: he leadeth me beside the still waters. He restoreth my soul: he leadeth me in the paths of righteousness for his name's sake. Yea, though I walk through the valley of the shadow of death, I will fear no evil: for thou art with me; thy rod and thy staff they comfort me. Thou preparest a table before me in the presence of my enemies: thou anointest my head with oil; my cup runneth over. Surely goodness and mercies shall follow me all the days of my life: and I will dwell in the house of the Lord forever." Psalm 23:1-6

Jehovah Raah/Rohi is the God who possesses all things, and is the creator of the heavens and earth and all that is within them. He spoke into being the sun, the moon, the galaxies, the constellations of stars and heavenly bodies, and stationed them in their perfect positions, pathways and orbits.

He oversees the times and seasons, of seedtime and harvest, and of day and night. All the wealth and resources in existence were made by Him and for Him. He therefore never runs out of provision, might or power to supply the needs of His people, or the ability to save, heal, deliver and bring Jubilee into their lives.

As the Good Shepherd, He knows His sheep, what they want and what they need, and can supply their every need from His boundless resources. Jesus is that Great Shepherd, and when His people submit to Him as their Lord and Master, He leads them into green pastures and settles them beside still waters, for their sustenance and nourishment. He creates amazing opportunities for them, and administers the grace, ability and resources necessary for their fruitful living.

The Shepherd is also very much in tune with the flock, and is keenly aware of the tests, trials and difficulties they encounter in their lives. Nothing takes Him by surprise, and nothing escapes His watchful eye. He is ever present to help them, save and deliver them, minister to their needs, and to equip them as required.

The great Lord, our Shepherd, also guides His people. Following His guidance and leadership is the only sure way for His people to get to the place where they are insulated from hunger or thirst, and from predators.

The victorious child of God is the one that is led by the Spirit of God. Jesus, the Good Shepherd, declared that His sheep hear His voice and are sensitive to His leading; they will not follow the voice of another. Whereas Jehovah Rohi leads His people beside still waters and into places of serenity, the devil leads people into terror, danger and destruction.

"All that ever came before me are thieves and robbers: but the sheep did not hear them. I am the door: by me if any man enter in, he shall be saved, and shall go in and out, and find pasture. The thief cometh not, but for to steal, and to kill, and to destroy: I am come that they might have life, and that they might have it more abundantly. I am the good shepherd: the good shepherd giveth his life for the sheep." John 10:8-11

The people of God must not lean on their own understanding, but must rather acknowledge the sovereignty, supremacy and leadership of God in all their ways, and He will direct their paths. He will direct them away from the predators, thieves, and robbers lying in wait to destroy.

When Jehovah Rohi shows up, He does not only meet the physical needs of His people but the spiritual as well. Jesus, the Good Shepherd, is the way, the truth and the life, and He came to impart the life of God, eternal life, to humanity; that is, the salvation of God from sin, hell, death and eternal judgement. He came to present fruitfulness and an all-encompassing abundant life to humanity.

He is the restorer of our souls, that eternal part of our being. He leads us in the paths of righteousness for His name's sake. Jesus shed His blood to make atonement for our souls. His blood redeems the spiritually dead soul, which is alienated from God, and restores him back to his Maker in righteousness.

He can lead us into righteousness because He is Jehovah Tsidkenu, the Lord our Righteousness. He became sin who knew no sin, that we might become the righteousness of God. Jehovah Rohi, the Great Shepherd, guides, teaches, and instructs the sheep - God's people - in the way of living right with Him and with man. He injects into the flock, the enabling power, desire and life-giving force for holy and righteous living. He does this for His name's sake, that His name will be esteemed, exalted, honored and worshipped, and not blasphemed.

The Good Shepherd also awakens and revives the oppressed, depressed, broken and discouraged soul by the power of the Holy Spirit, and reinvents or remolds him into a bold, courageous, triumphant saint.

The Lord, with His rod and staff in His victorious hand, drives fear and evil from the hearts of His saints as they navigate the most treacherous terrains of life, the valley of the shadow of death. His rod of correction, which brings molding and inspiration, and His staff, which speaks of His authority and the power of His name, serve as the defense and protection of the sheep, preserving them from any form of defeat or horror. They offer comfort, assurance, stability, and a hope that never disappoints.

The name of the Lord is a strong tower; the righteous run into it and are safe (Proverbs 18:10). The name of the God of Jacob is our defense.(Psalm 20:1).

Jehovah Rohi, our Shepherd and our Captain, also sets a victory banquet for His flock. He prepares a table before His people in the presence of their enemies. He rises up as the Warrior King and fights their enemies, conquers them, holds them captive, and makes a public show of them (Colossians 2:15).

The shepherd pours fresh oil on the sheep's heads, and that oil heals the wounds of the sheep and flushes out all insects or parasites that torment them. So does Jehovah Rohi anoint the heads of His people. The anointing is the flow and manifestation of the Holy Spirit. The Holy Spirit is our helper and comforter, and He empowers us to break the rule and power of the devil in any given circumstance.

Through the anointing, God Almighty breaks any foul spirit or demon that fights the peace of mind of His people. He delivers them from the powers that chastise their peace, and He sets them free from the spirit of fear, granting to them the Spirit of love, power and a sound mind (2 Timothy 1:7). The oil and the anointing on the head breaks every yoke and lifts every burden (Isaiah 10:27). Any hurdle or mountain in the way of the believing one is removed, not by might nor by power, but by the Spirit of the Lord (Zechariah 4:6).

The Good Shepherd, the Lord Jesus, even Jehovah Rohi, is always ready with the anointing oil, the supply of the Spirit without measure, to push back and roll back satanic activities on behalf of His Church. When the enemy comes in, like a flood the Spirit of the Lord will lift up a standard against him (Isaiah 59:19).

Those sheep who are continually and consistently connected to, and are under the covering of, Jehovah Rohi, the great Lord and Master, will undoubtedly experience that unregulated and unceasing outpouring of His goodness and mercies upon them all the days of their lives. David declared that goodness and mercy would follow him all the days of his life, and added an important key - that he would dwell in the house of the Lord forever, a God-chaser.

May that be your cry and your desire too, that you will be a God-chaser. Hold on tight to Him, and never let Him go. He will also never let go of you, for you are His beloved treasure. To derive the very best from God, His people ought to be part of the sheepfold, the body of Christ, and not neglect the assembling of the saints, and must fully participate in the activities and worship in God's house. That way, they can readily access, by faith, the supernatural provisions of God, daily drawing from the treasure chest of Jehovah Rohi.

# Chapter 15

## JEHOVAH JIREH – THE LORD OUR PROVIDER

Jehovah Jireh is interpreted "The Lord my Provider." This name showcases the omniscience and magnanimity of the Lord Most High who sees ahead and knows every need of His people, and who provides for them in ways that are inexplicable, beyond comprehension, and beyond natural means. He unlocks His supplies by supernatural means, and does things outside the mould of human wisdom, skills, talents or abilities.

Let us not forget who He is - He is the Lord who called forth existence and created all things; as creator, therefore, He is able to bring into existence things that do not exist. He is also the possessor of all things, has the wherewithal and limitless resources and all it takes to supply or provide for His people. He is a God of miracles, and He expects those who walk with Him to implicitly trust Him and expect miracles, those things which defy logic and go beyond explanation.

The person God chose to make His name "Jehovah Jireh" known to humanity was His friend Abraham, and the vehicle through which he communicated His purpose was through an offering and sacrifice.

Offerings (rendered "qorban" in Hebrew) and sacrifices were designed by God as the means by which man could approach the holy God, and were the ways carved out to bring man closer to Him in covenant. Typically, those sacrifices and offerings would be of livestock. The shedding of the blood of animals and burning them up as acts of worship and offering to God were temporal ways God formulated for His people to be able to approach Him.

However, this time around, God told Abraham to go to Mount Moriah and offer his only son, Isaac, as a burnt offering to Him. The expectation was that Isaac would be killed and totally burnt to ashes.

This was probably the hardest thing that God could have asked Abraham to do. It is important to note that Isaac was himself a miracle, born because of God's own supernatural provision. Abraham was ninety-nine years old, and Sarah, his wife, about ninety years when Isaac was conceived and born. Isaac was the best thing that ever happened to them, an answer to prayer when they had all but given up. He was Abraham's most precious heir to carry on His name. Realistically, therefore, it would have been an exceedingly difficult thing for him, and even inconceivable, to sacrifice Isaac to God as a burnt offering of worship.

It was as if all of that did not matter to God, and it even sounded counterintuitive that God would give Isaac to Abraham and then ask him to give Isaac back to Him. But the omniscient God obviously wanted Abraham to prove the extent to which he would trust Him and be obedient to His instructions.

There may be times in our walk with God where He would require us to give away or give up or present to Him in worship, the things we value most, for example, our money, jobs, relationships, dreams, goals, amongst others, for the purpose of fostering a deeper relationship with Him.

We need to understand that these all-important possessions in our lives which God may require of us were supplied by God Himself. It is He who gives seed to the sower. Whatever we have to give to God in worship was already provided by Him and belongs to Him. Considering this fact, offering sacrifices and giving to God in worship and for His work is really about giving back to God what already belongs to Him.

As children of God, we must never begrudge Him or view our giving to Him as depletive or destructive to us because, when we obey Him, He will give us something that is more precious or even greater than, or will set us up for a multiplication and acceleration of blessings for, all those things which we sacrificed.

Abraham's heart was unflinchingly loyal to God. He dared to obey Him. He believed that God is the God of life, not death, and that, even if he sacrificed Isaac, God, having made promises to him and His seed, would bring him back to life again. He knew that whatever he gave to God would be restored to him in an even better state. He therefore readied himself to sacrifice his son.

"And Isaac spake unto Abraham, his father, and said, My father: and he said, Here am I, my son. And he said, Behold the fire and the wood: but where is the lamb for the burnt offering? And Abraham said, My son, God will provide himself a lamb for a burnt offering: so they went both of them together." Genesis 22:7-8

Abraham's trust in God and his obedience shows his heart for God and the hunger in his heart to draw even closer to Him. He did not hold back. He prepared the fire and the wood. He tied up Isaac. He drew his knife to slaughter him, and then came the divine intervention. An angel called from heaven and stopped him from slaying his son.

The Lord registered his full approval of Abraham as a person who feared God, and who accorded God's word reverence and finality, and who would fully obey the Lord.

Because of Abraham's heart of worship, offering, sacrifice, obedience and love for God, Isaac's life was spared, and God supernaturally provided a ram for the burnt offering.

"And Abraham lifted up his eyes, and looked, and behold behind him a ram caught in a thicket by his horns: and Abraham went and took the ram, and offered him up for a burnt offering instead of his son. And Abraham called the name of that place Jehovahjireh: as it is said to this day, In the mount of the LORD it shall be seen. And the angel of the LORD called unto Abraham out of heaven the second time, And said, By myself have I sworn, saith the LORD, for because thou has done this thing, and hast not withheld thy son, thine only son: That in blessing I will bless thee, and in multiplying I will multiply thy seed as the stars of the heaven, and as the sand which is upon the sea shore; and thy seed shall possess the gate of his enemies; And in thy seed shall all the nations of the earth be blessed; because thou hast obeyed my voice." Genesis 22:13-18

This shows how so much beauty and satisfaction came out of what initially presented itself as a potentially horrific event, and how God's treasures were poured on Abraham:

- The life of Isaac was preserved.
- God supernaturally provided a ram for the burnt offering.

- God revealed his covenant redemptive name Jehovah Jireh to Abraham.
- God made an oath to bless Abraham and multiply his seed as the stars of heaven and like the sand of the sea.
- God promised Abraham that his seed shall possess the gate of his enemies.
- God instituted a blessing for all humanity, that all nations of the earth will be blessed through the seed of Abraham.

Therefore, we must rest our faith in Jehovah Jireh, for when we give to Him what He has given to us and blessed us with, He will give it back to us exponentially, in multiplied blessings. Tremendous rewards came to Abraham from God because of his obedience.

Highly significant is the fact that Abraham's obedience to sacrifice Isaac, his only son, unleashed and set in motion the foreordained irrevocable redemptive plan of God; it served as the important prelude to what was to come in the fullness of time. It moved God's hand and paved the way for Him also to give His only begotten Son, even Jesus, as the lamb of God that takes away the sin of the world (John 1:29). Jesus is that seed of Abraham through whom salvation would come to all who believe (Galatians 3:13-14, 28-29).

The ram that was caught in the thicket and which Abraham ultimately used for the burnt offering was a type, shadow, or prelude to the actuality whereby God would provide Jesus as the ultimate sacrifice. The sacrifices of animals were non-permanent ordinances that could not sustain the depths of God's plan to unite with humanity. The fullness of God's intent could only come through the redemptive, reconciliatory price that Jesus paid by pouring out His own blood at Calvary's cross for the salvation of the world, and God fine-tuned the emergence of Jesus, and set it all up to perfection.

Until the effectuation of that plan, however, God continued to miraculously provide for His people Israel because of Abraham. By divine providence, He took them from Egypt, and divided the Red Sea before them so they could cross on dry land. He mounted up the River Jordan like a tree, brought water out of a rock, and fed them with manna and quails. He beat up their enemies before them and brought them into the promised land, the land flowing with milk and honey.

When the time was right, God sent His Son who was "made of a woman", meaning that, although He was born by a human, He was not of human descent. Jesus was conceived by the Virgin Mary through the power of the Holy Ghost. The prophet Isaiah spoke about the virgin birth of Jesus (Isaiah 7:14).

Mary was espoused to Joseph, but before they could come together, she was found to be with child. This was a surprise to Joseph, so he considered putting her away privately without disgracing her and making her a public example. The angel of the Lord however appeared to him and revealed that Mary was with child by the Holy Ghost. He told Joseph that Mary would bring forth a son who would be called Jesus, and that Jesus was destined to save His people from their sins. With this understanding, Joseph was not intimate with his wife until she brought forth Jesus (Matthew 1:18-23).

"But when the fulness of the time was come, God sent forth his Son, made of a woman, made under the law, To redeem them that were under the law, that we might receive the adoption of sons." Galatians 4:4-5

This is the wonder of God - miraculously sending a Savior through a virgin. Jesus is referred to as the seed of the woman, made of a woman, and not the seed of man (Genesis 3:15). Essentially, Mary gave birth to Jesus without knowing a man. Wow! Jesus was transported by the Holy Spirit through the virgin into this natural world. Thus, Jehovah Jireh moved beyond the realm of reason, logic and the natural laws of reproduction to bring forth Jesus.

Jesus was, and is, God's supernatural supply of a Saviour, Redeemer and Messiah, the lamb of God that would pay the price for our salvation, that would suffer, bleed and die to redeem humanity from the horrors of sin, hell and eternal condemnation.

"For God so loved the world, that he gave his only begotten Son, that whosoever believeth in him should not perish, but have everlasting life." John 3:16

Faith in Jehovah Jireh, the Lord our Provider, and obedience to Him will bring us into the realm of the unlimited resources of heaven, financial freedom, and the abundant life through Christ Jesus (John 10:8-10). Salvation and redemption become accessible to all who acknowledge Jehovah's presentation of Jesus as Messiah, believe with their hearts that He died as the lamb of God, and confess with their mouths that God raised Him from the dead (Romans 10:8-10).

There are several keys that will position us to access and receive the creative, miraculous provision of God, that which goes beyond what our own efforts could ever procure for us, and that which will assure us of victorious Christian living:

- Develop a reverential fear of God and walk in obedience to His word (James 1:22-25)
- Present yourself to God as a living sacrifice, holy and acceptable to God, in Christian service and worship (Romans 12:1-2)
- Give to God and to His work as an act of holy spiritual worship, and expect a multiplied harvest of blessings back into your life (Luke 6:38, 2Corinthians 9:6-15)
- Have unshakeable faith in God's covenant promises (Genesis 22:16-17)
- Be prayerful and persistent in prayer. (Matthew 7:7-10, John 14:13-14).
- Boldly declare and proclaim God's promises. God's power is set in motion by the declaration of His word (Hebrews 13:5-6, Mark 11:22-24, Proverbs 18:20-21)
- Maintain a lifestyle of thanksgiving, praise, and worship (Acts 16:24-25)

Here is our firm assurance. Jehovah Jireh gave the ram for the sacrifice when Abraham needed it. He gave Jesus, His Son, as a sacrifice when the world needed Him. That covenant provision to Abraham, and the more perfect and better covenant offering of Jesus to meet the demands of justice on the cross at Calvary, is our assurance that the Father God has always been, and will always be, faithful to His word, plan and agenda, and so we can trust Him.

Jehovah Jireh provides and supplies through miracles, signs and wonders. Creation and its sustenance by the Word of God is a miracle. The miraculous "Jireh" of a ram to Abraham was supernatural. The virgin birth of Jesus Messiah was a sign and wonder. Furnishing the world with a Savior through the life, death, resurrection, and ascension of Jesus was miraculous.

God is totally committed to the New Covenant enacted in the blood of Jesus. Since He did not spare Jesus, His only begotten Son, He will not withhold any good thing from those who love Him. He will supply all our needs according to His riches in glory by Christ Jesus. God is a wonder, and He is a miracle working God. Anyone who walks with Him should expect nothing short of a miracle. May there be an outbreak of the wonders of God in your walk with Him every moment of your life!

# Chapter 16

## THE ULTIMATE NAME OF JESUS

All the redemptive names or titles of God were packaged as they were for the easy consumption and digestion of man. They were released or made known by God to man at pivotal times and at the various points of their need. However, all those names were and are deeply revelatory of Jesus the Messiah.

An interesting observation is that, although each name identified and described a particular facet of God, for example, as the ever present One, or as the Healer, or as the Shepherd, or as our Peace, or as our Banner, or as our Righteousness, or as our Provider, each name was actually not a partial or incomplete revelation of Jesus, but a comprehensive and all-encompassing revelation of Him, the total package of "Genesis, the Cross at Calvary, and Us."

Put differently, the various names of God which were incrementally revealed to the people of Israel over the ages were not, as they seemed, discrete and insular expressions of His nature; each manifestation of God's name potently and patently embedded the full scope of God's plan for redemption.

Not only were the redemptive names of God a revelation of the person of Jesus Messiah, but they are also all wrapped up, merged, cohesively blended, into one name, the name of Jesus, which is the name that is above all names. In other words, they find full and complete expression in the name of Jesus.

To appreciate the wonder of His name, we must recognize that Jesus is the full revelation of the Godhead. It pleased the Father that the fullness of the Godhead should dwell bodily in Him (Colossians 1:19, 2:9-10). He is the radiance or brightness of God's glory, the appointed heir through whom all things are made. He is the express image of the invisible God (Hebrews 1:2-3).

The name of Jesus is the name of the creator of the ends of the earth. He is the Word that made all things (John 1:1-4). His name is packed with the forces of creation, loaded with the power of the Word that called into being, the angels, the planets, the galaxies of stars, the sun, the moon, and the endless cosmos.

That name is the strength which keeps them and guides them in their respective orbits. That name rules over the vast density of the oceans and keeps them at bay. It is that name that holds all things together, and that enables humanity to revel in the beauty of life, the thrills of the blue skies, the colorful vegetation, fresh springs of water, majestic waterfalls, the aura of the rockies and canyons, and the splendor of the mountains and the vales. O, the wonder and majesty, the glory and power of Jesus' name!

After creation, the greatness of the name of Jesus was demonstrated in an incredibly unique and unusual way. The Word was made flesh and came to dwell among us (John 1:14). The creator of the world took the form of the created. Prior to His arrival, the prophet Isaiah had prophesied about Him, saying:

"For unto us a child is born, unto us a son is given: and the government shall be upon his shoulder: and his name shall be called Wonderful, Counsellor, The mighty God, The everlasting Father, The Prince of Peace." Isaiah 9:6

Consider all these wondrous names assigned to Jesus some seven hundred to one thousand years before He was actually born! He is identified as the mighty God and the everlasting Father. Upon His birth, there was yet another supernatural dimension of His naming. An angel of the Lord instructed His parents that He was to be called Jesus (Yeshua), meaning rescuer or deliverer, and that He was, the Savior. As Isaiah prophesied:

"Listen, O isles, unto me; and hearken, ye people, from far; The LORD hath called me from the womb; from the bowels of my mother hath he made mention of my name. And he hath made my mouth like a sharp sword; in the shadow of his hand hath he hid me, and made me a polished shaft; in his quiver hath he hid me; And said unto me, Thou art my servant, O Israel, in whom I will be glorified." Isaiah 49:1-3

When He walked on the earth, His name was mighty. His disciples followed Him as He preached, and saw Him set the demoniacs free, restore blind eyes, cleanse the lepers, raise the crippled, and raise the dead. He sent His twelve disciples as well seventy of His followers to go out and do the same things in His name. They did, and recorded astounding miracles. They came back rejoicing, observing that devils were incapacitated and subjugated in the name of Jesus:

"And the seventy returned again with joy, saying, Lord, even the devils are subject unto us through thy name. And he said unto them, I beheld satan as lightning fall from heaven. Behold, I give unto you power to tread on serpents and scorpions, and over all the power of the enemy: and nothing shall by any means hurt you." Luke 10:17-19

Jesus authorized them to do the same things He did and even greater things in His name, and to expect signs and wonders to follow. The disciples were persuaded that if they used the name of Jesus, the very things He did in their presence would happen, and Jesus did not disappoint. Hallelujah!

When Jesus fulfilled His mission on earth by dying on the cross, paying the price for our sin, and resurrecting from the dead, another dimension of the greatness of His name was published. There was a heavenly coronation, so to speak. The Father highly exalted Him and conferred on Him the name that is above every name, at the mention of which every knee must bow and every tongue confess that Jesus is Lord to the glory of God the Father (Philippians 2:9-11).

"Wherefore God also hath highly exalted him, and given him a name which is above every name which is above every name: That at the name of Jesus every knee should bow, of things in heaven, things in earth, and things under the earth; And that every tongue should confess that Jesus Christ is Lord to the glory of the Father." Philippians 2:9-11

Jehovah God has thus vested, in the name of Jesus, the treasures, glory, authority and powers of the eternities. This is the name that contains and holds the sum of the powers of the Godhead - the Father, the Son, and the Holy Spirit.

The name of Jesus is the name which every spirit, power, force, disease, throne or dominion bows to and is subject. There is nothing known or unknown that is not subject to that name. The name rules in all three worlds – over angels and things in heaven, over created personalities, spirits and elements in the earth or universe, and over the satanic domain of the second heavens and realm of the demonic under-world. The elements, natural forces, and spiritual entities are all subject to this name. The name of Jesus is like no other name.

The name of Jesus is also the only name that holds the inherent power to save. Those who believe in, and call upon, the name of Jesus shall be saved. (Matthew 1:21)

"Neither is there salvation in any other: for there is none other name under heaven given among men, whereby we must be saved." Acts 4:12

"For whosoever shall call upon the name of the Lord shall be saved." Romans 10:13

"And it shall come to pass, that whosoever shall call on the name of the Lord shall be saved." Acts 2:21

Therefore, the gospel of Jesus must be preached, namely, that God, in His love for the world, freely gave us Jesus, so that anyone who believes in Him and His sacrifice on the cross to purge our sins, would be saved.

After Jesus' resurrection from the dead, He appeared to His disciples and told them what they had to do. He gave and willed to the Church, the unqualified use of His name. In legal terms, He gave us the Power of Attorney. A Power of Attorney is a written legal document given by a person - the principal, donor or grantor - to another, authorizing him/her to represent or act on their behalf in matters regarding their estate, business, finances, and/or any other issues and situations that may have legal implications. Jesus is that principal, grantor and donor who has authorized the Church to act on His behalf.

"And he said unto them, Go ye into all the world, and preach the gospel to every creature. He that believeth and is baptized shall be saved: but he that believeth not shall be damned. And these signs shall follow them that believe; In my name shall they cast out devils; they shall speak with new tongues; They shall take up serpents; and if they drink any deadly thing, it shall not hurt them; they shall lay hands on the sick, and they shall recover." Mark 16:15-18

This means that the Church is authorized and deputized to act as agents and representatives of Jesus, as ones who have received the Power of Attorney from Him. We have His permission to enforce and maintain His will, plan, purpose and design on earth (Matthew 28:18-20).

This is certainly not an empty delegation of power. As the apostle John stated, the Father God loves the Son Jesus, and has given all things into His hand, and Jesus has all power in heaven and on the earth. This power and authority has been transferred to the body of believers. Whatever we say, proclaim, decree, legislate and declare is backed by the endless and omnipotent power of heaven. Hallelujah!

After the Lord gave the disciples the Power of Attorney, that unqualified, unreserved use of His name, He was received into heaven.

After Jesus' ascension, the believers in the early Church who were witnesses to the grace, glory, authority, power and majesty with which He worked the works of God, had no cause to quietly fade into the background. Absolutely not. Rather, they continued His commission to them to go and do the same things He did to proclaim the Jubilee and its anointing to set humanity free.

They went everywhere and preached salvation in Jesus' name, and He was with them, working with them and confirming the word with signs and wonders following (Mark 16:19-20).

"And by the hands of the Apostles were many signs and wonders wrought among the people; (and they were all with one accord in Solomon's porch. And of the rest durst no man join himself to them: but the people magnified them. And believers were the more added to the Lord, multitudes both of men and women.) Insomuch that they brought forth the sick into the streets, and laid them on beds and couches, that at the least the shadow of Peter passing by might overshadow some of them. There came also a multitude out of the cities round about unto Jerusalem, bringing sick folks, and them which were vexed with unclean spirits: and they were healed everyone." Acts 5:12-16

As they went forth with the gospel, working wonders and miracles in the name of Jesus, it was as though Jesus was still present with them, physically doing the works.

The name of an individual represents his personality, nature, character, possessions, stature, power and authority. What the apostles and disciples did in ministry was therefore not by their own power; everything was accomplished in the name of Jesus who was at work in them.

There is an all-important key to grasp here about the power of Jesus' name, which is that, because of His name, there is no difference between His spiritual and physical presence. His name bridges the gap between the spiritual and physical divide, and so they are one and the same thing.

The realm of the spirit is as real as the realm of the natural. All this is to say that, although Jesus was no longer physically present, He was still right there through His name and His Spirit. That remains the same for us today. He is always present with us. The Lord Himself promised: "I am with you always, even to the end of the age."

It is also particularly important to highlight the fact that the name of Jesus is that key that grants us access to the Father in heaven and to all His unlimited resources. His name unrestrictedly opens to us all that the Father has. There is a dual purpose to God lavishing His good treasure upon us.

First, Jesus grants us all our petitions and supplications and requests that we ask in His name so that the Father God is glorified. We must get this, that it is very important to Jesus that we do not hold back in asking Him for anything, because our asking and our receiving from Him throws the floodlights on God's glory without fail, as we, the receivers, give honor and praise to God. Jesus said:

"Verily, verily, I say unto you, He that believeth on me, the works that I do shall he do also; and greater works than these shall he do; because I go unto my Father. And whatsoever ye shall ask in my name, that will I do, that the Father may be glorified in the Son. If ye shall ask anything in my name, I will do it." John 14:12-13

As well, our petitions, supplications and requests made to the Father in Jesus' name are answered because Jesus wants His people to be happy, ecstatic, and full of joy. It pleases Him immensely when His people are liberated and break out in exceeding and unspeakable joy.

"And in that day ye shall ask me nothing. Verily, verily, I say unto you, Whatsoever ye shall ask the Father in my name, he will give it you. Hitherto have ye asked nothing in my name: ask, and ye shall receive, that your joy may be full." John 16:23-24

When Jesus said, "And in that day, ye shall ask me nothing", He was referring to the day He would be physically absent from His disciples and when they could no longer bring their petitions to Him. In that period, He said, they would now have direct access to the Father through His name. What He is saying to us is that we now have the key which opens the door to the Father's throne room and storehouse. We are now children who can cry out to Him, "Abba Father."

Responsible parents meet the needs of their children. They work hard to provide for their children, to relieve them of any stress, struggle or concern. Some of them may not have all the resources to meet all the needs of their children, but they certainly put in their best. They would do anything in their power to address their children's needs, making sure they are blessed, safe and secure.

If earthly parents can be so gracious, how much more the good and perfect Father in heaven whose loving kindness and tender mercies endure forever? He never runs out of resources and supplies, and He is ever ready to open up His good treasure to those who ask of Him and trust Him.

The name of Jesus turns open the lock to the treasure chest of the Father. All things are ready and available in the bank and barns of the heavenly Father. When the child of God comes to the Father in the name of his Holy Child Jesus and asks or makes requests and petitions, he will receive what he asks for.

The Father sees the tears in the eyes of every child. He knows and understands our worries, pain, sorrow and desperation. He hears our cracking, weary voices, and knows all about our tests, trials and tribulation in the world. He is full of love and compassion.

He says to us: "You are home now. Weep not, child, for my Son, the first begotten from the dead, the first born among many brethren, paid the full price on your behalf. You are here in His name; therefore, my treasure box is open to you. Take all you need or desire. All things are ready, and all things are yours."

Therefore, let the Church arise now, more than ever before, to herald the victories, triumphs, glories and power of this majestic name "Jesus" which brings salvation to the lost, deliverance to the bound, release to the oppressed, and provision and fulfilment to humanity.

In this name are the sick healed, the dead raised, lepers cleansed, and devils cast out. At the sound of this name, demons flee, the cripples leap for joy, dumb tongues are loosened, and deaf ears are unstopped.

Child of God, whatsoever ye desire, when ye pray, believe that ye receive them, and ye shall have them (Mark 11:24). Jesus wants your joy to be full. There is a miracle ready for you today, a miracle prepared for you always. Grab it by faith today and expect the manifestation in due season. The name of Jesus does it all.

# Chapter 17

## THE PROCLAMATION OF THE JUBILEE

As the preceding Chapters show, the Jubilee was proclaimed in Israel through multiple mediums and formats. It was a production like no other, staged through creation. It was expressed through the various Sabbaths of Israel. It was also decreed as an ordinance under the Law through Moses. It was further dramatized through the feasts of Israel, and was unraveled through the redemptive names of God. Through the ages, it became a pseudohistorical celebration. The prophets of God alluded to it as they received inspired words from God.

The prophet Isaiah stands out in making some deep prophetic proclamations about the Jubilee and its connection to the anointed One. He said:

"The Spirit of the Lord GOD is upon me; because the LORD hath anointed me to preach good tidings unto the meek; he hath sent me to bind up the brokenhearted, to proclaim liberty to the captives, and the opening of the prison to them that are bound; To proclaim the acceptable year of the LORD, and the day of vengeance of our God; to comfort all that mourn; To appoint unto them that mourn in Zion, to give unto them beauty for ashes, the oil of joy for mourning, the garment of praise for the spirit of heaviness; that they might be called trees of righteousness, the planting of the LORD, that he might be glorified." Isaiah 61:1-3

All of Israel understood that this was a Messianic scripture, foretelling the advent of the promised Messiah. Then comes Jesus on a special Sabbath day to a synagogue in His hometown of Nazareth, some seven hundred to one thousand years after Isaiah. He stood up to read a scripture from the prophets, and the scroll of the prophet Isaiah was handed to Him:

"And there was delivered unto him the book of the prophet Esaias. And when he had opened the book, he found the place where it was written, The Spirit of the Lord is upon me, because he hath anointed me to preach the gospel to the poor; he hath sent me to heal the brokenhearted, to preach deliverance to the captives, and recovering of sight to the blind, to set at liberty them that are bruised, To preach the acceptable year of the Lord. And he closed the book, and he gave it again to the minister, and sat down. And the eyes of all them that were in the synagogue were fastened on him. And he began to say unto them, This day is this scripture fulfilled in your ears." Luke 4:17-21

Essentially, in declaring that the scripture was this day fulfilled, Jesus was connecting His very being, identity and mission with Isaiah's prophecy about the Messiah. He was saying that He is the Jubilee.

This absolutely incensed His hearers who thought He was being blasphemous. They were livid, and sought to throw Him down a hill, but He quietly made His escape.

It is interesting that the people of Israel were eagerly awaiting the advent of the Messiah who would deliver and set them free. Nonetheless, when He appeared and presented Himself to them as such, they were outraged and failed to recognize Him, and pointed to his antecedents as Joseph's son.

Note that the people's palpable outrage, rejection and resentment did not, and could not neutralize, change, rebrand or redefine the truth Jesus sought to convey, namely that He is the "I am that I am", and the Jubilee. This is just as true for the world today. Although many reject Him as the Savior of the world, that does not make Him any less the Savior, nor does it alter God's redemptive plan for humanity. In other words, Jesus' Lordship is not a binary or bifurcated truth moderated through people's views, preferences and philosophies. It is a given, a constant, and an unequivocal and eternal fact.

In making the proclamation regarding the acceptable year of the Lord, therefore, Jesus presented Himself as the very embodiment and fulfillment of the acceptable year of the Lord, the year of Jubilee. His declaration showed that He is the Christ, the anointed, appointed One to atone for sin, redeem humanity, set them free from the dominion of darkness, and translate them into the kingdom of God (Colossians 1:13).

Let us now go on the remarkable journey of deciphering and decrypting all that Jesus declared and proclaimed about the acceptable year of the Lord.

# Chapter 18

## THE SPIRIT OF THE LORD IS UPON ME

"The Spirit of the Lord is upon me ..."

Jesus proclaimed in the synagogue in Nazareth that the Spirit of the Lord was upon Him and had anointed Him to fulfill His purpose and to proclaim the acceptable year of the Lord, the Jubilee. What we see here is that the Jubilee is inextricably intertwined with, and dependent on, the anointing of the Spirit. In other words, it is the anointing that brings and releases the Jubilee freedom package.

The anointing is the manifest power, flow or activity of the Spirit of God. Jesus Christ is the Messiah. "Messiah" means "the Christ", which also means "the Anointed One and His anointing."

Jesus was heavily anointed by God, and this is a theme that runs through His entire life and ministry. He was conceived by the power of the Holy Spirit (Luke 1:34-35). His mother Mary was overshadowed by the power of the Holy Spirit. Therefore, even though He was born in the likeness of men, He was not of human descent, but God incarnate. Through His birth, God united with man, but Jesus never lost His deity or divinity, in that the Father dwelt in Him.

In His ministry on earth, however, He did not operate in that capacity as God. Rather, He emptied Himself of His divinity and ministered and functioned in His humanity, at the level of man and as the last Adam. As a man, though, He was anointed in the fullness of the power of the Spirit, and He demonstrated that Holy Ghost anointing and power.

The prophets, priests, kings, apostles and Biblical writers had the anointing from God by degree, and the measure of the Spirit was commensurate with their divine assignments and work. Likewise, Jesus, because of His mandate as the Messiah, was given the fullness of the Spirit for His redemptive activities.

Just look at the Messianic job description. The Messiah was ordained by God to break the power of sin, to forgive sin, to preach good news to the poor, heal the sick, cast out devils, heal the broken-hearted, to die for mankind, to destroy the devil and all his works, to overcome death, hell and the grave, to be the first begotten from the dead, and to lead the Church in triumphant procession from glory to glory. These far-reaching works of God could not be accomplished without God's Spirit, without the empowerment of the anointing.

Since Jesus was tapped by the Godhead to fulfill these eternal purposes of the Jubilee, it was imperative for Him to be endowed with the fullness of the Spirit and of power, and so God anointed Him with the Spirit without measure.

"For whom God hath sent speaketh the words of God: for God giveth not the Spirit by measure unto him." John 4:34

When God assigns a person any task, He equips and anoints that person, and causes the anointing to flow to accomplish His purposes.

At the beginning of Jesus' ministry, He was baptized by John the Baptist, and the Spirit of God descended on Him in bodily form like a dove and acknowledged Him as His beloved Son in whom He was well pleased (Luke 3:21-22). That was a wonderful endorsement from the Most High God.

He was then led, by the Spirit, into the wilderness to fast and pray for forty days and nights (Luke 4:1.) After this, He entered Galilee in the power of the Spirit, and His fame was broadcast all over (Luke 4:14). He went about doing good and healing all who were oppressed of the devil (Acts 10:38, Matthew 4:23-25). The Holy Spirit empowered Jesus to preach, teach, heal and work the wonders of God. His whole ministry was therefore by the Spirit. No one can be used of God without the Holy Spirit.

It is also the anointing of the Spirit that enabled Jesus to offer Himself as a sacrifice for sin. The ministry of offering sacrifices to God was reserved for the High Priest who, on the Day of Atonement, would swap his golden priestly robe for a linen robe, and would receive the sacrifices of the people. He would then take the blood thereof into the Holy of Holies to present it to God as atonement for the sins of the people.

Jesus is our eternal High Priest who presented the blood of the sacrifice to God in heaven, in the real Holiest Place. Like the earthly High Priest, He put off His golden priestly garments (His deity) when He emptied Himself and made Himself of no reputation. He put on the linen garments of the ordinary priests when he was fashioned in the likeness of men. He thus fully identified with humanity and went to the cross to pour out His own blood to pay the price for sin through his death (Philippians 2:5-9). He took that blood to the mercy seat to make atonement for the sins of the world. He could not have done that without the Holy Spirit.

"How much more shall the blood of Christ, who through the eternal Spirit offered himself without spot unto God, purge your conscience from dead works to serve the living God?." Hebrews 9:14

He had to be anointed for this all-important priestly ministry, and He was able to offer Himself to be crucified, to shed His blood, and to become the atonement for sin, only through the eternal Spirit.

The impact of the Spirit on Jesus did not end with His death. In fact, God raised Him from the dead by the Spirit (Romans 8:11). In His ascension also, He was received into heaven in the cloud of glory, which is the shekinah, the manifest presence of the Spirit of God (Acts 1:9).

Jesus was therefore never void of the help and presence of the Holy Spirit at any point in His life. His conception, life, ministry, death, resurrection and ascension into heaven were all marked by the deep work of the Spirit. He accomplished His duties on earth with the help of the Spirit.

Like the High Priest in the Old Testament who, after completing his duties on the Day of Atonement, would again put on his golden high priestly robes and would bless the people, Jesus has put on His robes of divinity, and is glorified and exalted to the highest place. Like the earthly High Priest did, He too comes with a blessing.

He blessed the Church and gave it the great commission to herald the gospel to all nations. He however required of them that, before they assumed this responsibility, they must wait for the promise of the Father, the Holy Spirit, to endue them with power from on high (Luke 24:49; Acts 1:8).

If Jesus needed the anointing of the Spirit to fulfill His ministry, then surely, the Church, His sentinel which must occupy till He returns, will require no less; she simply cannot function optimally and to her utmost potential without the empowering of the Spirit. Where the Spirit of the Lord is, there is liberty; yokes are broken and burdens lifted by reason of the anointing; mountains are removed, and the impossible is made possible, not by might nor by power, but by the Spirit of the Lord.

# Chapter 19

## JESUS ANOINTED TO PREACH THE GOSPEL

*"… because He hath anointed me
to preach the gospel …"*

As part of His Jubilee portfolio, Jesus reminded His hearers that He came to preach the gospel, the good news, to the world. In the three years of His ministry, He did this without fail. He preached and taught on a wide variety of topics, and in all of His teachings, He progressively and surely revealed Himself as the Jubilee.

He relayed the information to the people through multiple channels and in diverse settings. He taught through plain discourse or parables, through formal or informal means, in the synagogues, in the wilderness, in homes, at the seaside and lakeside, from city to city, and in small intimate settings with His disciples, in large gatherings, using every opportunity as a teaching moment. Some of the foundational tenets He preached and taught are discussed below.

## 1. THE GOSPEL OF THE KINGDOM

God gave to Adam and Eve, dominion and rule over all the earth; they were the original rulers of the kingdom of this world (Genesis 1:26-27). However, Adam submitted himself to the devil when he disobeyed God by eating of the forbidden fruit of the Garden. He thereby transferred the kingdom of this world to the devil, and the devil became the god of this world (Luke 4:5-6).

Once the devil's kingdom of darkness took over the affairs of this world through sin, he introduced and released sickness, disease, poverty, bondage, demonic spirits, torments, oppression and affliction, leading multitudes to damnation in hell.

For this reason, God Almighty sent Jesus to bring down into the earth, His heavenly kingdom, to diffuse the darkness, dispel the blindness, and to repair the destruction Satan brought into this world. Everything Jesus stood for, and everything He said and did, was to enforce the kingdom of God over the powers of darkness. He was manifested so that He would destroy all the works of the devil (1 John 3:8).

God's kingdom is here. It was presented and entrenched by Jesus, not only in His teaching and preaching, but also in the effective release of kingdom power and dominion over every sickness and disease among the people, the exercise of authority over demonic spirits, and the enforcement of the deliverance and liberty of those bound and oppressed.

"And Jesus went about all Galilee, teaching in their synagogues, and preaching the gospel of the kingdom, and healing all manner of sickness and all manner of disease among the people. And his fame went throughout all Syria: and they brought unto him all sick people that were taken with divers diseases and torments, and those which were possessed with devils, and those which were lunatick, and those that had the palsy; and he healed them."
Matthew 4:23-24

When Jesus cast out devils, He presented it as compelling evidence that the kingdom of God is here now on earth. (Luke 11:20). He said:

"But if I cast out devils by the Spirit of God, then the kingdom of God is come unto you." Matthew 12:28

Freedom from demons and sicknesses, as demonstrated by Jesus or by the use of His name, indicates the activity of heaven upon the earth.

God is not only the God of heaven but also of the earth, and the God of all things He has created. He is alive in the earth today, enforcing the power of His kingdom and breaking the powers of the devil against humanity.

Jesus came proclaiming the message of the kingdom of heaven. That message is the gospel that declares forgiveness of sins to the repentant heart, and the atonement and propitiation through the sacrificial work of Christ on the cross, providing redemption and the reconciliation of man to His creator. Jesus Messiah is God's offering for salvation to restore communion and fellowship between man and God.

There is nothing humanly possible that sinful man could ever do to attain God's righteousness, that right standing with Him. Man could not develop, refine or refurbish himself through any form of penance or religious medium to recover from his fallen state, for all have sinned and come short of the glory of God (Romans 3:23).

Neither could the monarchs, rulers and kingdoms of this world do or institute anything to obtain righteousness for their subjects. They may have dominion over their geographical jurisdictions, yes, but they have no power over sin, Satan, hell, death and the grave.

Jesus, on the other hand, by the power of His kingdom, which is the kingdom of heaven, reigns supreme eternally in every realm - the natural and spiritual. He rules in heaven, on earth, and under the earth, and all things are subject to Him (Philippians 2:8-10). Salvation and righteousness could therefore only come from the kingdom of heaven, that kingdom which holds all power, dominion and authority (Romans 5:17, Romans 6:23). The healing of the sick and casting out of devils are a major and integral part of the presentation of the gospel.

Jesus dissolved the power of sin to present righteousness to humanity. He took the sting of death, which is the penalty for sin, to offer eternal life to the world. He overcame sin, hell and death. The grave could not hold Him. Therefore, all who come to Him will experience the truth that sets them free, and righteousness and life eternal are imparted to their spirits (John 3:1-6, 16; John 14:6).

The gospel of the kingdom is God's foreordained plan, premeditated scheme, and predestined purpose to provide eternal redemption for lost and sinful humanity. It is totally an act of God, cooked, baked and set up from heaven to reach to souls on earth who hear the word of God, come under the convicting power of the Holy Spirit, and call on God for His mercy, for salvation and restoration.

Jesus is "Immanuel" which, by interpretation, means that God is with us and is united with humanity. He is with us always, presenting to us, the unqualified access to His kingdom.

Whosoever will, may come. All who receive Him will find their way into God's kingdom, for He is the way, the truth and the life. His light shines in our hearts, restoring to us righteousness, peace and joy in the Holy Ghost (Romans 14:17).

The good news, the gospel, is the very ticket for the flight to freedom, to Jubilee's destination.

## 2. REPENTANCE

Jesus taught on repentance from sin and forgiveness. Repentance takes place when a person is convicted of his sin or experiences the awareness of his error or wrongdoing, and regrets it with godly sorrow. It is a willingness to have a change of heart and mind.

"From that time Jesus began to preach, and to say, Repent: for the kingdom of God is at hand." Matthew 4:17

God is a holy and righteous God who cannot countenance sin; sin breaks fellowship and communion with Him (Isaiah 59:1-2). Out of the depths of His love for humanity, however, He made provision for the remission of sin through repentance, for without repentance, all will perish and none will be saved (Luke 13:1-5). The coming of Jesus was the intervention of God's kingdom in the earth to bring liberty and redemption to man through repentance.

Through the atoning work of Christ on the cross, and through the power of the Holy Spirit, the repentant person cuts off the dominion of Satan and sin, and garners the ability to overcome temptation to sin and to lead a pure, godly life through prayer.

Repentance generates the loss of the desire to sin or slip back into the works of the flesh or worldly lusts.

Jesus did not come to condemn the sinner but to atone for their sin. He did not come for the righteous but to call sinners to repentance (Luke 5:31-32). The essence of God's kingdom is to liberate humanity from sin and all of its effects.

"And he said unto them, Thus it is written, and thus it behooved Christ to suffer, and to rise from the dead the third day: And that repentance and remission of sins should be preached in his name among all nations, beginning at Jerusalem. And ye are witnesses of these things." Luke 24:46-48

Jesus suffered, bled, died and rose again on the third day to pay the price for the remission of sin, and that remission of sin is attained through repentance. When sinners confess their sins to God and bury them at the cross of Christ Jesus, He saves them. His life and light is then expressed through the new heart received by the enabling power of the Holy Spirit.

Jesus came to proclaim and establish the kingdom of God. Salvation through Him brings this kingdom rule into the heart of a person. The way to experience the kingdom and its provisions of remission of sin and escape from the judgement of God is through repentance.

### 3. LOVE

Jesus spoke a lot about love and was Himself love in action. He taught that love embodies and fulfils the law and the prophets; it is the key that unlocks everything under the law and the prophets. Love is the sum of the commandments of the holy and righteous God.

"Master, which is the great commandment in the law? Jesus said unto him, Thou shalt love the Lord thy God with all thy heart, and with all thy soul, and with all thy mind. This is the first and great commandment. And the second is like unto it, Thou shalt love thy neighbour as thyself. On these two commandments hang all the law and the prophets." Matthew 22:36-40

The God-kind of love (Greek: Agape) which Jesus proclaimed is the type that is without dissimulation. That kind of love is sacrificial; it is not only for the friend, but is also for the enemy, and it streams out to persons who are good to us as well as to those who unkindly or improperly treat us. Jesus said:

"Ye have heard that it hath been said, Thou shalt love thy neighbour, and hate thine enemy. But I say unto you, Love your enemies, bless them that curse you, do good to them that hate you, and pray for them which despitefully use you, and persecute you; That ye may be the children of your Father which is in heaven: for he maketh his sun to rise on the evil and on the good, and sendeth rain on the just and on the unjust. For if ye love them which love you, what reward have ye? do not even the publicans the same? And if ye salute your brethren only, what do ye more than others? do not even the publicans so? Be ye therefore perfect, even as your Father which is in heaven is perfect." Matthew 5:43-48

The vast majority of people are usually only good to those who are good to them. However, Jesus taught that to be loving only to those who do us good places us in the class of the publicans who were reputed to be corrupt and insincere, and who overburdened the masses with taxes, and only showed love to persons in their fraternity. Jesus taught that a person is only better than a publican when he loves all.

It is clear, then, that it is the love of God reigning in our hearts that distinguishes the saint from the sinner. God Himself modeled that love for us when He gave His Son, Jesus, to bring us salvation. Jesus is God's love gift to the world. Jesus revealed His love through His teachings, His life, and His death. It was love that went to the cross and paid the price for sin to bring redemption to humanity.

We ought to imbibe God's character of love and to love all. Love will forever remain the golden rule, and will stand the test of all time and eternity. "Love the Lord thy God with all thy heart, with all thy soul, and with all thy strength and with all thy mind, and love your neighbor as thy self" (Luke 10:27, Mark 12:30-31). Operating the love of God is what demonstrates to the world who we are in Christ.

## 4. FORGIVENESS

Jesus preached again and again on forgiveness and showed how imperative this is in our walk with God and our devotion to Him. Forgiveness is the conscious and deliberate decision a person makes to release another who has inflicted harm, pain, offence or hurt, from feelings of resentment, anger, animosity or revenge.

Jesus explained that we ought to forgive others their trespasses even as the Father forgives us our trespasses. Our prayers to God are blocked when we are unforgiving. In fact, as Jesus relayed through parables, our lives become open season to tormentors, and are subject to bondage and spiritual warfare when we are unforgiving (Matthew 6:12-13, Mark 11:24-26, Matthew 18:21-35).

When He was asked how many times a person ought to forgive, He said seventy times seven. The Jubilee connection is right there in that algorithm, because 70 x 7 = 490. That product of 490 follows Jubilee computations, and is symbolic of the Jubilee season where all debts are cancelled, and the bound go free. This was therefore Jesus' way of saying that we cannot be legalistic, and that we must forgive always.

Forgiveness is therapeutic. Although it is a demonstration of mercy towards the one who has done wrong, it is also greatly beneficial to the one who has been wronged. It releases the heart from toxicity, and saves, heals, and throws the door wide open to freedom, love and reconciliation.

## 5. PRAYER

Prayer is central to the life of the follower of Christ. In fact, our first baby steps toward God to build a relationship with Him are taken through the prayer of salvation through Jesus (John 1:12-14).

Prayer opens the heavens. After Jesus' baptism by John, He came out of the water praying, and the heavens were opened. The Spirit of God descended upon Him like a dove, and a voice came down from heaven saying, "Thou art my beloved Son, in thee I am well pleased" (Luke 3:21-22). There would be no fuel or spiritual fire power in the life of the saint without prayer.

Jesus imparted various insights on prayer. He reoriented people's minds about the sanctity and purpose of the House of God. When He saw that it was being used as a marketplace, He reprimanded the moneychangers and those buying and selling, reminding them that the House of God is the House of prayer, and not a den of robbers (Mark 11:15-17). By this, He was trying to instill the importance of sanctified corporate prayer in the Temple. The Temple is the place where the people of God bring their sacrifices and prayers to Him. This is where they ought to gather and seek God in prayer.

Jesus also instructed His followers on the way they ought to pray. He taught "The Lord's Prayer" which communicated and modeled what prayer should entail (Matthew 6:9-13). He urged that, when we stand praying and we hold something against another person, we should forgive that person, so that the Father will forgive us our trespasses also (Mark 11:24-26).

He also warned people not to be like the hypocrites or Pharisees when they prayed. He explained that prayer was not an opportunity for them to publicly show off or demonstrate their eloquence and righteousness; prayer must come from the depths of the heart in humility (Matthew 6:5-8).

Jesus sought to inculcate, in His hearers, certain disciplines in prayer. He taught the attributes of perseverance, persistence, importunity, and humility in prayer (Luke 18:1-14). People ought to pray always, and not faint; they must believe God to see the impossible become possible. Praying through to the breakthrough is the major key to the outbreak of the supernatural. Jesus gave the assurance that prayer would always yield results.

He drew parallels between our earthly fathers and our heavenly Father to stress and establish that the Father God knows even better how to give good things to His children. He therefore encouraged God's children to ask, and that they would receive, to seek, and they would find, and to knock, and the door would be opened (Matthew 7:7-8).

Jesus Himself exemplified a persistent, robust prayer life, and that is the believer's example for prayer. He rose early, a great while before day, and went to the mountains to pray (Mark 1:35). Led by the Holy Spirit, He separated Himself for forty days and forty nights, fasting and praying (Matthew 4:1-2). He prayed fervent prayers of agony in the Garden of Gethsemane (Hebrews 5:7; Mathew 26:36-46). And when He was dying on the cross, He prayed intercessory prayers of forgiveness to the Father.

May God lift the drooping hands and strengthen the weak knees, for this is the time to cry out to Him! Let the people of God rise in prevailing prayer for miracles.

## 6. FAITH

Jesus cursed a fig tree that had no figs to teach the disciples lessons in faith. By the next morning, that tree was dried up from its roots, totally shriveled. Peter was amazed, and called Jesus' attention to what had happened to the tree as a result of the words spoken against it the day before. Jesus replied, "Have faith in God" (Mark 11:22).

By these words, Jesus was conveying the pivotal truth that the people of God must have and demonstrate the God-kind of faith. This is the faith that is released through the words that we proclaim, decree and declare. God released His creative power through His spoken word. He made all things by the word of His power (Hebrews 11:3). He called the things that be not as though they were, through words (Romans 4:17).

To see miracles, signs and wonders, and to experience the full breadth of Jubilee, we must have and exercise that same kind of faith through our bold declarations. That faith is not unattainable faith; on the contrary, Jesus declares, it can be as small as a mustard seed.

"And the apostles said unto the Lord, Increase our faith. And the Lord said, If ye had faith as a grain of mustard seed, ye might say unto this sycamine tree, Be thou plucked up by the root, and be thou planted into the sea; and it should obey you." Luke 17:5-6

Jesus further revealed that, when we speak to a mountain to be removed and cast into the sea and do not entertain doubts in our heart, but believe that those things we say shall come to pass, we will have whatsoever we say (Mark 11:23, Matthew 17:20-21).

The mountain refers to any hindrance, opposition, struggle, burden, or any need imaginable; these are all subject to the words spoken in faith without doubting. All things are possible to them that believe (Mark 9:23).

Therefore, rise up in faith. Speak to your mountain. Tear down the strongholds in your mind, and bind the powers of the enemy. Command diseases and evil spirits to leave. Call forth the blessings of the Lord.

Jesus assures us: "Therefore I say unto you, what things so ever ye desire, when ye pray, believe that ye receive them, and ye shall have them" (Mark 11:24). Child of God, proclaim, by faith, freedom and Jubilee now, in the name of Jesus.

## 7. GIVING

Giving is very important to God. He demonstrated it when He freely gave Jesus to the world. If He did not hold back His only Son, Jesus, then we can rest in the assurance that He would, together with Jesus, freely give us all things (Romans 8:32). Jesus explained:

"For God so loved the world, that he gave his only begotten Son, that whosoever believeth in him should not perish, but have everlasting life." John 3:16

This kind of selfless giving from God is our example. Jesus impressed on His followers that they must cultivate the right attitude towards giving. He cautioned people not to sound an alarm when giving, simply to get the approval, applause and respect of men. He urged them to give their alms in secret, assuring them that the Father who sees in secret will reward them openly (Matthew 6:1-4).

Essentially, Jesus was communicating that giving is not "show biz." It must be done with the right heart and motive. When it is done with the correct mindset and motivation, the giver is rewarded by the faithful God.

Jesus also promoted cheerfulness and generosity in giving. He taught the law of giving and receiving, which is a spiritual law that can be activated in faith. He said:

"Give, and it shall be given unto you; good measure, pressed down, and shaken together, and running over, shall men give into your bosom. For with the same measure that ye mete withal it shall it shall be measured to you again." Luke 6:38

Giving in faith and in good conscience for a good cause triggers a harvest. God's watchful eyes are on us when we give, and He sees our attitude and our faith in action. When He is pleased by our giving, our faith and our attitude, He moves on the hearts of others to work on our behalf. Men will return the favor; they will give back to us and open unimaginable doors of opportunity to us.

Jesus used the widow's mite as a teachable moment on giving. One day, He sat at the treasury in the Temple during offering time. He observed the people giving their offerings. Some gave out of their abundance, but were not happy about giving to God. They gave grudgingly, and not with pure motives or cheerful hearts. The widow gave the smallest offering that day.

In the eyes of Jesus, however, she gave the greatest offering because she gave out of her insufficiency, and not out of her abundance. Proportionally, she gave a hundred percent because that was all she had. She gave in faith, likely not knowing where the next meal was going to come from. She had no husband to help her. There is also no indication that she had anyone in her life to support or motivate her. Yet, she gave all she had into the Temple treasury.

Jesus, who knows the hearts of people, was watching. He observed her faith, intentions, motives, and commended her for her great giving even though, in reality, the amount she gave was the smallest (Mark 12:41-44).

Your giving too may gain that quality which pleases God if it is done in faith and with a genuine heart towards God and His work. Its size does not matter; it may be the greatest giving in His sight. He who sees in secret will reward you openly.

Giving is like a seed you sow. Expect a harvest. May God grant you a bountiful harvest in all your sacrifices made and seed sown into His kingdom.

## 8. HIS SECOND COMING

Before His ascension, Jesus spoke about the signs of the end-times and His second coming. He addressed these matters to stoke alertness, preparation and readiness amongst His people (Matthew 24:4-31).

He forewarned that there would be wars and rumors of wars; nation would rise up against nation, and kingdom against kingdom. There would be catastrophic events like famines, earthquakes, and pestilences hitting the earth in diverse places.
He also warned that there would arise false Christs and false prophets who would deceive many. Iniquity would abound, and the love of many for God and the things of God would wax cold. There would also be persecution in the Church. There would be betrayals, and many would be offended. The gospel of the kingdom will be preached in all the world as a witness to all nations, and then will the end come.

Jesus presented the silver lining, namely that those who endure to the end shall be saved. He told the disciples that He would be received into heaven, and that He was going to prepare a place for the believers. Once that mission is complete, He would return to receive His Church, His bride, onto Himself, that where He is, there we may be also (John 14:1-3). Upon completing His work on earth, Jesus ascended on high and took His place at the right hand of God, the Father.

The second coming of Jesus is going to be simply glorious. It will be like lightning flashing and shining from the east to the west. He will appear in clouds of glory and power, and all eyes shall see Him. At the sound of the trumpet blast by the angels, the elect of God shall be gathered from the four winds of the earth, from one end of heaven to the other (Matthew 24:4-31).

Jesus is getting our mansions ready, saints of God! That is exciting news. Not only is Jesus preparing the mansions in heaven, but He is also refining His bride, the Church in the earth today. He is coming back for a purified, sanctified, glorious Church without spot or wrinkle.

The walk of faith is not always going to be rosy. However, the Church needs to be strong, tough, single-minded, grounded and rooted in faith, and must not waver in difficult and testing times. Spending eternity with the Father, Jesus, the Holy Spirit and the believers in glory, is the hope and anchor of every child of God. Get ready, for soon and very soon, we are going to see the King.

# Chapter 20

## JESUS PREACHES THE GOSPEL / GOOD NEWS TO THE POOR

*"He hath anointed me to preach the gospel to the poor..."*

Poverty is a state of insufficiency, deprivation, lack and want. It often subjects people to deplorable, inhumane, or substandard living conditions, and deflates or strips them of their human dignity. It is, unfortunately, an endemic reality of the vast majority of people. Please, please, please get this - poverty is not synonymous with humility, holiness or spirituality, as some people believe. It is the work of the devil, and it is a demonic spirit that plagues lives and holds people in bondage to oppressive task masters.

Jesus' manifesto, which He read out from Isaiah 61, stated that He was anointed to preach good news to the poor. This means that poverty was an area that He was destined and ordained to specifically deal with and eradicate. A number of points are worthy of note.

The first consideration is this - what is that poverty that was to be addressed by Jesus? Some have grappled with the question of whether the good news to the poor is only a reference to spiritual poverty, or is a reference to material poverty. The Bible persuasively shows that Jesus was not only speaking about spiritual poverty; He also came to break the back of material poverty.

With respect to spiritual poverty, there is no question that Jesus came to deal with it. When God created Adam and Eve, He blessed them and told them to be fruitful and to multiply, and to replenish the earth and subdue it. Man was given total dominion over the resources, riches, and wealth that God deposited in the earth (Genesis 1:28).

However, the devil stealthily came in. He tempted Adam and lured him into sin, thus introducing sin into the world. The result was that he stole that dominion, prosperity and blessings that belonged to man, and the earth was cursed with sickness, poverty and death.

Jesus, the Word, came to earth as the second Adam. He was manifested as the Son of God and anointed to destroy all the works of the devil; therefore, His focus necessarily would have included poverty which is definitely the work of the devil (1 John 3:8). The devil comes to steal, to kill and to destroy, the Bible says, but Jesus has come so that we would have abundant life (1 John 3:8; John 10:10).

He fulfilled that mandate as He destroyed and overcame the devil and all his troops and arsenal, and made a public show of the enemy, triumphing over them in the grave. Once the spiritual was dealt with, every hindrance was cleared for the release of material blessings from God.

With respect to material poverty, it is important to be pragmatic and to inject some realism here. Practically, what would represent good news to the poor? By every stretch of the imagination, good news to the poor is that which would cause them to come out of lack, want, insufficiency and poverty.

This is actually what was done whenever the Jubilee was celebrated in Israel. When the trumpet of Jubilee was sounded, people who were in debt had their debts forgiven, and those in bondage were relieved of their obligations and were set free. They came out of servitude, and their properties were returned to them. They were also furnished with an abundance and overflow of supplies. Therefore, the poor, at Jubilee, came away with great provision, and came into a place where they were no longer constricted and plagued by want, lack, and insufficiency.

This was a shadow of that which was to come. Rationally, then, since Jesus was speaking about the Jubilee, and since He came to fulfil that Jubilee, then, according to the pattern that had been preset during the traditional celebration of the Jubilee, the good news to the poor that He brought had to be expressed along the same lines, yielding such material provision for the people, and even better.

We must therefore appreciate the fact that Jesus came to tackle the problem, not only of spiritual poverty but also material poverty. He is Himself the Word, the trumpet (shofar) of Jubilee, and the Jubilee personified, and He is blasting the joyful sound of the shofar, breaking the spirit of poverty, and releasing provision in excess to the believing one. When the anointing is released, the trumpet blast at the Jubilee emits good news to the poor that breaks the back of poverty.

On a more generic level, there are some who maintain that the salvation and abundant life that Jesus brings is only spiritual, that He only brings us spiritual riches. They hold that the gospel has nothing to do with prosperity, and that all the blessings God promises are spiritual.

This is only half the truth. Jesus preached to the multitudes in the wilderness, feeding them spiritually, after which He miraculously multiplied loaves and fish to physically feed them. On another occasion, He used Peter's boat to preach, after which He asked Peter to launch his net into the deep; Peter drew in such a great catch of fish which his boat was unable to contain. These show that Jesus is just as interested in our material well-being as in our spiritual.

In fact, His ministry was characterized by miracles, signs and wonders. Ministering to people's physical and material needs was a staple of His ministry. If He were only interested in the spiritual things, He would not be the very present solution to the many needs of the people amongst whom He dwelt.

The case of John the Baptist is instructive. While he was imprisoned at the order of Herod, he sent his disciples to inquire of Jesus, who was also his cousin, if He was the Messiah, or if they should look for another. Why he would ask such a question is rather surprising as he was the very same prophet who had baptized Jesus, and who had earlier prophesied that Jesus was the lamb of God, the Messiah, who takes away the sin of the world.

Now in prison, however, his faith was shaken; he was despondent, discouraged and unsure, and most likely depressed and oppressed. He also might have wondered why Jesus, if He was the Messiah, had not intervened miraculously in his situation to release him from the oppressive rule of Herod. Things were obviously not going the way John expected, so he began to doubt his own true prophetic revelation of who Jesus was. Jesus' response to John the Baptist's query is insightful:

"Jesus answered and said unto them, Go and shew John again those things which ye do hear and see: The blind receive their sight, and the lame walk, the lepers are cleansed, and the deaf hear, the dead are raised up, and the poor have the gospel preached to them." Matthew 11:4-5

As the forerunner of the Messiah, John the Baptist would have been well aware that the Messiah's ministry was to fulfil the Jubilee; in that respect, the Messiah would demonstrate the miraculous, supernatural power of God to set humanity free. So Jesus just sent him a reminder about the unique things happening that would credibly and persuasively authenticate and affirm that He was the One - namely, the miracles, signs and wonders. He told John's disciples to go and tell him what they did see and hear.

The point that should stand out here is that the signs and wonders through Christ – the blind, lame and deaf being restored, lepers being cleansed, the dead coming back to life, and the poor hearing the good news - were not only spiritual, but were palpable, tangible and real occurrences, and were manifest for all to see. Good news to the poor, then, could not only be spiritual, but also that outward demonstration of the poor coming out of their predicament into wealth and prosperity.

There are still others who reject the message of prosperity and subscribe to the view that the prosperity teaching is false. Let's face the uncomplimentary truth - some Bible teachers have over-stretched the truth of the success and prosperity message and have at times given it a spin that allows for manipulation, extortion, and deception.

Notwithstanding these failings of man, however, the integrity of God's word remains unassailable and irrefutable, and the truth is that God blesses holistically - spiritually, physically and materially – and He prospers His people.

The Bible, which is the inspired word of God, is a revelation of His will for both spiritual and material blessings for His people (Deuteronomy 28:1-14). It is replete with prosperity scriptures. It says: "Beloved, I wish above all things that you will prosper and be in good health, even as thy soul prospers" (3 John 2). The Bible also tells us that Jesus came so that we may experience abundant life (John 10:10); that God has pleasure in the prosperity of His servants (Psalm 35:27); that the blessing of the Lord makes us rich and adds no sorrow to it (Proverbs 10:22); and that a good man leaves an inheritance to his children and to his children's children (Proverbs 13:22).

In the foreordained and predestined plan of God, therefore, every person is supposed to experience prosperity and abundant life. Every soul has a portion in the resources of the earth which far exceeds all that they can ever ask or think. God gives us a shadow of that reality, using His people Israel. He promised to bring them into a land flowing with milk and honey, and that spells abundance of provision.

He required that when they came into the promised land, the land was to be divided equitably amongst all of Israel and her tribes as their inheritance for them to enjoy. Moreover, He put a program in place amongst His people, commanding that the rich should help the poor. By that token, the poor would have their needs met, and the helpers of the poor would also be blessed and would prosper in all their ways. He said to the people of Israel:

"If there be among you a poor man of one of thy brethren within any of thy gates in thy land which the Lord thy God giveth thee, thou shall not harden thy heart, nor shut thine hand from thy poor brother: But thou shall open thy hand wide unto him, and shalt surely lend him sufficient for his need, in that which he wanteth. Beware that there be not a thought in thy wicked heart, saying, the seventh year, the year of release, is at hand; and thine eye be evil against thy poor brother, and thou givest him nought; and he cry unto the Lord against thee, and it shall be sin unto thee. Thou shalt surely give him, and thine heart shall not be grieved when thou givest unto him: because that for this thing the Lord thy God shall bless thee in all thy works, and in all that thou puttest thine hand unto. For the poor shall never cease out of the land: Therefore I command thee, saying, Thou shalt open thy hand wide unto thy brother, to thy poor, and to thy needy, in the land." Deuteronomy 15:7-11

God set forth specific instructions in His word to relieve and alleviate poverty. He was not speaking about spiritual poverty in the above passage but about physical and material needs. He commanded that His people should open their hands wide to help the poor, and to lend to those who were in need, and He attached special blessings to helping the poor - He promised to bless the givers in all their works and in whatever they would undertake.

Surely, then, God is a God who unequivocally wants all of our needs met, and He puts structures and things in place for that to happen. He has no plan to make anyone poor; neither does He intend for anyone to remain poor.

Some have misconstrued a statement Jesus made about the poor when He stated: "For the poor always ye have with you: but me ye have not always" (John 12:8; Matthew 26:11). They interpret it as an endorsement of the inevitability of poverty. But that is not the import of the message Jesus was trying to get across. It is just that the New Testament did not really bring out the full quotation.

Contextually, Jesus was referring to Deuteronomy 15, discussed above, where God required the people to be generous to the poor at all times. They were not to hold back from the poor or harden their hearts at any time, and were to refrain from banking on the fact that the Jubilee would roll around upon the completion of the seven-year cycle, at which time they would be obligated to forgive debts and set the poor free, anyway.

The purpose of His statement, therefore, was to ignite the right response of generous giving from those able to assist because it is more blessed to give than to receive, and there was coming a time when He would no longer be physically on earth. He certainly did not mean that the poor should continue to live in poverty, and/or that nothing should be done about it. That would have been antithetical to the word of God, and to what He did, what He stood for, and what He came for.

In fact, the poor but believing person can himself open up the anointing of prosperity blessings and come out of poverty by functioning according to Biblical principles. God said to Joshua:

"This book of the law shall not depart out of thy mouth; but thou shalt meditate therein day and night, that thou mayest observe to do according to all that is written therein: for then thou shalt make thy way prosperous, and then thou shalt have good success." Joshua 1:8

Hence, the poor can partner with God through His word to come into abundance and wealth. Notwithstanding, giving is also a divine and Spirit-led key that God gave to the people of Israel and to the early Church as well to break the back of poverty.

Ministering to the physical needs of people has remained front and centre in the history of the Church. In the first century Church, there are records showing that the people sold their excess possessions, brought their surplus together, had all things in common, and ministered to the necessity of all. The result was that none had any need among them, and need and poverty were driven out the door and eradicated (Acts 4:34-35). Many Churches, charitable organizations and philanthropists around the world today still do the great job of fighting poverty, and the have-nots receive help from those who are in a position to help.

It must be firmly riveted in our hearts that the law of giving is an eternal powerful tool that God has placed in the hands of men to enable them to be a blessing to others, and thereby to be also blessed. The best analogy is when a man puts his seed in the body of a woman; she brings forth children, and this is replicated as the children bring forth grandchildren, and this goes on interminably. One seed therefore produces a multiplication of children from generation to generation. The same is true of the seed of plants, animals and many other living organisms.

The word of God compares our giving to a farmer sowing his seed. He expects a harvest. God has pre-programmed, packed and computed within a seed, the life and the capability to produce and reproduce after its kind in a multiplied harvest and bounty. Nonetheless, the seed needs to be sown to yield that harvest. The seed abides alone if it is not sown. As Jesus taught:

"Verily, verily, I say unto you, Except a corn of wheat fall into the ground and die, it abideth alone: but if it die, it bringeth forth much fruit." John 12:24

Our giving represents the seeds we sow in other people's lives, in places of need, or in genuine ministries that preach the truth of the gospel. Those seeds will definitely generate a harvest. God spoke about the inherent dynamic correlation in these terms:

"While the earth remaineth, seedtime and harvest, and cold and heat, and summer and winter, and day and night shall not cease." Genesis 8:22

"Give, and it shall be given unto you; good measure, pressed down, and shaken together, and running over, shall men give into your bosom. For with the same measure that ye mete withal it shall be measured to you again." Luke 6:38

"There is that scattereth, and yet increaseth; and there is that withholdeth more than is meet, but it tendeth to poverty. The liberal soul shall be made fat: and he that watereth shall be watered also himself." Proverbs 11:24-25

"Now he that ministereth seed to the sower both minister bread for your food, and multiply your seed sown, and increase the fruits of your righteousness;) Being enriched in every thing unto all bountifulness, which causeth through us thanksgiving unto God." 2 Corinthians 9:10-11

We must therefore expect a choice harvest and exponential increase in return when we help the poor. The beauty of it all is that God deposits on our faith and cheerful giving, His life, anointing and power to create wealth, and He releases an unstoppable harvest of blessings in return. According to the unchanging principle of His word, the cheerful giver will always be replenished and refreshed, and will enjoy the increase and bountiful harvest of whatever they sow.

In the end, the awe-inspiring truth is that giving and receiving are integrally woven or built into the Jubilee, as conceived and ordained by God. It is always Jubilee for the receiver, and an even greater Jubilee for the giver, bringing liberation to all.

Witness that, at the joyful sound of the trumpet of Jubilee, the shofar, the needy who had become bondservants by reason of poverty were released by their masters, free to go back to their respective homes to be reunited with their families. Those who had had their lands and properties forfeited or taken away from them because of debts they owed received them back from the creditors. All debts owed to creditors were cancelled. Essentially, the burdens of poverty, sorrow, lack, want and insufficiency were rolled away. What a great time of freedom and liberty this was!

At Jubilee, the anointing on the gospel runs over into abundance and prosperity for the poor. God wraps His favor around the poor and sends them help from the least expected places. He grants them favor for debt cancellation and opens fruitful doors of opportunities. He activates and endows them with the skills, talents, innovation and creativity to prosper.

Great news! Jesus has come, and He is the substantiality of the ever-present, never-ending Jubilee. In Him, no one has to wait for forty-nine years to hear the trumpet of freedom from poverty. He is the shofar, and the blower of the Jubilee, and He has come to restore and to give life, even life more abundantly.

He is the anointed One, and His anointing is flowing now, addressing every need and want. He assures us:

"I am the door: by me if any man enter in, he shall be saved, and shall go in and out, and find pasture. The thief cometh not, but for to steal, and to kill, and to destroy: I am come that they might have life, and that they might have it more abundantly." John 10:9-10

Jesus, our Jubilee, is the Great Shepherd and the door to green pastures. He is anointed to break the back of poverty, and has come to address spiritual poverty, material poverty and poverty in any area of human life. He has come, not only grant us spiritual provision, but also to supply all our needs according to His riches in glory (Philippians 4:19).

He who made all things out of nothing is able to address every need and meet it. All the resources, health, success and inheritance which are your portion in the earth are released through Him. The silver and gold belong to Him. He owns the cattle on thousand hills. His perfect and overarching will is for you to prosper and be in health, even as your soul prospers (3 John 2). He has come to impart to us eternal life, everlasting life, the very life of God.

May we respond to the trumpet of Jubilee that is blasting loud and clear. May we rise up in renewed faith and prayer and behold the banqueting table that Jesus, our Jubilee, has laid out before us! May His Holy Spirit grant us favor and send us to the right places to meet the right people and connect us to our destiny helpers. May He open doors of opportunity and give us clear guidance about, and stimulus in, our vocations, trades, businesses or commerce. May He launch us out in power to possess our inheritance of true financial freedom. May the Lord of Jubilee rain abundance and prosperity on us.

Receive the blessing and anointing to break the spirit of poverty and to prosper now!

# Chapter 21

## JESUS SENT TO HEAL THE BROKENHEARTED

*"He hath sent me to heal the brokenhearted …"*

"Brokenhearted" is the term used for someone in a state of extreme sorrow, sadness, disappointment or disillusionment, which may sometimes lead to the point of extreme or clinical depression. It is a state where the inner person or the human spirit is crushed, with the consequent inability to respond to, or function in, faith and hope. The Book of Proverbs observes that a merry heart produces a cheerful countenance, but the spirit of a person is broken by a sorrowful heart (Proverbs 15:13).

There is a wide spectrum of events in life that opens the door to broken heartedness. To name a few, it could be the result of a broken marriage, a broken home, the break-up of an intimate relationship, the loss of a loved one or close relative, a traumatic event, rejection, anxiety, abuse, addiction, a failure to achieve dreams or to attain a certain position in life, or the loss of a business, livelihood or monumental wealth. The list is endless.

These situations often bring people to the point of hopelessness and helplessness. The heart and soul is gripped with fear, fatigue and failure. Defeat is then written on the soul and imagination of the individual. The inner person gives up and throws in the towel, emptied of any amount of strength to fight. The broken heart is a crushed spirit, a depressed soul, and a sick person.

A broken heart is also a broken life, in that it is a life bereft of motivation, drive and focus, and it is void of vision and the ability to dream. It is, as it were, the life of a living person who is not alive. This has a direct correlation to the condition of the body. When the inner man is sick, the whole person becomes sick and chained to the spirit of oppression.

There may be demonic spirits behind certain types of depression and oppression. In fact, Satan, the arch enemy of God and man, is more often than not the architect of most of these issues.

Many who are plagued with diverse physical ailments, sicknesses and diseases are unable to respond well to medical treatment or recover speedily where the root of their diseases is a broken heart lodged within their spirits and the souls. As Proverbs 17:22 explains, "a merry heart doeth good like medicine: but a broken spirit drieth the bones."

Those who are brokenhearted desperately need healing and wholeness, and Jesus understands this better than any other. He was labeled "a man of sorrows, and acquainted with grief", the Hebrew translation of which meant our sicknesses and diseases. As Isaiah explained:

"He is despised and rejected of men; a man of sorrows, and acquainted with grief: and we hid as it were our faces from him; he was despised, and we esteemed him not. Surely he hath borne our griefs, and carried our sorrows: yet we did esteem him stricken, smitten of God, and afflicted. But he was wounded for our transgressions, he was bruised for our iniquities: the chastisement of our peace was upon him; and with his stripes we are healed." Isaiah 53:3-5

Because a broken heart is seated within the soul and spirit of a person, any healing for that condition must necessarily begin in the spirit and soul of the individual.

Jesus, our Jubilee, took upon Himself the chastisement of our peace, bearing the burden thereof. He came to heal the brokenhearted. That healing is the restoration of the inner spirit and the renewal and reinvigoration of the soul and mind of that person, and this comes through the salvation and joy which Jesus alone brings to humanity.

"He healeth the broken in heart, and bindeth up their wounds." Psalm 147:3

"The Lord is nigh unto them that are of a broken heart; and saveth such as be of a contrite spirit." Psalm 34:18

Salvation is the work of God in the human spirit. Any person who hears the gospel of salvation and receives Jesus as Lord and confesses Him as the Savior, and who acknowledges Him as the One who died and shed His blood to atone for his sin, and who was raised from the dead for his justification, is saved and born again, and becomes a New Creation (Romans 4:25; 5:1-5; 6:23; 10:8-10).

That New Creation is the brand new inner spirit that God puts within man (2 Corinthians 5:17, Ezekiel 36:25-27). It is the regenerated spirit which is free from the baggage of sin and the oppression of Satan. Old things pass away, and all things become new.

The New Creation is also equipped with the power of God to overcome all the power of the enemy and is ushered into a place of freedom, for it was for freedom that Christ set us free. There is absolutely no assumption of risk here; there is only a download of the unquantifiable benefits of victorious Christian living to the one who accesses salvation through Christ. Hallelujah!

Not only does Jesus bring us salvation, but He also administers joy to the believing one as an antidote to a broken heart. Jesus' Jubilee mantle and package brings the oil of joy for mourning. Concerning the work the Messiah would accomplish, Isaiah prophesied that He would come:

"To appoint unto them that mourn in Zion, to give unto them beauty for ashes, the oil of joy for mourning, the garment of praise for the spirit of heaviness; that they might be called the trees of righteousness, the planting of the Lord, that he might be glorified." Isaiah 61:3

The oil symbolizes the anointing; joy is therefore an anointing of the Holy Spirit that breaks sadness, grief and mourning. It breaks the spirit of heaviness (depression, brokenness) and supplies beauty for ashes, so that the heavy-hearted and broken person can laugh, sing and dance again. This is deliverance; it is freedom; it is Jubilee.

Jesus came to do all that. He came to supply the oil-anointing of joy to turn the captivity and mourning men into dancing.

The nexus between joy and salvation is powerful; through His salvation, Jesus gives us joy unspeakable. King David petitioned God to restore unto him the joy of His salvation (Psalm 51:12). In God's presence is fullness of joy, and at His right hand are pleasures evermore (Psalm 16:11; 1 Peter 1:8). Joy therefore has the capacity to drive away the heavy burden of a broken heart.

Joy in the heart and soul is like good medicine applied to the entire human being. The Book of Proverbs declares that a merry heart (or a joyful heart) is as effective or potent as medicine, and makes a cheerful countenance (Proverbs 17:22; 15:13). Laughter born out of joy is therapeutic. Joy and laughter are directly linked to the wellbeing of a person, and produce health, liberty and freedom.

The people of Israel experienced this in real time. Their experience shows that hope that is delayed or deferred makes the heart sick, but when that which is desired comes, it is a tree of life (Proverbs 13:12). When God brought them out of Egypt with a mighty hand, they were ecstatic:

"When the Lord turned again the captivity of Zion, we were like them that dream. Then was our mouth filled with laughter, and our tongue with singing: then said they among the heathen, The Lord hath done great things for them. The Lord hath done great things for us; whereof we are glad." Psalm 126:1-3

Professional counselors, psychologists, psychiatrists and the medical profession play an important role and may be very helpful in bringing some meaningful, temporal relief when people suffer broken hearts or get into states of depression and anxiety. Nevertheless, where there are demonic indicators or flags, it takes the anointing of the Holy Spirit to break the oppression of the devil (Acts 10:38).

The Master healer of the brokenhearted is Jesus, the Anointed One and our Jubilee. The Spirit of the Lord was poured upon Him to bring healing and Jubilee to the brokenhearted. Through His anointing, therefore, every person who is brokenhearted in Zion is assured of this: they can be set free from captivity and oppression; they can enjoy the unending euphoric experience of deliverance; they can be optimistic again; they can laugh and sing as their joy is restored; they can begin to live again.

The Lord is right there with the brokenhearted, and He saves those that are of a contrite spirit. He heals them and binds up their wounds. May the brokenhearted become beacons of inspiration and living testimonies amongst the nations as they bear witness to the wonder of God's healing, salvation and deliverance, and declare the great and awesome things that the Lord has done for them. Praise the Lord forevermore.

# Chapter 22

## JESUS PREACHES DELIVERANCE TO THE CAPTIVES

*"He hath sent me… to preach deliverance to the captives…"*

The predicament of captivity (the state of bondage, subservience, servitude, slavery and subjugation to another) came upon humanity through one man's disobedience. God placed Adam and Eve in the Garden of Eden, gave them dominion over all His creation, and placed all things at their disposal. The only access that was withheld from them was to the tree of good and evil, from which they could not eat. However, the devil deceived Eve and got her to eat from that tree, and Adam willfully did the same.

Spiritually speaking, Adam's disobedience to the law of God in the Garden of Eden introduced sin into his heart, and that connected him indelibly to the devil because sin originated from the devil, and he transferred that sin nature to the human spirit.

"He that committeth sin is of the devil; for the devil sinneth from the beginning." 1 John 3:8

Through Adam's disobedience, sin was transmitted into the life of all men, without exception. The apostle Paul explained this situation, stating that "all have sinned and come short of the glory of God" (Romans 3:23).

The entrance of sin into the heart of man meant a number of things. First, there was a change of spiritual fathers. Fellowship with God was broken, and all mankind thus became the children of the devil, sealed with his birthmark of sin within their spirits and souls.

"Ye are of your father the devil, and the lusts of your father ye will do. He was a murderer from the beginning, and abode not in the truth, because there is no truth in him. When he speaketh a lie, he speaketh of his own: for he is a liar, and the father of it." John 8:44

"In this the children of God are manifest, and the children of the devil: whosoever doeth not righteousness is not of God, neither he that loveth not his brother." 1 John 3:10

Essentially, man was reduced from being a child of God to being only a creature of God, and the child of the devil. The nature of sin and the devil within a person is what separates him from God, his Maker.

Secondly, Adam's disobedience came with very serious consequences for humanity. It subjected the whole world to sin and eternal death, and the entire human race became the captives of the devil, and servants and slaves to sin. Man was imprisoned by sin and enslaved to Satan and the dominion of darkness.

"Wherefore, as by one man sin entered into the world, and death by sin; and so death passed upon all men, for that all have sinned." Romans 5:12

Sin, death are the essence of Satan's nature and character, and they rule in the heart and soul of the sinner, the one who is not regenerated in Christ. That person takes on the nature of sin and the devil within his spirit and soul, becoming a captive of sin and the devil, and condemned to eternal death.

Sin and death and the devil were destined by God to be cast into eternal damnation in the lake of fire. When Adam sinned, however, sin and death held the spirit and soul of man captive, and man was thus subject to, or prepared for, the same judgment of eternal damnation in the lake of fire (Revelation 20:14-15).

The devil, that wicked one, has trapped multitudes with his whoredom and idolatry. He holds many captive through false religions, witchcraft, wiccan beliefs, demon possession, sorcery, divination, psychic phenomenon, spiritism, occultism, secret societies, necromancy (communicating with the dead), use of tarot cards, reading of palms, reading of stars, drug, alcohol and sex addictions, emotional and mental breakdowns, and many more horrific issues of life, known and unknown.

All must understand this, that the sin problem of man cannot be resolved through rituals or religion; neither is there any escape from God's preordained judgment, which is the condemnation to hell and the lake of fire, because He is just.

But the loving God, who had foreknowledge of the fall of man, carved out, in His eternal counsel and before the foundation of the world, His plan of redemption of humanity, to set the captives free.

God showed glimpses and shadows and sent echoes of His mighty power to liberate His people throughout the history of Israel. He also gave precious promises to the people to deliver them from captivity or any form of oppression when they called out to Him.

When King Solomon dedicated the Temple he built to God, he specifically petitioned the God of Israel, that, when His people are taken into captivity and they go before the Lord in prayers of repentance, turning their hearts and eyes toward Jerusalem and the Temple, God should hear their prayers and release them from captivity (1 Kings 8:46-50).

In this inspired prayer of Solomon during the Temple dedication, it is evident that he knew the ways of the Lord, and how He would bring them out of captivity.

The sure precept of God for salvation, deliverance and release from captivity is for His people to repent from their sin. Repentance always precedes deliverance from captivity. In other words, repentance is the forerunner of God's forgiveness, reconciliation, restored fellowship, and healing.

"If my people, which are called by my name, shall humble themselves, and pray, and seek my face, and turn from their wicked ways; then will I hear from heaven, and will forgive their sin, and will heal their land." 2 Chronicles 7:14

Isaiah also spoke about the promise of God to set His people free when they were taken into captivity. God promised to have mercy on Jacob and yet choose Israel.

"That thou mayest say to the prisoners, Go forth; to them that are in darkness, Shew yourselves. They shall feed in the ways, and their pastures shall be in all high places."

"Shall the prey be taken from the mighty, or the lawful captive delivered? But thus saith the Lord, Even the captives of the mighty shall be taken away, and the prey of the terrible shall be delivered: for I will contend with him that contendeth with thee, and I will save thy children." Isaiah 49:9, 24-25

By the mercies of God and His compassions that fail not, and by reason of His unbreakable covenant with His people, He always comes through, bringing them out of their predicaments.

"For the Lord will have mercy on Jacob, and will yet choose Israel, and set them in their own land: and the strangers shall be joined with them, and they shall cleave to the house of Jacob. And the people shall take them and bring them to their place: and the house of Israel shall possess them in the land of the Lord for servants and handmaids: and they shall take them captives, whose captives they were; and shall rule over their oppressors. And it shall come to pass in the day that the Lord shall give thee rest from thy sorrow, and from thy fear, and from the hard bondage wherein thou wast made to serve." Isaiah 14:1-3

Israel was taken captive by the Babylonians. Yet, it was God's plan that Israel would not remain in exile but would return to the land of promise, free as a bird from the snare of the fowler. God brought them out with laughter and singing, and they moved their feet to begin to dance. The enemies who took His people captive were defeated and overpowered.

God's unfailing agenda is to set His people free from their captors and to flip the tables on those captors, causing them to become the captives of His people. Jehovah, in His mighty power, delivers His people and even causes their enemies to follow them to become their menservants and handmaids.

Here is the amazing truth. Long before the creation of man, before the deception of the devil, and before the start of any religion and the perpetuation of the fallacy that there are many ways to God, God had already mapped out the only way to free man from the captivity of sin and death, namely, total redemption through the shed blood of His Son, Jesus (Ephesians 1:7). Jesus was destined to be the Savior of the world, and He is the lamb of God that was slain before the foundation of the world (Revelation 13:8).

Although Jesus was God and in the form of God, He emptied himself of His deity and was fashioned as a man in order to fulfill His earthly ministry. Whatever He said and did on earth, He said and did as a man anointed by the Spirit of God for Jubilee. The Father gave Him all authority in heaven and on earth.

The demonstration of His authority under the unction of the Holy Spirit resulted in undisputed miracles that the opposing ecclesiastical order of the day could not contest. When He preached and taught, He exuded the authority of God. In His meetings, the power of God was present to heal.

Demons cried out in His presence, and at His word, they took their leave and souls were set free. He set the Gadarene demoniac free, and cast out seven evil spirits from Mary Magdalene. The blind saw, the lame walked, lepers were cleansed, and death heard His voice and the dead came back to life. He stilled the storms and calmed the raging seas. He mastered the laws of flotation and walked on the sea. Peter's boat could not contain the amount of fish he caught at Jesus' spoken word. Indeed, many are the great things which Jesus did that are not even recorded.

Jesus also became the ransom for our souls and spirits. He paid the price for our sin by laying down His life as the atonement for the salvation of the believing one. He came to set free from any entrapment, the spirit of man which was in captivity to sin, Satan and the domain of darkness. He came to set the captives free from eternal death in hell, to deliver them from the power of darkness, and to translate them into the kingdom of God and to eternal life in heaven (Colossians 1:13).

"But now being made free from sin, and become servants to God, ye have your fruit unto holiness, and the end everlasting life. For the wages of sin is death; but the gift of God is eternal life through Jesus Christ our Lord." Romans 6:22-23

It is manifestly discernible, then, that God's redemptive plan stipulates salvation for the whole person (1 Thessalonians 5:23). He brings deliverance and wholeness to every facet of the person - to their spirit, soul, mind, body, emotions, and material wellbeing. As can be seen from the works of Jesus, God does not only deal with our spiritual lives, forgetting those issues that affect or impact us in the literal sense; He delivers the whole person from captivity in the spiritual sense and also, literally. This same power, authority and grace is available to the captive, to the sick and the oppressed, today and always. Jesus is the same yesterday, today and forever (Hebrews 13:8).

Jesus Messiah is the answer to any form of captivity, and this is what He declared when He said He was sent to bring deliverance to the captives. He overcame sin, death, hell and the grave through His life, ministry, death and resurrection. He disarmed every demonic spirit, principality and power, triumphing over them; He made a public show of them (Colossians 2:15;

Hebrews 2:14). He breaks every chain and fetter, and He breaks every yoke and lifts all burdens.

He declared: "I am the way, the truth, and the life: no man cometh unto the Father, but by me." (John 14:6). There is one God and one mediator between God and men, the man Christ Jesus (1 Timothy 2:5).

Man desires to do what is wrong because of the nature of sin in him. However, when he acknowledges Jesus Christ as Savior, he receives the free gift of righteousness which is the nature and character of God. He then becomes clothed with the ability, desire and hunger to live right and act in obedience to God's word (Romans 5:17).

Jesus Messiah is here. It is Jubilee! He is sounding the Jubilee shofar to set the captives free from the dominion of sin and darkness. As Captain of our salvation, He has come to open the prison doors. He has issued the resounding, ever powerful, and unbreakable command for all those who hear His voice to come out of prison. He is the door and ticket out of satanic prison; He came to set the captives free.

To all who are held in darkness, in the doom, gloom and horrors of the satanic dungeon, hear the joyful sound of the Jubilee shofar! Our God delivers the prey of the terrible and sets free the captive of the mighty. The Lord contends with those who contend with you. He fights those who fight you, and when they come against you in one way, they will be scattered before you in seven ways. The battle is the Lord's. He always wins, and He cannot be defeated. He cannot fail, and they who put their trust in the Lord shall not be disappointed. You are more than a conqueror through Christ, the Anointed One and by His anointing (2 Chronicles 20:15-17; Romans 8:37; Deuteronomy 28:7).

Through Him, any spirit or power that holds you bound or captive loses its grip. As you call on His Name, they will be defeated and held bound by you, and you shall rule over them, for He gives His people dominion and authority over all the power of the enemy, and nothing shall by any means hurt them. Those things that hinder your progress are decimated as you sing and lift Jesus up in worship. Get out of all the things that seem to confine you, for the prison doors are open! Celebrate the victories God has in store.

No matter the strength of the enemy or the power of the oppressor, the Lord has promised His people rest from their sorrow, fear, and hard bondage. It is Jubilee! At Jubilee, God turns situations around, causing prisoners of war to go free, and bondservants to go home. Light comes to those who dwell in darkness, and they find their way to freedom. They are fed in the way as Jesus, the great warrior Shepherd, leads them into green pastures. Hallelujah!!!

Through Jesus who is our Jubilee, we are delivered from the power of darkness and translated into the kingdom of God, and we boldly jump onto the lap of a compassionate and merciful Savior. Burdens are lifted, chains are broken, diseases are healed, demons are cast out, and humanity springs out of darkness into the glorious light of liberty. The Lord alone is our deliverer, and He saves us, our households and all our generations (Acts 16:31).

# Chapter 23

## JESUS PREACHES RECOVERING OF SIGHT TO THE BLIND

*"He hath sent me ... to preach ... recovering of sight to the blind ..."*

Blindness is a state where there is a loss of sight, either partially or totally. In the Bible, it has a dual connotation, referring, not only to physical blindness but also, to spiritual blindness.

Jehovah God initiated His redemptive process for humanity by choosing the nation of Israel as His exemplar or prototype. He made a covenant with Israel, and foreordained that out of Israel shall come the deliverer, the Savior of the world. Jehovah's dispensational agendas were mapped out through the life and history of Israel.

He raised the priesthood, the judges, the prophets and the kings out of Israel. He handed to them the covenants of promise. They were also the recipients of the oracles of God - the holy prophets were inspired and moved by the Holy Ghost, and gave us the Holy Scriptures. Moreover, God fashioned out the celebrations of the Sabbaths and Feasts to stage, dramatize and articulate His eternal plans for the redemption of His people.

Throughout the ages, then, Israel was eagerly expecting the Messiah, the Anointed One who, according to the prophets, would save them from all their enemies and complete and consummate Jehovah's redemptive process in the life of His covenant children.

As promised, the Messiah came in the fullness of time. He came, first, to the lost sheep of Israel, for salvation is of the Jews. However, Israel had a temporal blindness regarding who this Messiah was. As such, they missed the redeemer when He came to town wrapped in swaddling clothes, lying in a manger amidst bleating sheep in a stable.

They failed to acknowledge Him when He taught and preached, and when He made bold and audacious declarations that none before Him had dared to make.

They failed to recognize Him when He worked miracles, signs and wonders amongst them. They failed to appreciate Him when He was nailed to the cross and died for them.

They failed to see Him revealed in His detailed actions in the ongoing writings of Israel's prophetic destiny, and did not fully grasp the role of the Savior to redeem and bless, not only Israel but also the Gentiles, through His declaration of the Jubilee-gospel to everyone who believes, to the Jew first, and then to the Gentiles (Romans 1:16-17).

That Messiah was none other than Jesus of Nazareth, the root out of the stem of Jesse, the Savior of the world. He came to His very own people, but they were blind to who He was and rejected Him.

"That was the true Light, which lighteth every man that cometh into the world. He was in the world, and the world was made by him, and the world knew him not. He came unto his own, and his own received him not. But as many as received him, to them gave he power to become the sons of God, even to them that believe on his name: Which were born, not of blood, nor of the will of the flesh, nor of the will of man, but of God." John 1:9-13

According to divine ordination, though, the blindness of the Jews was purposive and had to persist for a while till the grace and mercy of God was administered to the Gentile world. The apostle Paul spoke to King Agrippa about the opening of the eyes of the Gentiles to the message of the gospel, and pointed out that no one can see Jesus and acknowledge Him as Savior without their spiritual eyes being opened.

"To open their eyes, and to turn them from darkness to light, and from the power of Satan unto God, that they may receive forgiveness of sins, and inheritance among them which are sanctified by faith that is in me." Acts 26:18

The salvation of the Gentile world is being used by God to provoke and quicken the faith of Israel to come to Jesus Messiah. All is therefore not lost for Israel; their sight will surely will be recovered. As the apostle Paul explained:

"For I would not, brethren, that ye should be ignorant of this mystery, lest ye should be wise in your own conceits; that blindness in part is happened to Israel, until the fullness of the Gentiles be come in. And so all Israel shall be saved: as is written, there shall come out of Sion the deliverer, and shall turn away ungodliness from Jacob: For this is my covenant unto them, when I shall take away their sins. As concerning the gospel, they are enemies for your sakes: but as touching the election, they are beloved for the father's sakes. For the gifts and calling of God are without repentance." Romans 11:25-29

It is clear, therefore, that the rejection of the Messiah by Israel, the elect of God, worked to the advantage of the rest of the world. God grafted the wild olive branch, the Gentiles who come to faith in Christ, into the olive tree, Israel, to whom God's covenant of salvation was given. But Israel, the natural branch, will be grafted back in when Jesus restores their spiritual sight and they receive him as Lord.

For Israel and the rest of the world, spiritual sight can only be restored by the proclamation of the Jubilee by Christ Jesus, and the anointing that comes with it. Satan is the prince of darkness, and it is he who has blinded the spiritual eyes of the world with his false ideas and deceptive philosophies, such that they do not see the light of the glorious gospel (2 Corinthians 4:4).

Jesus came as the light to the entire world so that humanity would come out of darkness into the marvelous light of the kingdom of God. In Him, there is neither Jew nor Gentile, bond nor free, male nor female, for we blend together in Him as the Church (Ephesians 2:11-20, Galatians 3:28-29).

He came as the light of the world to diffuse the gross darkness that covered the world as a result of the entrance of sin, Satan and his diabolical activities. The gospel He brings is an open message to the world, to every tribe and tongue, nation and kindred. It is the water of life and salvation, and whosoever is thirsty may drink of it freely.

The Holy Spirit aids and abets the new birth of the believer. He reveals Jesus, and takes away the spiritual blindness so that people can come to the point of faith in Christ Jesus. The blindness caused by Satan and the power of darkness can only be broken by the anointing of the Spirit on the Messiah. Jesus turns men from darkness to light, and from the power of Satan to God.

If you are not saved, may you see the light as the Holy Spirit anoints your spiritual eyes and removes the blindness so that you can see Jesus who gave His life a ransom for your salvation. May you experience forgiveness of sins and Jubilee from the power of Satan and participate in the inheritance of the saints.

The New Testament manuscripts unveil the earthly ministry of Christ, and show His redeeming grace covering all aspects of the total needs of mankind, in their spirit, soul and body. Jesus ministered to the physical healing needs of the masses during His three years of ministry on earth, and He is still doing that today. The blind literally received their sight in His ministry.

The miraculous power of God is released at Jubilee to effect salvation ("sozo") that includes healing of the physical body. The healing ministry of Jesus continues as He sits on the right hand side of the majesty on high making intercession for us (Hebrews 7:25). Jehovah has not changed. Jesus has not changed; He is the same yesterday, today, and forever (Hebrews 13:8). God is still the healer of every disease and ailment, including recovering the sight of the physically and spiritually blind.

# Chapter 24

## JESUS, SETTING AT LIBERTY THEM THAT ARE BRUISED

*"... to set at liberty them that are bruised ..."*

Liberty is the state of being free from oppressive restrictions imposed by authority, or by the behavior, the world views, or the way of life of others. It also means to be pardoned or released from prison or confinement.

Accordingly, the ones who need liberty are those that are repressed, suppressed and oppressed, and who are restricted in their freedoms and limited in their free will to operate and function as they please. They find themselves locked up in a toxic environment that gives them no chance to flourish, to break out, or to be themselves or to be what God wants them to be.

To be bruised is to be pounded or crushed in a way that goes so deep and leaves a mark showing the area of damage. It suggests an injury with a blow. Persons that are bruised may feel imprisoned, helpless and hopeless when the bruises are inflicted on them by their oppressors.

This is the reality of the human situation - the devil, who comes with the sole agenda to steal, to kill and to destroy, orchestrates and sets up life events to squeeze the life out of people. He has dealt an injurious blow to the spirits, souls and bodies of many who find themselves bound, confined, damaged, and non-functional, and condemned, as he is, to eternal damnation.

There are myriad situations in life that bruise, a discussion of which would go well beyond the scope of this book. To mention a few, though, there are those bruised souls that are victims of the ungodly acts of their ancestors who were rebellious against God and His word, and who were haters of God. Others are bruised from their own consummate choices in life, and their hardheartedness towards God and His word.

There are also those who are crushed or bruised in their inner being because they have suffered various forms of abuse - sexual, physical, verbal, emotional, or through other means that bring injury to the heart and emotions of a person.

A high percentage of people who have habitual lifestyles of substance abuse and addictions, sexual promiscuity, criminality, gang involvement, anti-social vices, and who exhibit a ready resort and recourse to violence, may have suffered, one way or the other, from abuse from relatives, friends or people in authority. Rapists, pedophiles and physical abusers have broken the spirits of victims and inflicted bruises in the lives of so many, and those who suffer such abuse in their tender and formative years turn to act out their trauma later in their lives, living out their inner damage and brokenness.

Furthermore, evil projections and evil reports against people, false accusations, and hurtful or injurious words that malign and destroy reputations have devastated not a few. The words of gossips and talebearers are like wounds, and they go down to the innermost part of the belly (Proverbs 18:8-9). We need to be careful what we say to each other. Words can either make or break a person; they may build up or tear down.

Make no mistake, saints. The devil and his demonic empire is behind all of these egregious occurrences, and it takes a higher spiritual or governmental authority to pardon, and/or command or order the release of those who are bruised or imprisoned, and to set them at liberty.

That higher power is none other than Jesus Messiah. The Father God has delivered to the Son, Jesus, all authority in heaven and earth (Matthew 28:19). In His atoning and redemptive work on the cross at Calvary, Jesus paid the price for our transgressions and iniquities.

He is the answer to those who are bruised in any way, for He sets them at liberty. It is He who has spoken the word of emancipation. He has signed the release order with His shed blood at Calvary. He, as the highest authority in heaven, earth and under the earth, has granted and publicized and actualized our pardon (Philippians 2:8-10).

The bruises that Satan inflicts on humanity can only be healed, and will be healed, by the compassionate and merciful Savior who Himself, in His body and soul, absorbed those bruises. The Bible says:

"But he was wounded for our transgressions, he was bruised for our iniquities: the chastisement of our peace was upon him; and with his stripes we are healed." Isaiah 53:5

Note that Jesus' wounds were inflicted for our transgressions, whilst the bruises were meted out to Him to address our iniquities. The distinction is not at all cosmetic but is meant to relay some truths about the character of both forms injury that Jesus received.

Wounds are injuries which are usually more obvious, and which tear, cut, puncture or damage the epidermis of the skin. They typically heal much faster and much more easily. Bruises, on the other hand, are injuries in the blood cells deep beneath the skin, trapped under the skin and leaving the skin discolored. Bruises and contusions go deeper into the body and have the tendency to poison it if they are not given very serious attention.

Jesus was wounded for our transgressions. The sin of transgression is the direct disobedience to God's law, the overstepping of God's order, or the flouting or disregard of the guardrails or boundaries He has set for His people. Because of how wounds are, easily seen and easily healed, the symbolic relation here is to say that transgressions may be dealt with or broken off a person's life with much more ease.

Jesus was bruised for our iniquities. Iniquity is the demonstration of hatred for the Holy and righteous God by serving idols and submitting to false demonic activities of Satan, witchcraft, spiritism, occultism and such like, and the hitting against the authority and supremacy of God. God required of His people:

"Thou shalt have no other gods before me. Thou shalt not make unto thee any graven image, or any likeness of anything that is in heaven above, or that is in the earth beneath, or that is in the water under the earth. Thou shalt not bow down thyself to them, nor serve them: for I the LORD thy God am a jealous God, visiting the iniquity of the fathers upon the children unto the third and fourth generation of them that hate me; And shewing mercy unto thousands of them that love me, and keep my commandments." Exodus 20:3-6

Iniquity is also inherent in extreme acts of wickedness, such as murder and human blood sacrifices or abuse.

The repercussions for iniquity are very serious. The sin of iniquity cuts deep into the spirit and soul. It eats into the inner fabric of the heart and soul of men and keeps them captive. It tends to have a stronger hold and grip on people's lives, and lingers on for the longest time until deliverance comes.

Iniquitous actions may also be passed down to generations. Iniquity breaks fellowship with God and incurs His wrath and judgment. That judgment/punishment and the allocation of the burden for the deviance is passed down to generations as well. Iniquity blocks answers to prayer (Psalm 66:18). Iniquity also hinders deliverance (Isaiah 59:1-2).

But God, in His mercy, sets people at liberty when they repent and show their love for Him. He facilitated the deliverance and liberation of humanity by giving us the gift of His Son Jesus, through whose wounds and bruises, transgressions and iniquities are thoroughly dealt with.

Jesus was smitten of God and afflicted with our sins, wounds and bruises in His spirit, soul and body. He was broken, so that we would be remolded, damaged so that we might be renewed, crushed in spirit and soul so that we would be recreated, and His body mutilated and disfigured so that we would be healed and made whole.

He is the burden-bearer who carried our sin, shame, sorrow, affliction and addiction, and nailed them to the cross. The chastisement, disturbance and bruises of the spirit, soul and body were laid on him. He is the healer of all traumatic, psychological and emotional disorders. He is the deliverer from all mental issues and gives us, not the spirit of fear, but of love, power and of a sound mind (2 Timothy 1:7). By His stripes and broken body, we are healed, and He is the Prince of peace who keeps in perfect peace the one who trusts Him and whose mind is stayed on Him (Isaiah 26:3).

The Father God fashioned the sinless Christ into sin, that we might be made the righteousness of God (2 Corinthians 5:21). Through His wounds, our transgressions are forgiven. He forgives all iniquities and heals all diseases (Psalm 103:3). In His bruises, we are free from extreme acts of sin, wickedness, and habitual proclivities towards breaking the laws of God and incurring His punishment and generational judgment.

Jesus also dealt with all spirits or forces warring against the emotional and mental stability and wellbeing of His people. He dealt an eternally paralyzing and debilitating blow to the devil and his wicked hosts. He broke the spirits of fear, sin, death hell and the grave, and has handed over to us, the spirit of power, love and of a sound mind.

The Father God made Christ our Jubilee. He was anointed with an unlimited dose of the Holy Spirit to announce our Jubilee. He has eternally closed off to Satan, all the loopholes and inroads that he had into our lives. He blows the trumpet of Jubilee to set at liberty them that are bruised.

# Chapter 25

## JESUS PREACHES THE ACCEPTABLE YEAR OF THE LORD, THE YEAR OF THE LORD'S FAVOUR

### "To preach the acceptable year of the Lord"

Jesus declared, in the synagogue at Nazareth, that He was anointed by the Spirit of the Lord to preach the acceptable year of the Lord.

What is that acceptable year of the Lord? It is the year of Jubilee. It is the year of the Lord's favor, the year of the Lord's goodwill, the year of the Lord's good pleasure, the year of the Lord's benefits. It is also the day of salvation. All of these are interrelated and interwoven into a coherent package in Christ Jesus.

Israel heard the shofar sound of Jubilee every $49^{th}$ year, and they celebrated, from that point, a whole year of Jubilee into the $50^{th}$ year. Jubilee, from the time it was instituted by God, came up once every half a century. However, it was prophesying a future day when God would demonstrate the fullness of His goodwill and favor to His people. Until that blessed eventuality, the Jubilee cycle served only as a prelude to the real deal.

Although the nation of Israel celebrated the Jubilee as an event, they were actually celebrating a person when they went through all the traditions, motions, rituals and events. God, in His infinite mind, was setting the stage for the emergence and manifestation of Jesus.

Jubilee is actually a person, and that person is none other than Jesus, who came to fulfill every detail, symbol, emblem, facet, shadow, intent, and impact of the Jubilee. Thus, He is the Jubilee that they were celebrating, and the fullness thereof was consummated with His tangible appearance and manifestation into the realm of humanity.

Jesus came to put a stop to the wait time of half a century before God's people could experience the overstock and outpouring of His favor, salvation and freedom. On that blessed day, when He went into the Temple and read the scroll from the prophet Isaiah, He declared the year of Jubilee and boldly affirmed that this scripture was that day fulfilled in the ears of the listeners.

With that declaration, He ushered in the endless, uninterrupted, unrelenting overflow, and the outpouring and dispensation of the Lord's favor and salvation, and this continues until He sits down at the great marriage supper of the lamb in His Father's kingdom with His Church, the Bride, constituted of both Jews and Gentiles united in Him.

## 1. THE DAY OF SALVATION

Here is a deep truth – that the acceptable year of the Lord or the year of the Lord's favor is, in simple terms, the day of salvation. The year of the Lord's favor opens the pathway to salvation when people hear God's voice, the gospel, and do not harden their hearts.

"(For he saith, I have heard thee in a time accepted, and in the day of salvation have I succoured thee: behold, now is the accepted time; behold, now is the day of salvation)." 2 Corinthians 6:2

The "time accepted" and "accepted time", which mean the same as "the acceptable year of the Lord", signify or denote the coming of Jesus to pay the price for the redemption of humanity through His sacrificial work of the cross.

Through sin, man became alienated and separated from God. He fell short of the glory of God and could no longer enjoy fellowship with Him (Romans 3:23). Sin came with the punishment of spiritual death, for the wages of sin is death (Romans 6:23).

Jesus gave up His throne and took on the human form to pay the price for the sin of humanity by dying on the cross. The shedding of His blood at the cross was God's act to reconcile the world to Himself. Jesus broke the power of sin and cancelled its effects, nailing them to the cross, and He imparts eternal life to all who come to God through Him.

Jubilee, then, provides salvation, reconciliation, and the way for man to be reunited with God through Christ Jesus. That free gift of getting saved, with the consequent escape from eternal damnation and the entrance into the kingdom of God, is the greatest and the most important of all miracles, and through that, God has given to us all things that pertain to life and godliness.

In spite of God's lovingkindness, however, we ought to be mindful of the fact that there is a timeline to the day of salvation, and the clock is slowly ticking. The acceptable year of the Lord's favor, which brings salvation and redemption to all who believe and surrender to Jesus as their Lord, has been running from the time of Jesus' sacrifice on the cross, and will continue till He comes back again to rapture His Church.

This period, the Jubilee period, is marked by the patience and mercy of God, freedom from sin and its effects, deliverance from the power of darkness, and the translation into the kingdom of God's dear Son (Colossians 1:13).

However, after the second coming of Christ, and after the great tribulation and millennium, the day of God's vengeance and His judgment will come upon His enemies and on all who have not repented (John 14:1-3, 1 Thessalonians 4:16-18, Revelation 20:1-6).

Expressed another way, the period of the Lord's favor would lapse, and God will bring judgment on Satan and on all those who derided and despised His saving grace. Those who accept the salvation of the Lord will enjoy Jubilee on earth, and will also enter into the eternal and unending rest of God. But those who do not repent and seek the Lord will come under His judgment. Isaiah, the prophet, speaking about the Messiah, said He was anointed for this purpose:

"To proclaim the acceptable year of the Lord, and the day of vengeance of our God." Isaiah 61:2

After the rapture of the Church, the great tribulation period would be ushered in (Matthew 24:21, Isaiah 2:12, Daniel 12:9, Revelation 3:10; 13:16-18; 14:14-20). The reign of the antichrist would be seven terrible years of tribulation. It would be a time of suffering the likes of which have never been seen since the world began, and salvation, if at all, may come at a high cost, like martyrdom.

After these events will come the day of vengeance of our God. Satan, the antichrist, death and hell, and all those whose names are not written in the book of life will be cast into the lake of fire (Revelation 20:7-15). The day of reckoning is coming when no one stands the chance to repent or can repent. Those who died without Christ and those who never repented would spend the rest of their lives in eternal suffering in the fires of damnation.

But hear this loud and clear, that God never intended that any person should perish; rather, He made provision for all to come to the saving knowledge of God and have everlasting life (John 3:16, 2 Peter 3:9).

E.W. Kenyon sums up the salvation message in one statement: "The gospel is GENESIS, CALVARY and YOU." Adam's sin in GENESIS passed on to all men, such that all have sinned (Romans 5:12). CALVARY is where Jesus died and shed His blood to make atonement for your sin. YOU, as the free moral agent that you are, and as the only variable in the equation, must respond to what Christ has done. Are you, or are you not going to repent and accept Him as your Lord and Savior?

Jesus alone can present us holy and blameless to the Father God, for He is the way, the truth and the life, and no man comes to the Father except through Him (John 14:6). The day of repentance therefore is now.

"Seek ye the Lord while he may be found, call ye upon him while he is near: Let the wicked forsake his way, and the unrighteous man his thoughts; and let him return unto the Lord, and he will have mercy upon him; and to our God, for he will abundantly pardon." Isaiah 55:6-7

This is the period of the Lord's favor, this is the day of salvation. The trumpet of permanent Jubilee is being blown. God is saying it is Jubilee now and forever. He is saying to the lost, "Come home"; to the poor, "Trade your needs for abundant life"; to the sick, "Be healed"; to the broken hearts, "Be mended"; and to the captives, "Go free."

It is a new day for the New Creation to sing to our God, songs of thanksgiving, praise and worship, songs of salvation and victory, songs of deliverance and shouts of joy, songs of His goodness and mercies that endure forever. He is pouring out the river and water of life freely, and whosoever will, and whosoever believes, may drink of the water of life at no cost, without price. This day is this scripture fulfilled in your ears (Luke 4:21).

## 2. THE YEAR OF THE LORD'S FAVOR

Jesus has proclaimed, once and for all eternity, the acceptable, favored, Jubilee dispensation. Therefore, every minute, every hour, every day, every year, and every moment is the Lord's favored time.

Favor is the show of support, approval or preference for someone or something, an act of kindness that goes beyond that which is due or usual. The spirit of favor on a person or group brings them into a preferred position. They are given a choice place or portion in everything.

In most situations, those persons would not have done anything to deserve the place or opportunities given them, nor would they have worked to earn that preferred position or preferential treatment, but the acts of benevolence are just bestowed on them.

There are countless Biblical examples of people and groups who experienced the manifold favor and the overgenerous preferential treatment of the Lord. Each experience represents, displays, and mirrors the favor that we, the children of God, are endowed with, and even more so in the year of the Lord's favor.

## A. JACOB

Jacob started off in life with a name that labelled him as a trickster and a supplanting or overreaching character, and he began to exhibit those traits. With the connivance of his mother, he passed himself off as his elder brother, Esau, and received from their father, Isaac, the blessing and birthright that was legally Esau's.

When his duplicity came to light, a family feud began. Isaac was visibly shaken, Esau was incensed, Jacob was fearful for his life, and his mother was in torment for the men she loved. As a result, Jacob fled from his father's house and sojourned with his uncle, Laban, for a number of years.

When he finally left Laban to return to his homeland, he encountered the angel of the Lord, with whom he wrestled till daybreak. He prevailed with the angel, and the Lord changed his name from Jacob (supplanted) to Israel, meaning a prince (Genesis 32:24-30).

Jacob thereby experienced a transformation, a new identity, and this was the result of having favor with God and favor with man.

A new royal nation of Israel was birthed because of the favor of God.

The place of Israel in the history of mankind is so pivotal. Israel was chosen to be God's covenant people, and they received the oracles of God. The word of God was given to us through their prophets and apostles. Jesus, our Messiah, came out of Jacob-Israel, and salvation, indisputably, is of the Jews. In essence, God's redemptive plan was set in motion because of His favor on Jacob, who became Israel.

There is so much grace released and blessings poured out when a person is connected to the favor of God. It does not matter that you have an uncomplimentary background, a bad reputation, a complicated history or a negative profile. Once you encounter the Lord and open up to His mercies and salvation, He will curate and groom you and adorn you with His majesty, dignity and favor.

May we seek and receive the favor which God supplies to realign our destinies, and to change and transform us to fulfill His great purposes in our lives. May we find a new identity in Him.

## B. HANNAH

"He raiseth up the poor from the dust, and lifteth up the beggar from the dunghill, to set them among princes, and to make them inherit the throne of glory: for the pillars of the earth are the Lord's, and he hath set the world upon them." 1 Samuel 2:8

These words of Hannah, praising the Lord, come from a place of pain that was soothed and healed and radically transformed by the unleashed favor of God.

She was married, but barren for years. Barrenness was a reproach during her time, and even in many cultures today, it is reckoned a reproach not to have children. She was ridiculed, put down, and shamed by her rival and the community. She experienced firsthand what it meant to be in immense torment, broken, downcast or discouraged.

This is a familiar state for many who are poor and considered to be on the fringes of society, and who have few or no opportunities or supports in society. They are despised, disrespected, rejected and not recognized because they are perceived to be people of low esteem.

Jehovah heard the cry of Hannah for a child and opened her womb. She gave birth to Samuel, and to six others after him. She praised God who was her glory and the lifter up of her head. She recognized that man does not prevail in life because of his strength; she saw, in her own life, how the bow of the mighty and arrogant are broken, and how the Lord keeps the feet of His saints, and silences the wicked in darkness (1 Samuel 2:9).

God is full of grace and mercy. He is the one who knows how to elevate the poor and the beggars and to settle them among princes. When we put our trust in the Lord, as Hannah did, He can bring us out of nowhere, out of obscurity, out of nothing, and from afar off, and cause us to inherit the throne of glory. He sets us in places of prominence, authority, renown, wealth and riches.

Lord, our cry today is for you to let your favor lift us from the dunghill to inherit the throne of glory!

## C. ESTHER

Esther was a Jewish orphan who lived in Persia in the time of Ahasuerus, the great king, who reigned from 486 B.C. to 465 B.C. His kingdom was vast, stretching from India to Ethiopia, and covering over one hundred and twenty-seven provinces. Esther was raised by her uncle, Mordecai, after her parents died, and she grew into a beautiful young woman.

King Ahasuerus, after many days of celebrating and displaying the wealth, splendor and glory of his kingdom and majesty, asked Vashti, his queen, to parade before him and all the dignitaries gathered, to show her beauty. She refused to do so. Perceiving that to be a grave dishonor and insolence to him, he divorced her and sought her replacement.

Accordingly, a search commenced in the whole realm for beautiful young virgins for the king. Many virgins in the kingdom were assembled and brought under the care of the king's eunuch, who was to prepare them for twelve months, following which they could meet the king. They went through an intense beautification period - they were purified for six months with the oil of myrrh, and six months with sweet odors and beauty products.

At the end of the appointed period, all the ladies were poised, polished, beautiful and highly attractive, and they were presented to the king. Of all the numerous virgins, Esther was the one who found favor with the king and with all who dealt with and saw her. The king loved her more than all the other virgins, and she obtained grace and favor in his sight. He therefore set the royal crown on her head and made her queen in place of Vashti. Her ethnicity as a Jew was unknown to the king (Esther 2:15-17).

In the process of time, the king appointed and promoted Haman to be chief of all the princes in the province. Haman was ambitious and power-drunk, and he expected all the people to bow before him and give him reverence, but Mordecai, who brought up Queen Esther, refused to do so. That incensed Haman, who sought ways to punish Mordecai for his insubordination.

Haman learned that Mordecai was a Jew, and so he spun a scheme to eliminate all Jews from the province. He told King Ahasuerus that the Jews did not obey the laws of the land, and suggested that they should all be executed. The king bought into the malicious plan of Haman, and a decree went out to enforce this. Haman therefore built up gallows upon which the Jews would be executed.

A time was set for this to happen; however, Mordecai went to Esther and asked her to petition the king on this matter. After some initial reservations about approaching the king uninvited, Esther accepted the challenge and asked all the Jews to fast for three days and nights.

On the third day, she put on her royal apparel and went to the king's court, even though it was not lawful for her to do so without being summoned or invited by the king. She could have suffered serious repercussions for such effrontery. She still took the risk, though, and stepped out in faith with the backing of her Jewish brethren who were fasting and praying.

When the king saw Esther standing in his court, she again obtained favor in his sight. He extended his golden scepter to her. That was a gesture showing that, in spite of any breach of protocol on her part, she was accepted and welcome into his presence. She touched the scepter, and had free access to the king.

He did not just give her audience, but he invited her to ask him anything she wanted, even up to half of the kingdom. Wow! (Esther 5:1-3).

After hosting a feast for the king and Haman, she revealed her Jewish antecedents and what Haman had planned against them. The king finally woke up to the evil intentions of Haman, and sentenced him rather to the same fate that he had planned for the Jews. He reversed the decree made that all the Jews should be executed.

This is a great expression of favor. It is obvious that God set up Esther in the kingdom of Ahasuerus for such a time, so as to bring a great deliverance to the Jews (Esther 4:14). Through favor, God used her to persuade the king to withdraw the decree that went out that all the Jews were to be wiped out. Haman, the enemy of the Jews, was rather executed.

God is rallying modern day "Esthers" to change the tidal wave of intimidation and repression, and to shine bright in beauty and influence.

May the Lord's favor settle on His people, the Church. May all those who put their trust in the Lord God Most High experience a preferred and favored status in every arena of human endeavor. May we access the courts of our God, as well as the higher echelons of society and places of high esteem, without any sense of inferiority, reproach, unworthiness or limitation. May we, by the force of favor, revoke and reverse every decree the devil has written against us regarding our peace, joy, progress, livelihood, health and well-being. Hallelujah!

## D. DANIEL

Daniel and the people of Israel were taken into captivity in Babylon. He was amongst a small group of young men separated, by the order of King Nebuchadnezzar, to be groomed and educated in the Babylonian system. On the orders of the king, these young men were to be fed well with food from his own table and given the best education.

However, Daniel purposed in his heart not to defile himself with the portion of the king's food and wine, which was food offered to idols. That decision was likely going to put the prince of the eunuchs, who was in charge of Daniel and the other young men, in trouble. He faced certain death if it ever came to light that Daniel and the others had grown lean or had become emaciated or underperforming because they were not being fed the best portion of food that came from the king's table.

However, God granted Daniel immense favor with the prince of the eunuchs, who set Melzer over Daniel, Hananiah, Mishael, and Azariah. Melzer begrudgingly agreed to Daniel's proposal to allow them to feed on pulse and water for ten days, instead of eating the king's meat. After the ten days, they looked better, fairer and fatter than all the others who ate the king's food, and so Melzer allowed them to continue to feed as they requested.

God gave these four Hebrew youths, who did not defile themselves with food offered to idols, knowledge and wisdom and skill in all learning. Daniel also had understanding in visions and dreams as well. In all matters of wisdom and understanding, they were found to be ten times better than all the magicians and astrologers in the king's realm. Ultimately, Daniel became great in the land of Babylon, growing to, and continuing in, prominence from the reign of Nebuchadnezzar through to the first year of King Cyrus (Daniel 1:6-21).

God is the source of all the enlightenment, creativity, innovation, skill, knowledge, wisdom and understanding that anyone would ever need in life, and these blessings are released through the force of favor. Thus, even where a person is constrained, constricted and contained by life and circumstances, he/she can still flourish, blossom and bloom when the favor of the Lord is present.

Oh Lord, grant us all the favor in your realm of freedom and Jubilee to receive and operate in wisdom, knowledge, skill and understanding far above the people of this world. Grant that we would become creative and innovative geniuses in education, vocation, trade, business and commerce. Let the spirit of intelligence and excellence flow from within us daily in all we do, that we will succeed in, and surpass, all expectations, in Jesus' name.

## E. MARY, THE MOTHER OF JESUS

There has never been any part of history that is more important, more sacred, or more transformational than redemption's story. Jesus, the Word, entered this world as the One who would pay the price for the sin of humanity.

This glorious narrative and event all started with, and was wrapped in, the release of the extraordinary favor of God on the Virgin Mary.

The stage was set when Adam sinned, and he and the world became subject to the judgement for sin. But God, in His mercy and love, could not condemn man to eternal death and judgement, and put in place a plan for redemption. Sin could not redeem sin, and it was only perfect sinless blood which could set humanity free from sin.

It was therefore destined by God that Jesus, who knew no sin, would take on the form of human flesh. Ordinarily, to become human, He would have had to be born of the seed of man. However, if He were born of the seed of man, the sin of Adam would be transferred to Him, and He simply could not be the Savior who knew no sin.

As such, for the incarnation of the Messiah to be complete, God ordained that He would be born of the seed of the woman in the fullness of time (Galatians 4:4). Predictively speaking, He had told the serpent who beguiled Eve in the Garden that there would be enmity between his seed and the woman's seed, and that the woman's seed would bruise his head (Genesis 3:15).

The idea of the seed of a woman is biologically untenable. In terms of progeny, a woman does not have a seed. The seed comes from a man. However, in God's redemptive plan, it was imperative to maintain Jesus' sinless nature for the specific task of redemption He was to fulfil.

Accordingly, the Holy Ghost had to do that which was extraordinary, supernatural and miraculous, and the Virgin Mary was chosen by God to be the vector for this.

"Then said Mary unto the angel, How shall this be, seeing I know not a man? And the angel answered and said unto her, The Holy

Ghost shall come upon thee, and the power of the Highest shall overshadow thee: therefore also that holy thing which shall be born of thee shall be called the Son of God." Luke 1:34-35

"But when the fulness of the time was come, God sent forth his Son, made of a woman, made under the law, To redeem them that were under the law, that we might receive the adoption of sons." Galatians 4:4-5

Surely, then, Jesus was not of the descent of man. The Holy Spirit, who is the power of the Highest, administered and orchestrated His miraculous birth. He was transported from heaven by the supernatural workings of the Holy Ghost and planted in the womb of the Virgin Mary so that He could be born as a man.

Jesus' virgin birth was unexplainable and confounded procreative logic, bypassing and defying the natural, scientific and biological laws of reproduction (Matthew 1:18,23). It was a sign and a wonder spoken of and predicted by the prophets (Isaiah 7:14, 9:6, Matthew 1:22-23).

What we simply cannot miss or overlook is the fact that there were many virgins in Israel at the time of the consummation of God's eternal plan, but God chose Mary to be the vessel to carry the Son of God.

What is it that set her apart and eminently qualified her for this? The Bible gives the answer. It is that she was highly favored by God! The angel Gabriel appeared to her and declared to her how she was regarded by God: "And the angel came in unto her, and said, Hail, thou that art highly favored, the Lord is with thee: blessed art thou among women." Luke 1:28

Mary was therefore the receiver of the special grace, favor and benevolence from God, and she brought forth the Savior in due season. The angels rejoiced, delivering the glad tidings of great joy; the shepherds were struck with awe and rejoiced, and the wise men worshipped!

Once born, Jesus was clothed with, and soaked in, the favor of God. When the time was right, Mary and Joseph presented Him at the Temple to be dedicated to God according to the law. He grew strong both in stature and in spirit, walking in the wisdom and favor of God, and God was with Him.

"And Jesus increased in wisdom and stature, and in favor with God and man." Luke 2:52

The continuum of His life - His predestined advent to earth, His conception and birth, His ministry, and the consummation of His redemptive activity on the cross when He cried "it is finished" - represents the most important event in the history of humankind. Every facet of His life was totally engulfed in the high-level favor of Jehovah.

If the Son of God could only be unveiled to humanity through the outpouring of God's favor on Mary, and if He Himself needed the favor, grace and wisdom of God here on earth to fulfill His destiny, then we need no less.

May the Lord increase us in wisdom, strength, and favor with God and with man, so we can walk in the paths of righteousness, fulfilling His perfect will for our lives. May He favor us to become solution providers to humanity, as He did with Mary. May the Lord ignite the visions and dreams He has deposited within us, and preserve the purity of those visions and dreams;

and may He instill in us the discipline of waiting for them to come to pass, and cause us to bring them forth in the fullness of time by the power of His favor.

Favor with God is the blessing which changes or transforms lives for the better. When you have God's favor, He will be with you always, and will bring you to the place of great favor with man.

## F. THE CHURCH

The Church is the body of Jesus Christ, and He is its head. He gave His life to ransom the Church, and devolved and delegated all authority and power to it. In the ages to come, in the fullness of time, He will be reunited with her at the marriage supper of the lamb.

Spiritually speaking, there is a nexus or merger between Zion and the Church; Zion is the mirror image of the Church. Zion is the dwelling place of God, and so is the Church, which is the body of Christ, His temple and His dwelling place (Psalm 132:13-14, 1 Corinthians 3:16-17, 6:19).

The apostle Paul explained that we have come to Mount Zion, the city of the living God, the heavenly Jerusalem, the general assembly and Church of Jesus (Hebrews 12:22-23). The Church is represented in heaven as the heavenly Jerusalem. King Solomon, in his Temple dedication prayer, petitioned God that if any person came into the earthly Temple, the House of God in Zion, and lifted up his hands to pray, God should hear them from heaven, His dwelling place, and grant them their supplications and requests (2 Chronicles 6:28-33). Essentially, then, every blessing God pronounced on Zion is equally applicable to, and transmitted to, the Church. Prophetically, David had stated:

"Thou shalt arise, and have mercy upon Zion: for the time to favor her, yea, the set time is come." Psalm 102:13

When Jesus proclaimed the acceptable year of the Lord and its fulfilment in Himself, He was declaring that the set time of the Lord to extend the full devolution of His favor to the Church had come.

Accordingly, the Church is endowed with the favor of the Lord that beautifies and glorifies. As the blood-bought bride of Christ, washed by His word and blood, she is radiant, beautiful and glorious, holy, and without blemish, spot or wrinkle (Ephesians 5:26-27).

Through the outpouring of the favor of the Lord also, the Church is vested with the capacity and capability to attract and transform the world. It is a magnet for increase and the harvest of souls as the pillar of truth. Isaiah prophesied that the Gentiles would come to the light of God's people, and kings to the brightness of their rising (Isaiah 60:3).

Isaiah also spoke about the increase of the Messiah's government, and declared that there would be no end to it (Isaiah 9:7). The early Church operated in this blessing:

"Praising God, and having favour with all the people. And the Lord added to the Church daily such as should be saved." Acts 2:47

The believers shared fellowship daily in the Temple with one accord, breaking bread from house to house in unity and gladness of heart. Praising God was a key feature of their lifestyle. The Lord granted them favor with all the people. Many people got saved and the Church grew. The Lord will continue to build His Church, and the gates of hell will not prevail against it.

The great grace and favor of the Lord also enlightens the saints of God, and equips and enables them to walk the saintly walk on earth as He walked, to concurrently model the mandate and call of God on their lives (1 John 2:1-6).

Practically, however, life sometimes greets the saints with unexpected tests and trials, and their devotion, commitment and testimony come under massive pressure and attack. There are so many curveballs, bumps and bruises along the way.

The contemporary Church is confronted with adversity and rivalry from diverse sources – from religious leaders, politicians, and people who are driven by the spirit of the antichrist. There are also unceasing efforts and attempts from many opposing groups to shut the mouth of the Church and muzzle the spread of the word. In many places in the world today, the gospel is not allowed to be preached, and the Church operates underground.

The good news is that God is on the move against the maniacal terror and machinations of the enemy, tearing down political, religious and cultural barriers for His word to have free course. As the prophet Obadiah declares:

"But upon mount Zion shall be deliverance, and there shall be holiness; and the house of Jacob shall possess their possessions." Obadiah 1:17

God brings deliverance to the Church, and through Jesus, has given her authority to trample on snakes and scorpions, and to overcome all the power of the enemy, and nothing shall by any means harm His people (Luke 10:19). The Church will recover and reclaim everything that has been stolen from her, and possess her possessions.

Hey! The set time for Jehovah to favor the Church is now. Let the people of God rise up and ardently seek God for His favor. As truly as God lives, nothing can stop Him from filling the whole earth with His glory.

Lord, we pray Thee, increase your favor on your Church in these last days of the move of your Spirit. Grant that exponential growth of your Church in the earth today, for of the increase of your kingdom there shall be no end. Make your saints and your Church glide on your great grace and favor, and cause them to advance against the gates of hell with power, authority and dominion, and the gates of hell shall not prevail. Let us walk in your Jubilee so that we can minister Jubilee to the world.

## 3. WRAPPING IT ALL UP …

"For thou, Lord, wilt bless the righteous: with favor wilt thou compass him as with a shield." Psalm 5:12

The favor of the Lord changes everything, and dynamically impacts a person's situation, status, standing, placement, approval, connections, access, opportunities, abilities, fruitfulness, creativity; the list is truly endless. That favor has been released by the resounding, blasting, shofar-voice of Jesus Messiah through the preaching of the gospel of salvation, peace, healing and deliverance, and the proclamation of Jubilee to the nations of the earth.

That shofar blast of the gospel of salvation and the year of the Lord's favor belongs to all who believe and acknowledge Jesus as the Savior who died for their sins to set them free. The message of salvation and favor cuts across demographical, ethnic and cultural barriers, impacting every race, color, creed, gender and social class. It is for the young and old, rich and poor, nobles and servants, monarchs and subjects, the famous and the unknown, and no one is left out of its coverage.

This is an opportune time - if you have not met Jesus, the Redeemer, may I introduce Him to you now. Take a moment to thank God, the heavenly Father and creator of all things, for sending Jesus to the cross at Calvary to pour out His blood and His life to atone for our sins and to save us. Ask Jesus to come into your life and heart now, confessing with your mouth that He is Lord, and believing in your heart that God raised Him from the dead, and you will be saved (Romans 10:8-10).

This is the acceptable year of the Lord, the day of salvation, the year of the Lord's favor. Receive salvation now. Take the favor now. Bask in the explosion of the Lord's favor which surrounds us like a shield. Revel in that favor. It belongs to you!

# Chapter 26

## THE JUBILEE MANDATE

The Old Testament prophets and priests put their fingers on the very pulse of Jubilee. They prophesied, lived out and practiced the Jubilee once every seven Sabbatical years; it began on the tenth day of the Day of Atonement in the 49$^{th}$ year and run into the 50$^{th}$ year.

At each Jubilee, Jehovah God reset His divine action plan and template regarding salvation, freedom and deliverance. Jubilee resounded to the nation of Israel through the blasting loud sounding shofar. Sins were atoned for and forgiven, and righteousness and holiness was restored. Those who were estranged from God or from each other reconciled and bounced back into fellowship. Debts were cancelled; bondservants went home; lands and properties which served as collateral were released to their original owners with all price tags on them removed. The national economic slate was wiped clean, giving all a fresh start.

The liberty and freedom that the Jubilee year brought impacted, shaped and realigned the spiritual, economic and national course of life for the people of Israel for another fifty years, into the next generation.

We cannot even begin to imagine the spring and dance in the feet of multitudes! The cry of liberty was heard all over the land.

Many hands were thrown up towards heaven in thanksgiving, praise, worship and humble adoration, celebrating the goodness and victories of Jehovah. Many different voices - bass, tenor, treble, soprano, and probably other pitches that could never be discovered on any keyboard - sang songs of deliverance and uttered shouts of joy.

Jubilee was the joyful sound in the ears of all hearers. Joy had come to town "big time." Jubilee was, and is, good news, glad tidings to all. But ... Hmmm! Wait a minute. That sounds really really familiar ... Oooh, yes, it sounds like the gospel! Truly, Jubilee was, and is, and will forever be, the gospel.

The gospel is intrinsically wrapped up in Jesus Messiah. At His birth, the angels announced to the shepherds in the field, "good tidings of great joy, which shall be to all people. For unto you is born this day in the city of David a Savior, which is Christ the Lord. ... Glory to God in the highest, and on earth peace, good will toward men" (Luke 2:10, 11, 14).

Jesus Messiah was the arrival of the Jubilee in person. His arrival was that which the Father God had foreordained, predesigned, cooked, baked, and fired up in the crucible of eternity before time began.

"According as he hath chosen us in him before the foundation of the world, that we should be holy and without blame before him in love: Having predestinated us unto the adoption of children by Jesus Christ to himself, according to the good pleasure of his will." Ephesians 1:4-5

It was His arrival as Savior that the prophets had spoken about hundreds and thousands of years before it eventuated. They looked into, tapped and pulled out, God's blueprint for humanity's redemption. Inspired by the Holy Ghost, they prophesied about, and wrote down, the pathway to salvation, and emancipation from sin, judgment, death, hell and the grave.

Everything was narrowing down and counting down to the irrefutable fact that Jesus is the One all of creation awaited with bated breath, the new thing created in the earth, the Rod out of the stem of Jesse, the Rose of Sharon, the Lily of the valley, the Prince of Peace, Wonderful, Counsellor, everlasting Father, King of kings and Lord of Lords.

Jubilee is the story of Jesus who, made of the seed of the woman, showed up in human flesh in the earth in fullness of time (Galatians 4:4). He is the Word who was made flesh, the incarnate God, Immanuel (God with us), and deity united with humanity (John 1:14). These are infallible unassailable truths, that:

- Jesus came, not only to declare the Jubilee; He is Jubilee.
- Jesus came, not only to show us the Father; whoever has seen Him has seen the Father.
- Jesus came, not only to teach the truth of the way of life; He is the way, the truth, and He is the life.
- Jesus came, not only to atone for our sins; He has the power to forgive sins.
- Jesus came, not only to declare peace; He is peace.
- Jesus came, not only to show us the kingdom of God; He is the King of the kingdom.
- He is God, the Word.

- He is the creator of all things.
- He is the Sabbath, the Lord of the Sabbath.
- He is the personation of the Feasts that were celebrated.
- He is the Trumpet/shofar that sounded the Jubilee.
- He is the High Priest who went into the Temple to present the blood of the sacrifice.
- He is the sacrifice that was offered up to God.
- He is the Atonement for the sin of the people.
- He is the name that is above every other name.
- He is the one who broke the back of enslavement, bondage and servitude to the devil to set the captives free.

Based on all of the above, there is not a shred of doubt that He alone was eminently qualified to announce the Jubilee and to proclaim its various facets and manifestations. This Jesus came to tell the Jubilee story, live the Jubilee, and demonstrate the Jubilee. He is the Jubilee personified, the Jubilee fulfilled, the very embodiment of its totality.

But the message does not end there.

Jesus, the Jubilee, is seated at the right hand side of the Majesty on High. He has passed on to us, His people, the fullness of His authority, that is, the Jubilee baton, the Jubilee torch, and the Jubilee mantle.

He has given to us the JUBILEE MANDATE!

This is the Jubilee Mandate – that Jesus has authorized every believer to carry out and extend His mandate of preaching the gospel, to turn men from darkness to light and from the power of Satan unto God, that they might receive forgiveness of sins, everlasting life, and an imperishable inheritance among them that are sanctified.

## 1. THE JUBILEE MANDATE OF JESUS

Jesus Himself had a mandate to fulfill. A mandate is an official order or commission that gives someone authority to act a certain way; it means to appoint, nominate or empower someone to carry out a specific assignment.

The Father God chose, appointed, assigned and anointed Jesus to come to earth with the comprehensive mandate:

- To reveal the Father;
- To bring the intervention of God's kingdom in the earth;
- To preach the gospel to the poor;
- To heal the broken hearted;
- To preach deliverance to the captives;
- To preach recovering of sight to the blind;
- To set at liberty them that are bruised;
- To preach the acceptable year of the Lord;
- To lay down His life as the lamb of God who takes away the sin of the world;
- To conquer sin, death, hell and the grave;
- To conquer Satan, disarm every principality and power, and triumphantly make a public show of them;
- To lead those who believe in Him and who confess His Lordship, and who believe in His death and resurrection,

into the experience of the new birth, so that they can enter the kingdom of God;
- To ascend to heaven and to send the promise of the Holy Ghost;
- To come again to rapture His perfect bride, the Church, to heaven, to His Father's house where there are many mansions.

Jesus Himself confirmed that He was sent by the Father to fulfill the Father's mandate. So did John the Baptist who affirmed the mandate of Jesus Messiah as the lamb of God which takes away the sin of the world. Jesus stated:

"For God so loved the world, that he gave his only begotten Son, that whosoever believeth in him should not perish, but have everlasting life. For God sent not his Son into the world to condemn the world; but that the world through him might be saved." John 3:16-17

"Verily, verily, I say unto you, He that heareth my word, and believeth on him that sent me, hath everlasting life, and shall not come into condemnation; but is passed from death unto life." John 5:24

In His own words, Jesus said He proceeded from the Father and came to do the Father's will; He did not come of His own accord or to perform His own wishes. He represented the Father and came to reveal Him, so that those who heard Him would believe in the Father who sent Him. He spoke the words of God.

Jesus was not sent out without divine enablement. He received from the Father God, all that He needed to perform and accomplish His mandate. As He observed, the Father loves the Son and has given all things into His hand. The Father showed Him all the things that had to be done, and He, the obedient and loving Son, followed the Father's expectations to the letter, even to death on the cross.

"But Jesus answered them, My Father worketh hitherto, and I work. Therefore the Jews sought the more to kill him, because he not only had broken the sabbath, but said also that God was his Father, making himself equal with God. Then answered Jesus and said unto them, Verily, verily, I say unto you, The Son can do nothing of himself, but what he seeth the Father do: for what things soever he doeth, these also doeth the Son likewise. For the Father loveth the Son, and sheweth him all things that himself doeth: and he will shew him greater works than these, that ye may marvel." John 5:17-20

Jesus walked in the Spirit and was led by the Spirit, and His duties and activities were revealed to Him by God, through the Spirit. His ministry began with two baptisms – His water baptism, and the Holy Spirit baptism. When He was baptized in the River Jordan by John the Baptist, the heavens opened, and the Holy Spirit descended on Him in bodily form like a dove. The Spirit then directed Him into the wilderness where he waited on God, fasting and praying for forty days and nights.

Anointed by the Spirit without measure, He obeyed and worked the works of God. All His teaching, preaching, and marvelous miraculous works were under the auspices of the Father's authority, the Father's mandate.

Noteworthy is the fact that, whilst on earth, Jesus ministered in His humanity, and not as deity. In coming to the earth, He emptied Himself of His deity and was made in fashion as a man (Philippians 2:5-7). In His humanity, He could only walk in the will of God through the ministry and power of the Holy Spirit. Therefore, the workings and operations of the Spirit were integral and of utmost importance during His ministry on earth. He moved in the Spirit, walked in the Spirit, and was empowered by the Spirit.

He also operated in the spirit of full disclosure and candidly let His listeners know that those who believe on Him, the Son, would have everlasting life; conversely, those who choose not to believe on Him would not see life, but would come under the wrath of God (John 1:29, 3:34-36).

He could only come to announce the year of Jubilee by the anointing of the Holy Spirit. Jesus, who was tasked with the Jubilee mandate of God, addressed, in every prism and facet of His life and ministry, the matter of freedom, liberty and Jubilee. He administered it. He went about doing good and healing all who were oppressed of the devil, for God was with Him (Acts 10:38). He fulfilled the Jubilee through and through.

## 2. THE JUBILEE MANDATE OF THE DISCIPLES

We know that the Father sent, authorized and anointed Jesus to establish His purposes in the earth, to bring Jubilee to humanity. Jesus, without reservation, transferred this self-same mandate to His disciples.

"As thou hast sent me into the world, even so have I also sent them into the world." John 17:18

The disciples' obedience to this call had to begin with faith in the Father God and faith in His Son, to go forth to accomplish the works of God. They were to continue Jesus' mission in the same Spirit and in the same vein as He, and to do nothing less than He did. In fact, they were to do even greater works than He did.

"Verily, verily, I say unto you, He that believeth on me, the works that I do shall he do also; and greater works than these shall he do: because I go unto my Father." John14:12

"And he said unto them, Go ye into all the world, and preach the gospel to every creature. He that believeth and is baptized shall be saved: but he that believeth not shall be damned. And these signs shall follow them that believe; In my name shall they cast out devils; they shall speak with new tongues; They shall take up serpents; and if they drink any deadly thing, it shall not hurt them; they shall lay hands on the sick, and they shall recover." Mark 16:15-18

Jesus did the works of his Father, drawing faith, strength, power, authority and the anointing from Him. He was in the Father and the Father was in Him (John 14:11). Likewise, Jesus assured His disciples that, if they abide in Him, and He in them, they would have all the enablement, power, and anointing to do the works that He did, and even more, because He has gone to the Father.

It is important not to miss the element of being sent. Christ, which means "the Sent One", was sent of the Father. It was therefore critical for the disciples to identify with, and have faith in, Him as "the Sent One" from the Father with the mandate of the Father.

Consequently, coming under the mandate of the Christ, the Sent One, meant that they were also drawing from the same authority that Christ received from His Father, culminating in the logical projection that they could also work the works of the Father. As God sent Jesus, so Jesus sent His disciples.

"And when he had called unto him his twelve disciples, he gave them power against unclean spirits, to cast them out, and to heal all manner of sickness and all manner of disease"

"And as ye go, preach, saying, the kingdom of heaven is at hand. Heal the sick, cleanse the lepers, raise the dead, cast out devils: freely ye have received, freely give." Matthew 10:1, 7-8

Jesus did the work of the soul-winner. He went to all the cities, villages, and synagogues, preaching the gospel of the kingdom. He was also engaged in healing every disease and sickness, casting out devils, and setting at liberty those who were bound.

He led by example, and His disciples saw what He did. It therefore fell on them to also go to all the world and preach the same good news, lead people to salvation in Christ, minister deliverance to the captives, cast out devils, heal the sick, and baptize the saved into the body of Christ. They did, and God endorsed their ministry by confirming the word with signs following (Mark 16:20).

There was a direct transmission of the Jubilee Mandate from the Messiah to the disciples. They embraced that mandate with zeal and passion, and they were deputized, authorized, and thoroughly equipped to carry out the ministry of Jubilee.

## 3. THE JUBILEE MANDATE OF THE APOSTLE PAUL

The apostle Paul was neither a disciple nor follower of Christ when Christ was on the earth. He still was not a follower after Christ was received into heaven. In fact, he persecuted the Church, and it was in pursuance of that same agenda that he had a life-altering, destiny-changing, encounter with the Lord Jesus on his way to Damascus.

From that point of his submission to Christ, he came under the authority of a higher power, and he was tasked with the mandate from Christ to preach the gospel. He was consumed by his passion to preach. As he saw it:

"For though I preach the gospel, I have nothing to glory of: for necessity is laid upon me; yea, woe is unto me, if I preach not the gospel!." 1 Corinthians 9:16

Paul recognized that he was under a divine injunction to preach the word. It was a burden laid upon him, and he reckoned had no choice, nor could he be free, until he sent the message across to the lost. He therefore devoted his entire life and ministry to obeying the call to preach to the lost, and so should every one of us.

His attitude and commitment to the mandate to preach the gospel is inspiring, and his insight into the word is revelatory and worth emulating.

First, he was not ashamed of the gospel, and unabashedly declared it. He viewed it as the power of God to transform lives. He boldly preached the gospel, declaring that it is the power of

God that brings salvation to all who believe, and that the preaching of the cross is foolishness to those who are perishing (Romans 1:16-17, 1 Corinthians 1:18).

Paul tapped into a deep revelation that no one experiences God's power and remains unchanged. The power of the gospel changes people in their character, conduct, choices and speech. When people submit their hearts and minds to the word of God, they are renewed, transformed and conformed into the image of God. The gospel does not only renew lives, but also effects a spiritual translation or transition from the dominion of sin, darkness and the power of Satan, into the kingdom of God (Colossians 1:13).

Paul was also committed to, and advocated, the preaching of the full gospel of God. That full gospel is the message that comes in the demonstration of the miraculous power of God.

"For I will not dare to speak of any of those things which Christ hath not wrought by me, to make the Gentiles obedient, both by word and deed, Through mighty signs and wonders, by the power of the Spirit of God; so that from Jerusalem, and round about unto Illyricum, I have fully preached the gospel of Christ." Romans 15:18-19

He fully preached the gospel, and the body of Christ must take a cue from this. It must not deliver the gospel in a half-hearted manner. It must awake to preach a balanced gospel, not a half-baked, watered down, or "feel good only" gospel, but the gospel that fully declares the counsel of God. This effort must engage the Church's full energies.

Paul was also very careful about the manner in which he communicated the gospel to people. As a person under the authority of God, he recognized that it was imperative for him to convey the gospel in a way that was not enticing. His strategy was to deliver the word in a way that shifted or deflected people's focus from his human eloquence and the captivating power of his persuasion; instead, he wanted their faith to be established in the power of God. He stated:

"And my speech and my preaching was not with enticing words of man's wisdom, but in demonstration of the Spirit and of power: That your faith should not stand in the wisdom of men, but in the power of God." 1 Corinthians 2:4-5

Paul did not present the wisdom of men or the ideas and philosophies of men. He was also not concerned about the rudiments of this world or preoccupied with political and cultural correctness. Rather, he was full of the Holy Ghost and declared the word of God with the manifestation of the explosive, dynamic power of the Spirit everywhere he went.

His ministry was marked by mighty signs and wonders by the enablement of the 'dunamis', the outbreak and surge of the power of the Holy Ghost. Beginning from Jerusalem and round about Illyricum, his hearers experienced the power and saw the miracles, and therefore, they became obedient to the faith, both in word and deed.

He could only accomplish this by declaring the unadulterated word and demonstrating the power of the Holy Spirit, and not by resorting to, or utilizing, the words of man's wisdom.

Paul also recognized that there were many out there who had not heard the gospel, and who were yet to be reached for Christ. Therefore, rather than going to places where the gospel had already taken root, he went to the heathen, the lost who had never heard the gospel, to make Christ known.

"Yea, so have I strived to preach the gospel, not where Christ was named, lest I should build upon another man's foundation." Romans 15:20

Throughout the history of the Church, though, there have been some troubling trends. In today's world, especially, there is the largely illegitimate conduct of building on other's foundations. Christians are like recycled goods amongst ministries. Churches scramble for the same souls, and people move from Church to Church. However, there is a massive harvest of souls out there, people who have not been reached with the gospel and who could be won for Christ and brought into the Church.

Related to this is the very unsavory situation of Church splits and divisions and betrayals in the house of God and amongst the people. There are so many in the body of Christ who sow discord in ministries. They divide Churches, take with them the members who are already saved and plugged in to the local assembly, and launch out to start their own Churches and ministries, often claiming to be doing this under God's leading.

The truth is simple - God is not a God of confusion and division; neither will He endorse anything that is fundamentally contrary to His ways and His word. Division and discord in the body of Christ is anathema to God, and there are many repercussions that come along with such ungodly behaviors. The Bible says:

"These six things doth the LORD hate: yea, seven are an abomination unto him: A proud look, a lying tongue, and hands that shed innocent blood, An heart that deviseth wicked imaginations, feet that be swift in running to mischief, A false witness that speaketh lies, and he that soweth discord among brethren." Proverbs 6:16-19

Those who deceive others who are already saved and urge them to align themselves with them do so purely out of self-interest and self-gratification. They use them to start Churches, not because they are being led by the Spirit as they often claim, but because they want the easy path to ministerial success, and because they want others to congregate around them to get money and fame. These I call the "stomach direction preachers", for their god is their belly, and they have nothing to offer.

Church breakers are wicked and unreasonable men who literally dismember the body of Christ. They have no faith or calling to initiate any new work, and so they resort to "divide and rule" tactics (2 Thessalonians 3:1-2). They seek to build their own empires by undermining authority, and through deception, manipulation and sweet talks. Their agenda is not to build the Church but their own kingdom. Unfortunately, many fall for such misguidance, and others get disillusioned or feel spiritually abused.

Church breakers have no zeal or passion for the lost. They just set back the work of God and hinder its advancement and wound the body of Christ. The apostle Paul viewed this very seriously, and sternly addressed this matter, saying that such people should be marked out, that is, clearly identified, and avoided; that we must steer clear of them because they do not serve Jesus. He urges:

"Now I beseech you, brethren, mark them which cause divisions and offences contrary to the doctrine which ye have learned; and avoid them. For they that are such serve not our Lord Jesus Christ, but their own belly, and by good words and fair speeches deceive the hearts of the simple." Romans 16:17-18

The Church must address these issues prayerfully and with sound Biblical instruction, and not gloss over such matters. Moreover, Christians must understand that it is dangerous to follow Church breakers, or to endorse them by attending their gatherings, programs and fundraisers and the like, and by having misplaced sympathy towards them. Doing so may mean partaking in other people's sins, which could expose them to a share of the Lord's judgement.

People are free to worship wherever they want. However, they must also understand divine ordination - that God specifically places people in certain local Churches because He has a destined purpose for them there. It is the place where they can thrive, flourish, prosper and be a blessing, and they are there to encourage the work. It is therefore important for them to insulate themselves from the deception of divisive people who are full of greed and blind ambition, who mislead them or alter their spiritual destiny.

There are legitimate protocols and principles to follow where a person is leaving a particular local assembly or Church organization for God's true purpose. He/she must do so out of a pure and genuine heart, and should leave with the peace and blessing of the leadership and whole body. And for those who are minded to follow that person or leader who is departing in a peaceful way, they must be peacefully released by the leadership as well. If anyone needs Christians from another Church to come and help their Church, they must get permission from those people's leadership, and not just entice them to cross over. All of these steps will ensure love, unity and strength in Christendom.

The body of Christ needs to follow Paul's mandate - go out there and preach the gospel to the unsaved, adding them to the Church, instead of deceiving people who are already serving the Lord and offering support to their local assemblies. He enunciates, in Acts 20:20, his "2020-VISION", which is God's ordained strategy to reach the unsaved and unreached:

"And how I kept back nothing that was profitable unto you, but have shewed you, and have taught you publicly, and from house to house." Acts 20:20

It appears as though the Holy Spirit divinely orchestrated Acts 20:20 to give sight and vision to the Church. 2020 vision measures visual acuity, and refers to the perfect sight of the human being. Clear sight enables people to have an appreciable spatial awareness, to reach their destinations safely by avoiding pitfalls, dangers and misguidance, and to accomplish their goals.

This is equally applicable to the Church. Acts 20:20 impresses on the Church that it must function with perfect spiritual sight and perceive that the harvest is ripe. The people of God must launch their nets into the deep for a great haul of souls for the kingdom of God. The Church must stay on course to attain the vision of the kingdom of God, which is to increase the kingdom by reaching the unsaved.

The apostle Paul engaged crowds in public meetings and presented the kingdom message. He also moved from house to house, ministering the gospel to families. He ministered in mass evangelism, as well as one- on-one evangelism, to Jews, Gentiles, kings, politicians, the great, rich or poor, and to people from all walks of life. He became everything to everybody so that there would be no lost opportunity, and he might save some.

Paul received this from none other than Jesus. Jesus spoke to the multitudes, thousands of them at a go. Yet, He made time for Lazarus, Mary and Martha on a personal level. He went to the house of the centurion, the man of authority. He saw Zacchaeus, the corrupt tax collector, in a tree, and went to his home to preach the word and minister grace. He helped people he met people on the road. He ministered to the woman at the well. He went everywhere.

Soul-winning was Paul's heart, his cry, and his life. He felt a strong charge over his life to do that, and he perceived himself as having no other choice, but to preach the gospel. He did not want to incur God's displeasure.

This very same cry and zeal should be the heart-cry of the Church, that of every believer, every saint. When the Church adheres to the 20:20 Vision, it will grow in greater strength and power to overcome obstacles and to advance God's purpose in the earth. When people get all busy serving the Lord, leading souls to Christ, discipling them and promoting God's kingdom, there will be no room left for dissension, splits, division and man-made self-church empires. Let the Church arise and proclaim the Jubilee. Rescue the perishing, and care for the dying.

## 4. THE JUBILEE MANDATE OF THE CHURCH

From the inception of the Christian Church, its mandate and mission has always been that which was entrusted to Christ and

His disciples by the Father God. That baton, mantle and mandate from Christ to His disciples has now been passed on to the entire body of Christ, the Church.

The Church must, in like manner, go into all the world equipped with the same power and authority, and must preach the same good news, lead people to salvation in Christ, minister deliverance to the captives, cast out devils, heal the sick, and baptize the saved into the body of Christ.

The urgency of this mandate cannot be underplayed because the fate that awaits the lost is simply horrendous. The prophet Joel sends out the warning of God:

"Let the heathen be wakened, and come to the valley of Jehoshaphat: for there will I sit to judge all the heathen round about. Put ye in the sickle, for the harvest is ripe: come, get you down; for the press is full, the fats overflow; for their wickedness is great. Multitudes, multitudes in the valley of decision: for the day of the Lord is near in the valley of decision." Joel 3:12-14

The imagery in this passage relays the decadent and decrepit state of the world, and the fact that it is on the cusp of judgment. The ripe harvest refers to the multitudes of the unsaved, the heathen, whose wickedness is great and overflowing. These are they who are without God and godless, who have sinned and have not repented, and who have maltreated God's people, Israel. They have not come to faith in Christ Jesus, and they are lost.

The stage is set for justice to be meted out. These multitudes are at a place of decision, for at the end of the millennial reign of Christ and the Church, they would be assembled in the valley of Jehoshaphat for God's judgment. They are slated for destruction by the sickle, a handheld semicircular farming and harvesting instrument.

The valley of Jehoshaphat is the same as the valley of decision, or the valley of judgment, and it is the place where God judges. Jehoshaphat means "Yahweh judges". Some have interpreted the passage to mean that the multitudes are the ones to make the decision, but that is not so. God is the one to make the decision on the fate of the unrepented masses in the valley.

God is a God of judgment, and He will dish out His eternal judgment on the heathen. He will sit on the great white throne and judge the nations. At the end of days, the devil, the beast and the false prophet will be cast into the lake of fire. The sea, death and hell will also give up the dead that are in them.

The books will be opened, including the book of life. Death, hell and all those whose names are not written in the book of life will be cast into the lake of fire. They will be tormented day and night forever. There will be eternal damnation, a state of perpetual suffering, weeping and gnashing of teeth, unending torment and affliction in the ever-increasing heat of the lake of fire. This will be God's eternal verdict on those without Christ (Revelation 20:10-15).

As real as the coming judgment of God is, though, there is also the good news of escape from His wrath. No one, according to God's plan and purpose, should be eternally condemned. It is for this reason that He sent Jesus to pay the price for sin and to atone for eternal damnation. His will is that none should perish, but that all would come to the knowledge of the truth and have eternal life (John 3:16, 1 Timothy 2:4).

With that provision of Christ, there is absolutely no reason why there should be multitudes in the valley of Jehoshaphat, that valley where, at the end of days, God would make the decision to pass eternal condemnation on those without Christ.

It is this knowledge - that there is a way of escape for the world - that should animate and fine-tune the agenda of the Church. It is important for the Christian Church to be filled with the compassion of Jesus towards the lost and dying, and to rise with the sense of urgency and zeal to get people saved and restored to righteousness and fellowship with God. The Church must preach the word with intensity and with mercy, snatching some from the fire of judgment, and hating any clothing stained with the corruption of the things of the flesh (Jude 1:23).

Most Christians today have lost their zeal to reach the unsaved. Crafted Church programs are no longer tailored to bringing salvation to the lost but, rather, to entertaining people. As a result, there are many who self-identify as Christian, but who have not experienced true salvation because they have never heard or assimilated the pure message of the gospel.

The culture of this present world is also filled and contaminated with antichrist ideologies, false religions, secular humanism, heathenism and witchcraft, and these have blinded the spiritual eyes of many, and have caused them to disparage the gospel.

The Church must understand that the preaching of the gospel that brings light and awakening to the multitudes which are lost cannot be achieved through human efforts or the flesh, or by using the bait of entertainment that is based on worldly standards, or by importing worldly activities into the Church to attract and entice people.

The ministry of Jesus was not accomplished through fleshly or human efforts, but in the power of the Holy Spirit. The early Church, in the book of Acts, also did not employ the tactics of the world or worldly entertainment to bring souls into the Church. They preached the gospel, endued with the power of the Holy Spirit. Jesus shows us the unadulterated way to reach souls:

"And he said unto them, Thus it is written, and thus it behooved Christ to suffer, and to rise from the dead the third day: And that repentance and remission of sins should be preached in his name among all nations, beginning at Jerusalem. And ye are witnesses of these things. And, behold, I send the promise of my Father upon you: but tarry ye in the city of Jerusalem, until ye be endued with power from on high." Luke 24:46-49

"But ye shall receive power, after that the Holy Ghost is come upon you: and ye shall be witnesses unto me both in Jerusalem, and in all Judea, and in Samaria, and unto the uttermost part of the earth." Acts 1:8

With the power of the Holy Ghost, the early Church witnessed conversions, and crowds joined the Church. Their ministry was characterized by signs and wonders and diverse gifts of the Holy Ghost (Hebrews 2:4).

The modern Church needs no less of the Holy Spirit to accomplish the Jubilee mandate. The late evangelist, Reinhard Bonke, articulated his mission as being to "empty hell and populate heaven." This statement sums up the mandate of the Church. Every believer who is saved and born again must stand up and be counted, and must rise up and run with "Pentecost Fire" in their bones, and be unstoppable in reaching the perishing with the good news of salvation, healing and deliverance.

At Pentecost, the fire of the Holy Spirit fell on the disciples, and they were filled with the Holy Ghost and spoke in other tongues. The different ethnic groups who had gathered in Jerusalem at the time heard the disciples in their own languages declaring the mighty works of God.

Peter's message of repentance and salvation that day brought three thousand souls to Christ. The gospel was preached under the power of the Holy Spirit, and the hearers were cut to the heart, convicted, and eager to know what they could do to be saved.

What a big difference it would make if Christians learned to follow the Spirit-led life! What a glorious change that would bring. And what a great impact we would make in our world if the sermons preached, the songs written and sung, the books authored, and all ministry assignments and projects undertaken, were fueled, oiled and energized by the Spirit! No one could even imagine the explosive glory and grace that would fall on the Church which, in turn, would influence the world with the gospel.

Jesus sent His disciples and the entire Church to go and preach Jubilee to the world, that is, the word, the good news, the gospel, which is the power of God unto salvation for all who believe. This all-important assignment and mission echoes through the ages and generations.

The disciples who followed Jesus encountered the very Word of God who was made flesh. They saw Him, heard Him and touched Him. They had tangible interactions and personal relationships with Him. They watched and listened to Him preach and teach the word of God. They saw the miraculous and supernatural take place when people received the word and believed. They witnessed His grace, authority, power and dominion in all things and over all things. The apostle John relays these experiences, stating:

"That which was from the beginning, which we have heard, which we have seen with our eyes, which we have looked upon, and our hands have handled, of the Word of life; (For the life was manifested, and we have seen it, and bear witness, and shew unto you that eternal life, which was with the Father, and was manifested unto us;) That which we have seen and heard declare we unto you, that ye also may have fellowship with us: and truly our fellowship is with the Father and his Son Jesus Christ." 1 John 1:1-3

These disciples preached the word when Jesus was on the earth, and also after His ascension into heaven. They went out there showing Him forth through their preaching so that others would come to the knowledge of the Word of life, the gospel of their salvation, and be joined with them in fellowship. They knew that preaching this word was the only hope of salvation and redemption for humanity. They experienced the explosive power of God in signs and wonders.

The Church has been given the same mandate to deliver the word, and as was the case with the disciples, Jesus will confirm the word with signs following. It is absolutely fascinating that, although most of the Church world would never have seen or touched or walked with Jesus physically, as did the disciples, they have received no less of the amazing thing.

The Church, like the disciples, still has a real experience of the person of Jesus and His being because He is the Word, and His name is the "Word of God" (John 1:1; Revelation 19:13). He came down to dwell among us, revealing the good news which is the gospel. He came to show the will of the Father to the world and to bless the world with the outpouring of the Holy Spirit. All that He was, and is, and will ever be, and all that He did, and does, and will do, and all that He has, fills His word, the Bible, and the Church is armed with the Bible.

The apostles relayed to us what they had seen and heard and touched. Before then, the prophets of old spoke the word of the Lord. All Scripture is God-breathed, and given by the inspiration of God (2 Timothy 3:16). Jesus declared that the words He spoke are spirit and life. (John 6:63, Proverbs 4:20-22). Thus, the word of God is packed with the breath and life of God.

"For the word of God is quick (alive), and powerful, and sharper than any twoedged sword, piercing even to the dividing asunder of soul and spirit, and of the joints and marrow, and is a discerner of the thoughts and intents of the heart." Hebrews 4:12

Jesus is that word which the prophets were moved by the Holy Ghost to prophesy. Thus, when they declared, "Thus saith the Lord...", it was really Jesus Messiah, the Lord, who was speaking through them. When Jesus came to earth, He did not have to speak through the prophets, but spoke with authority saying, "verily, verily, I say unto you...", revealing that He was the Word in person, the Word made flesh dwelling among men. (John 5:24, 10:1, 12:24, 1:14).

Our job is to go forth to proclaim His word and win souls. Not our word, not anybody's word, not the philosophies and rudiments of this world, not even the traditions of Church denominations, but the word of the living God, which is Jesus. That word which we preach is unchanging, and it is loaded with power to produce what it promises. The word is equipped with the unique capability to save, heal, deliver, and to release signs and wonders, even Jubilee.

God has lifted His word above His names or His titles. (Psalm 138:2). When His word goes forth, it does not return void but accomplishes that which He pleases and prospers in what it was sent out for. (Isaiah 55:11). The word is so powerful.

"The voice of the LORD is upon the waters: the God of glory thundereth: the LORD is upon many waters. The voice of the LORD is powerful; the voice of the LORD is full of majesty. The voice of the LORD breaketh the cedars; yea, the LORD breaketh the cedars of Lebanon. He maketh them also to skip like a calf; Lebanon and Sirion like a young unicorn. The voice of the LORD divideth the flames of fire. The voice of the LORD shaketh the wilderness; the LORD shaketh the wilderness of Kadesh. The voice of the LORD maketh the hinds to calve, and discovereth the forests: and in his temple doth every one speak of his glory." Psalm 29:3-9

The word that is preached, heard and received will bring salvation, eternal life, righteousness and transformation, and will establish humanity in the kingdom of God.

Church, let us go preach it, proclaiming the joyful sound of Jubilee, freedom and liberty. Let us fill the whole earth with the knowledge of God's impregnable word! Let us exercise faith and demonstrate our corporate authority that is backed by the exceeding greatness of God's power, and break the hindering barriers to the proclamation of the good news in this post-modernist culture.

The convicting power of the Holy Spirit will surely move through the preaching of the Church, and will remove spiritual blindness and roll back the gross darkness that covers the multitudes. The glorious light of the gospel will penetrate the darkness, and will bring people to faith and salvation in Christ Jesus.

The glory of the latter house shall be greater than the former, the Bible declares. The Church is the latter house, that glorious Temple of God, and it must exude that greater glory, and with boldness, must permeate the darkness of this world with the Jubilee message that sets humanity free. God has promised that heaven must receive Jesus until the time of restoration and restitution of all things. There is a far greater working and operation of the Holy Spirit in the earth today, and the Church ought to wake up, and arise to fulfill the call of the Jubilee Mandate.

# Chapter 27

## JUBILEE MANDATE KEYS – BE FULL OF THE HOLY GHOST

The prophets, priests, judges and kings of Israel ministered to the spiritual, politico-legal and socio-economic needs of the nation of Israel through its redemptive history. As we see inscribed in the Old Testament records, they were men and women who were consecrated, separated, and powerfully anointed by the Holy Spirit to establish a theocracy in Israel and to bring divine direction and godly administration into life and governance.

They led in battles against the enemies of God's people. They facilitated the interventions of Jehovah against the foes that came against them. In times of adversity and in times of joy, they were rallying figures providing leadership and direction. They injected faith, assurance, discipline and stability into spiritual discourse and into the heart of the nation.

The operation of the leadership ranks of Israel was ostensibly restricted to the nation of Israel; in other words, everything they did was insular, and had to with their national pride as God's chosen people in their identity, their history, their burdens, their victories, and the whole gamut of their lives.

As leaders, they were also periodically, intermittently and functionally anointed by the Spirit of God to accomplish that which they had to do; the Spirit would come upon them.

There are recorded impartations of the Holy Spirit, for example, when kings were anointed for office and for battle. Priests were anointed and consecrated for ministry. The bands of the prophets who followed the lead prophets prophesied from time to time when the Spirit of the Lord came upon them (1 Samuel 19:20; 2 Kings 2:2,16; 2 Kings 4:38). God also took the Spirit that was on Moses and imparted the same onto the elders of Israel, and also on Joshua, in Moses' day (Numbers 11:16-30). All such impartations were generally selective and occasional.

A major chunk of God's work under the Old Testament relates to His dealings with Israel, but it also portrays His perspective on Israel *vis-a-vis* the rest of the world. Thus, when the revelatory layers are peeled off, we see that these prophets, priests and kings of Israel were a prototype or model of the New Testament believers through Christ, and the anointing and power they exuded provided a glimpse of the even greater things God would do with the New Testament believers through the Holy Spirit.

A new day dawned in the history of mankind when the Church was born on the day of Pentecost, right after the death, resurrection and ascension of Jesus. There was a visitation of the Holy Spirit in a way and manner that was so profound and so unlike anything that individuals, people, nations, and the world at large had ever experienced. The Jubilee Mandate became fully operational and fully global.

In that New dispensation, there was the outpouring of the Sprit without measure upon those who believed, and they were anointed as a chosen generation, a royal priesthood and a holy nation, and God's own people. In other words, they became the anointed prophet, priest, judge and king, all rolled into one comprehensive fireball of the power and authority of God to release Jubilee to humanity (1 Peter 2:9).

The Jubilee Mandate can only be fulfilled and accomplished in God's strength, might and Spirit. It is virtually impossible to rely solely on human energy to achieve the excellent purposes of God embedded therein. The Holy Ghost is the person in the Godhead who enables the people of God to do that work of the ministry.

Throughout history till the present, no one has fulfilled their call or spiritual destiny without being equipped by the Holy Ghost. He is the one who speaks, teaches and provides guidance as to what God wants done at any given time. The Holy Ghost knows the mind of God, and communicates that to us and empowers us to accomplish God's will.

After His resurrection and before His ascension into heaven, Jesus revealed Himself in many ways to His disciples, teaching them and showing them things that pertain to the kingdom of God. He commanded them to go and preach and teach, and to make disciples of all nations.

But He issued an important caution that they were not to start this ministry and mandate without the visitation of the Holy Ghost. He told them to wait in Jerusalem until the promised Holy Spirit came upon them, whereupon they would receive power, and would be His witnesses from Jerusalem, and through all Judea, into Samaria, and to the uttermost parts of the earth (Luke 24:49; Acts 1:1-8).

At the first advent of the Holy Spirit recorded in the Book of Acts, one hundred and twenty men and women gathered in the upper room were filled with the Holy Spirit, and they began to speak in tongues as the Spirit gave them utterance. They were understood by the many different tribes and ethnic groups from the different nations that had gathered in Jerusalem (Acts 2:1-11).

Peter, on that day of Pentecost, reminded his hearers that what they were witnessing was that which the prophet Joel had prophesied about, regarding the last days when God would pour out His Spirit upon all flesh (Joel 2:28-29). He preached a fiery gospel and declared that the gift of the Holy Ghost is for all those who repent, for their children, and for all those afar off, even as many as the Lord or God shall call (Acts 2:38-39).

The descent of the Holy Spirit at Pentecost ushered in a new era where Jehovah remained the God of Israel, but also showed Himself as the God of all nations, extending His covenant beyond Israel to as many as would receive Jesus Christ as Savior and Lord. Such persons would become part of the covenants of promise, part of the commonwealth of Israel, part of the body of Christ, and part of the Church.

In this new season, God is anointing, not only the Levites, prophets, kings and judges, but ALL who come to Jesus; they are all eligible to drink of the Spirit and to be baptized in the Spirit. Jesus has indeed come to fulfill the promise of the Father to pour out His Spirit upon all flesh, the Jews, Gentiles, Levites, non-Levites, ministers, laity, and all those near and far.

In these last days (which actually began from the outpouring of the Spirit on the day of Pentecost), God continues to raise apostles and prophetic companies from every corner of the earth who are speaking the oracles and the word of the Lord and working the works of God; He continues to raise pastors, evangelists and teachers to build up the saints for the work of the ministry (Ephesians 4:11-14).

In these last days, gigantic waves of the Holy Spirit are moving yielded men and women of every tribe and tongue from around the world to see visions, dream dreams, prophesy, lead souls to salvation in Christ, heal the sick, cast out devils, and raise the dead (Joel 2:28-29). In these last days, this move of God in the earth is growing from year to year and from decade to decade, and it is exponentially increasing in intensity and momentum.

Jesus is, at this time, sending out, not only the apostles who were with Him during His earthly ministry, but also, all who come to Him in faith. They are to go and preach the word to every creature, fortified in the assurance that He will confirm the word to those who believe with signs and wonders. They will lay hands on the sick and they shall recover; they will cast out devils; and if they are poisoned, it will not hurt them. The believer's authority and anointing is simply nuclear, and has been imparted to all who believe.

The Holy Spirit's activities recorded in the Book of Acts lay the foundation of what God has done, is doing, and will do in the New Testament Church. They set the pace and the guardrails for the operation of the Holy Catholic Church, which is the Universal Church and body of Christ around the world.

As the experience of the early Church shows, there is no infilling of the Holy Spirit without prayer. When the disciples were threatened not to preach or teach in the name of Jesus, they corporately prayed, and their gathering place was shaken, and they were all charged up and filled with the Holy Ghost and continued to preach with boldness (Acts 4:31).

Satan and his agents always work tirelessly through the world systems, the prevailing culture, deception, and falsehoods to prevent and oppose the preaching of the gospel and the salvation and discipling of souls. That kind of resistance is torn down, not by human strength or power, but by the infilling and capability granted by the Holy Spirit.

"Not by might, nor by power, but by my Spirit, saith the Lord of hosts." Zechariah 4:6

The Church needs to soak in more and more of the anointing of the Holy Ghost, and even go beyond the saturation point, in order to be a formidable and irresistible force, and to break down barriers, flush out demons, and to open the hearts of the heathen to the gospel.

Jesus instructed His disciples to wait for the Holy Spirit of promise before they embarked on ministry. They were to be endued with the power of the Holy Spirit before they took off, and this is still the case today.

"And, behold, I send the promise of my Father upon you: but tarry ye in the city of Jerusalem, until ye be endued with power from on high." Luke 24:49

To be endued means to be endowed, equipped, supplied with, or furnished with ability, capability, competency or resources. Such endowment and equipping of the saints with the ability and resources required for the ministry can only come from the Holy Spirit. The Church must understand that the spiritual work assigned by Jesus is to be done, not in the flesh or by human ability or skill, but in the Spirit and by the Spirit.

Jesus also assured His disciples that they would receive power when the Spirit fell upon them, and they would be witnesses unto Him from Jerusalem and to even the remotest part of the earth.

"But ye shall receive power, after that the Holy Ghost is come upon you: and ye shall be witnesses unto me both in Jerusalem, and in all Judaea, and in Samaria, and unto the uttermost part of the earth." Acts 1:8

The word "power", as used here, is the word "dunamis" in Greek. It is the same word for "dynamite" which is used in connection with explosives. What this connotes is that the Holy Spirit supplies explosive spiritual dynamite to the people of God, which equips them with spiritual explosives to wreak lethal damage to all the works of the enemy.

That same power also furnishes them with the supernatural ability to be witnesses of Christ to the ends of the earth. To be a witness of something or someone is to give evidence about, or show proof of, what one has seen, heard and knows, a personal observation or experience. To be a witness unto Jesus is to show proof or give evidence or testify about the fact that He is alive from the dead, and that He is still setting humanity free from sin, sicknesses, disease, and setting at liberty those who are oppressed of the devil.

To be able to give proof or evidence about the living Messiah that could be adjudged compelling, credible and trustworthy, the disciples were endowed and vested with the power of the Holy Ghost, and they preached Jesus and worked many miracles, signs and wonders in His name. When the believers did what Jesus did in His name, they gave proof or evidence or bore witness to the fact that He was forever alive.

The gospel is not just a story or anecdotal account, nor is it a theory about best practices. It is the living message of the living Messiah, whose power is demonstrated in His mighty name. Jesus is alive today and forevermore in the heart of every believing one; therefore, every person who has believed and received the grace of salvation ought to be out there as well, bearing witness and working the works of God.

The Church must also understand that, without the deep workings and operations of the Spirit, ministry efforts may yield very little or no results; the ministry, without the Spirit, cannot bring freedom or Jubilee.

Many in Christian ministry today are operating with their human skills and capabilities without the Spirit. Some even have large followings, but are not necessarily bringing salvation, transformation or deliverance to the masses. As the apostle Paul noted, there are those who may have the form of godliness but deny the power thereof, and he sounded the warning that we should turn away from such people (2 Timothy 3:5).

There are many fine and well-meaning people sitting in the Church who are still bound in sin, addiction and demonic oppression, and who are suffering diverse diseases and torments. The Holy Spirit is the person who administers liberty, freedom, and Jubilee.

"Now the Lord is that Spirit: and where the Spirit of the Lord is there is liberty." 2 Corinthians 3:17

The Church must know the person of the Holy Spirit, and understand His place in ministry, in the lives of individuals, and also in the corporate body of Christ.

Jesus referred to the Holy Spirit as "another Comforter" that would lead His people into all truth (John 14:16-18). In other words, the Spirit's presence with the saints of God is the same as Jesus being with them - just as Jesus was with them, helping, teaching, healing and guiding them, so would the Holy Spirit be with them. The Comforter is the One called alongside to help. He is the ever-present Friend who abides with God's people and lives inside of them.

The Comforter is the Spirit of truth. He reveals Jesus, testifies of Him, glorifies Him and brings understanding about all the things that Jesus would want to show to His Church (John 15:26-27; 16:1-15). The Spirit also reveals truth about life and heaven, and about the devil, the spirit world and hell. He arms the Church with the truth of the Jubilee that must be declared and demonstrated to the world.

Let us welcome the Spirit into our lives and into the Church. Let us seek His ways and give Him pre-eminence in our worship and service to God. The flesh profits nothing, but the Spirit gives life (John 6:63).

When believers are full of the Spirit, the Church will explode with the glory of God, and will be positioned and equipped to transmit that glory and Jubilee to their communities and the nations of the world.

Holy Spirit, we welcome you. Sanctify us and consecrate us. We thirst for you. We want to drink of you, to be satiated till we explode with your power. We crave your fellowship, friendship and communion. Show us your personality so that we can be sensitive to who you are, and follow your ways and be guided by you. Holy Spirit, reveal to us the Word; show us Jesus, and lead us into the glorious presence of the Father.

We, your Church, seek a new wave of your love, your power and presence. Quicken us, make us alive, and elevate us to heights unknown, that we might emit and exude your freedom, liberty and Jubilee, and demonstrate your greater glory in all the earth, for as truly as you live, the whole earth shall be filled with the glory of the Lord (Numbers 14:21).

# Chapter 28

## JUBILEE MANDATE KEYS – CORPORATE PRAYER IN THE CHURCH

The early Church exhibited the dynamism of the nature and character of Jesus, preaching His name, working miracles in His name, and asserting that He is alive from the dead. A known cripple who begged for alms at the Beautiful Gate of the Temple was healed in the name of Jesus, by Peter and John. That forty-year old man who had never walked rose up walking, leaping and praising God.

This notable and undeniable miracle of healing caused a stir as the people were filled with wonder and amazement. Whilst the masses were still puzzled, Peter started preaching Jesus and His resurrection from the dead. The Priests, the Captain of the Temple and the Sadducees were infuriated by this, and therefore detained them till the next day. They were then brought before Caiaphas, the High Priest, so that they could be queried on the authority and power by which they had worked the miracle and preached the gospel.

They answered that it was all done in the name of Jesus of Nazareth, whom they crucified and whom God had raised from the dead (Act 4:9-12). The religious authorities did not subscribe to the resurrection of Jesus, nor to the fact that He is the Savior, and so Peter and John were warned never again to preach in that name.

Upon release, they went to the rest of the disciples and recounted all that had taken place, whereupon the company of saints lifted up their voices in corporate prayer to deal with the intimidation the authorities sought to bring:

"And when they heard that, they lifted up their voice to God with one accord, and said, Lord, thou art God, which hast made heaven, and earth, and the sea, and all that in them is"

"And now, Lord, behold their threatenings: and grant unto thy servants, that with all boldness they may speak thy word, By stretching forth thine hand to heal; and that signs and wonders may be done by the name of thy holy child Jesus. And when they had prayed, the place was shaken where they were assembled together; and they were all filled with the Holy Ghost, and they spake the word of God with boldness." Acts 4:24, 29-31

In this situation, the religious establishment came against the commission Christ gave to His disciples; the ranks thereof wanted to impede God's move and His plans to bring, salvation, healing, deliverance and Jubilee to the oppressed. It is not uncommon for the devil to find and use people who are seemingly spiritual to oppose the work of God. In fact, there are people in the Church whose hearts are not set on the advancement of God's agenda, but on their own self-gratification and promotion, and they stall the grace and purposes of God.

The believers saw this as an act of spiritual warfare, and they knew they could not resort to natural or social tools to address these spiritual battles, so they called for the whole company to raise the spiritual weapon of prayer. They lifted up their voices to God, all voices roaring and thundering into the heavens with the same prayer focus and in one accord.

Their prayer literally shook the grounds of their meeting place; obviously, these warriors were penetrating the spirit realm, binding demonic spirits, bombarding principalities and powers with Holy Ghost fire, rolling back the powers of darkness, and rendering their work ineffective and harmless.

Personal devotions and prayer are indispensable to the believer's spiritual development, and must be pursued diligently and consistently. However the coming together of God's people in united prayer is next level dynamite. It projects a much higher level of spiritual energy and power that competently addresses adverse situations in a way that solo intercessions and "whispering on the couch" prayers may be unable to. In other words, there are certain activities of Satan and demons that require the efforts of the host of spiritual warriors to breakthrough.

The political establishment also persecuted the Church. King Herod killed the apostle James, which immensely pleased the Jews, and so he sought to kill Peter as well. Peter was arrested and thrust into prison. He was under the watch of four quaternions of soldiers (sixteen), and was slated to be executed right after the feast.

"Peter therefore was kept in prison: but prayer was made without ceasing of the Church unto God for him. And when Herod would have brought him forth, the same night Peter was sleeping between two soldiers, bound with two chains: and the keepers before the door kept the prison. And, behold, the angel of the Lord came upon him, and a light shined in the prison: and he smote Peter on the side, and raised him up, saying, Arise up quickly. And his chains fell off from his hands." Acts 12:5-7

Peter did not stand a sliver of a chance to break free from those chains, outmaneuver the two soldiers, open the locked prison doors, and defeat the sixteen armed soldiers. He was a simple fisherman, untrained in martial arts, and ill-equipped, humanly speaking, to deliver himself from his predicament.

However, the Church prayed without ceasing for him. United in prayer, they prevailed against the wicked intentions of Herod and the demons working to kill Peter. God sent his angel to bring Jubilee to Peter. The chains fell off, the doors were opened, and he was miraculously led by the angel out into the street.

The whole experience was surreal for Peter; he thought it was a vision. It only became real when the angel brought him into the street and left. When God moves by His Spirit and power, He breaks every chain, literally and spiritually, and it is often like a dream. And so it was when He turned the captivity of Zion; He filled their mouths with laughter and their tongues with singing (Psalm 126:1-3).

The Church, obviously, has the power to reverse the destructive agenda of Satan and the wicked intentions of men. When she battles in unceasing prevailing prayers, God intervenes, miracles break out, and multitudes are delivered and set free.

The early Church made it a point to come together regularly, and travailing, prevailing warfare prayer featured prominently in their gatherings (Acts 2:42). They were full of the Spirit and power because of their relentless, warring attitude in prayer. There is always unlimited grace and power released by the praying Church.

In order to preach the gospel and do the works of God in signs, wonders and diverse miracles, and in order to experience the glory of the latter house, participate in the latter and former rains, and haul in and minister restoration to the greatest harvest of souls yet, we have to be involved in real offensive prevailing prayers, the kind of prayers which shake the heavens and the earth.

The time of weak, emaciated or no prayers at all in the lives of nations, individuals and the Church is way past. Come on Church! On we "ka be!" That means we should start praying in tongues, in the power and might of the Spirit!

This is a clarion call to the Church. The effectual, fervent prayer of a righteous man avails much (James 5:16). The people of God are enlisted in God's army as soldiers of the cross. If they awake in these end times to repentance and purity, and seriously invest dedicated fervent, corporate intercessory warfare prayers to the Lord, He will move in greater glory and greater waves of His Spirit, crushing and tearing down, and rolling and pushing away the dark demonic spirits leading our world to destruction and damnation. The Church will take territories, regions and nations by the power of the gospel, and thereby transmit Jubilee to our world.

# Chapter 29

## JUBILEE MANDATE KEYS – BOLDNESS OF THE CHURCH

Boldness is that quality in a person that demonstrates courage, confidence and fearlessness in the face of uncertainty or danger. Bold people are not intimidated by adverse circumstances or scared off by bullies, dictators or terrorists, or by the merciless actions of the wicked. They are daring, innovative, willing to take risks, and take initiative. They do not wait for doors to open for them, but put themselves out there to knock on doors to get them opened.

It takes boldness to function effectively in every field of human endeavor, and it is the bold and strong who are often able to advance their agenda. The Church absolutely needs boldness to access and transmit the Jubilee Mandate.

- **Boldness of the Lion of Judah**

A snapshot of life shows that there is the adversary, the devil, who always prowls around like a roaring lion, seeking whom he may devour. He comes to steal, kill and destroy. There are many mountains the people of God must surmount, and valleys they must go through. There are waters that try to overwhelm, and fires that try to consume.

In the world of today, there are enemy forces, internal and external, spiritual and physical, social, political, economic and cultural, working overtime to hinder the advancement of the gospel and the increase of God's kingdom on earth. Not surprisingly, the Church has been crippled, muted, and even decimated, in some places and cultures.

But this is not the time to weep in despair, or cower in hopelessness or helplessness. The Church must not keep silent, and must obey God rather than man. It must not succumb to the tantrums of ungodly political and religious agendas which seek to legitimize sin, which open up the freeway for false hope and demonic activities, and which only set humanity up for delusion, bondage and destruction. It must break out of fear and rejection, and must not yield to the intimidating forces of modern society trying to shut down the freedom and liberty to send out the Jubilee message of salvation.

This is the blessed assurance the Church possesses, that the Lion of the tribe of Judah, even Jesus Messiah, has prevailed! He has overcome the world, and the kingdoms of this world have become the kingdoms of our Lord, and of His Christ, and He shall reign forever and ever.

"And one of the elders saith unto me, Weep not: behold the Lion of the tribe of Judah, the Root of David, hath prevailed to open the book, and to loose the seven seals thereof." Revelation 5:5

The lion is known for its courage, strength, fearlessness and invincibility. It is anecdotally referred to as the king of the jungle in many cultures, and it operates as a king with a kingdom and domain. It is the symbol of leadership, royalty, authority and majesty. It is the strongest among beasts, can attack any animal, and does not run from any, no matter their size. The lion is indomitable, and full of power. It has fierceness in its eyes, and it sizes up and attacks its enemies and prey. The lion is always in control, in charge, and never subdued.

All these qualities and aptitudes are amalgamated in the New Creation, which is made in the image and likeness of Jesus Messiah, who is the Lion of the tribe of Judah. He is the king of the pride, His Church and Bride, and the ultimate sovereign. His kingdom and authority is above all kingdoms and authorities, and it is He who has charged us with the mandate to declare His kingdom's message to all nations.

The righteous, even the people of God, are as bold as a lion, the Bible declares (Proverbs 28:1). Boldness is very much needed in the work of the Christian Church today. We have territories to take, the enemy to overcome, and the heathen to possess, in order to bring them to the saving knowledge of Messiah. We cannot do this without boldness, without fearlessness, without showing leadership, and without demonstrating the indomitable unbreakable spirit of the Lion of the tribe of Judah, Jesus the Christ.

Boldness was one of the important characteristics that the early Church exhibited. It was first on the list of the travailing prayers of the early Church, to proclaim the word with all boldness. They asked God for boldness, and they got it. And sure enough, they were bold in doing God's work without fear.

It takes prayer to release the vitality, energy and fire that will infuse the Church with boldness. Paul asked the Church in Ephesus to pray for him so that God would give him utterance, so he could boldly open his mouth to preach.

"Praying always with all prayer and supplication in the Spirit, and watching thereunto with all perseverance and supplication for all saints; And for me, that utterance may be given unto me, that I may open my mouth boldly, to make known the mystery of the gospel, For which I am and ambassador in bonds: that therein I may speak boldly, as I ought to speak." Ephesians 6:18-20

Intensive prevailing prayers release boldness (Acts 4:31, Psalm 138:3). Upon reflection, it is entirely possible that it may be the absence of such prayers and intercession that accounts for the lackluster soul-winning efforts amongst many Christians today. We need to awake in prayer.

The fullness of the Holy Spirit in the believer's life also generates boldness (Acts 1:8, Acts 4:32, Luke 24:49). A deeper, closer walk with Jesus, and the work of the Holy Spirit upon and within the believer, will embolden him to speak the word of God. As well, the ingraining of the word of God will outfit the Church with boldness. We must remind ourselves daily that the word of God is a living being; it is alive and powerful, and sharper that any two-edged sword. It is also the sword of the Spirit which we employ to fight, ward off, and overcome every device of the enemy. It must be believed, declared, proclaimed, confessed and spoken to release its inherent power and capability. We are deputized and authorized to do this, saints. Let us muster strength, boldness and courage, and launch out in the same Spirit as the Lion of Judah, armed with His authority, power, majesty and grace, and see His will done on earth, as it is in heaven.

- **Boldness through Persecution**

Although counterintuitive, persecution also results in boldness. A natural instinct in man is to give up or cower in times of adversity, but those who are totally sold out to God and to His call can rise up from the ashes in boldness. Paul was sorely tortured, beaten up, and put in prison. Yet, those things which happened to him did not deter or subdue the other Christians; rather, they were empowered all the more to preach the gospel with boldness.

"And many of the brethren in the Lord, waxing confident by my bonds, are much more bold to speak the word without fear." Philippians 1:14

The early disciples suffered many atrocities at the hands of the religious people of their day, rulers and governments, and yet, they did not crumble under the pressure. They were bold in the profession of their faith and the preaching of the gospel even though they went through terrible situations like being imprisoned, stoned to death, sawn to death, burned alive in the fire, and being fed alive to animals. They were strong and bold, and had imprinted on their hearts, the Lion of Judah. They were invincible, unstoppable.

Let the people of God not be discouraged or afraid of trials and persecution but rather be emboldened to preach the gospel in season and out of season, cultivating a closer walk with Jesus, and maintaining the fullness of the Spirit through travailing prevailing prayers. We must work whilst it is day, for the night cometh when no man can work (John 9:3).

- **Boldness to Approach the Throne of God**

There is another important aspect of boldness that the Father God would have us cultivate and operate in. He wants us to come before Him with boldness.

"Let us therefore come boldly unto the throne of grace, that we may obtain mercy, and find grace to help in the time of need." Hebrews 4:16

This is the boldness to approach the Most High God. That kind of boldness does not connote going into the Father's presence with the warring, defiant lion's heart, as though going against the powers of darkness, but rather, with an overwhelming appreciation of the Father's invitation to come before Him with confidence, not in our own righteousness but in the righteousness of Christ, without any sense of inferiority or condemnation.

Many do not feel the sense of worthiness to appear before the Holy God. They may confess their sins the whole day and yet, never feel forgiven; they have a debilitating sin-consciousness. But Jesus loved us and washed us from our sins in His own blood (Revelation 1:5). He shed His blood to atone for those sins. He fully paid the price for our sins - a hundred percent. If we confess our sins, He is faithful and just to forgive us and to cleanse us from all unrighteousness (1 John 1:8-9).

You must accept God's forgiveness by faith when you sincerely confess your sins, and must have the assurance that you are cleansed to stand before God in the very righteousness of Christ which has been imparted to you. Through the washing of the blood of Jesus you are reconciled to God and have renewed fellowship with Him. God has accepted you in Christ, the Beloved (Ephesians 1:6). As a New Creation, you can now approach the Father without fear of rejection or unacceptance, but with confidence, assurance, faith and boldness, just as any child who has a good relationship with their father would do.

When the children of God enter His throne room with boldness, certain things happen. Faith is activated and comes alive. Any person that comes to God must believe that He is, and that He is a rewarder of them that diligently seek Him (Hebrews 11:6). God acknowledges living faith in the heart of His saints. He is a God who moves by faith and who is moved by faith and pleased by faith.

Again, those who connect to God by boldness and confidence obtain His mercy and compassion. God is seated on His throne, on the mercy seat, which is a place of divine access and communion, and His mercies are renewed every day, inexhaustible and custom-made or tailored to address every situation of their lives.

Further, those who access the throne room boldly find grace to help in time of need. God makes His grace abundantly available as He is the ever-present help in any time of need. He gives power to the faint, and to those that are weak, He increases strength. He delivers the oppressed. He lifts the poor out of the dunghill and sets them among princes. He turns mourning into dancing, and weeping or sorrow into joy. We are saved by grace. The Father God is ever faithful, ever merciful, and ever gracious, and cannot fail anyone who comes to Him.

When we boldly go into God's presence also, we can more readily hear from Him, and it becomes easier to think like Him, talk like Him, and make bold proclamations of the unchanging, unfailing promises of His word.

"Let your conversation your conversation be without covetousness; and be content with such things as ye have: for he hath said, I will never leave thee nor forsake thee. So that we may boldly say, The Lord is my helper, and I will not fear what man shall do unto me." Hebrews 13:5-6

This prevails upon us, the need to boldly (not timidly, sheepishly or fearfully) repeat after God, what He has said. When God says something, we must also boldly say what He says. This means that our confessions, declarations, conversations, actions and beliefs must be based on what the word of God and His promises declare to us.

Saints of God, we need to get this - the word of God, which we have on our minds and in our hearts, must be spoken boldly. Our mouths must be fully engaged in this. Remember that we get saved by believing in our hearts the death and resurrection of Jesus and His redemptive work, and confessing with our mouths that He is Lord. With our hearts we believe unto righteousness, and with our mouths, confession is made unto salvation (Romans 10:8-10).

Jesus, our High Priest, has passed into the heavens (Hebrews 4:14). He is the High Priest of our confession (what we profess) and of our sacrifices of thanksgiving, praise and worship. Just as the people of Israel spoke over their sacrifices, following which the High Priest would present the sacrifices on the altar to God, Jesus, in His work as the High Priest in the heavens, presents our confessions, declarations and sacrifices of worship to the Father God. What we say, therefore, is what He submits at the altar of God.

When God finds our bold, faith-filled confessions and proclamations on the mercy seat, as presented by Jesus, He creates the content of those confessions and proclamations for us. Words have creative power. God calls the things that be not as though they were. He brought non-existence into existence by the words He spoke. He created all things by the power of His word, and controls all things by His word (Hebrews 1:3, Hebrews 11:3, Romans 4:17). Therefore, He uses our bold, word-aligned confessions and declarations to work signs and wonders on our behalf.

In the same vein, we can be taken captive or ensnared by what we say when we affirm, through our murmuring, complaining and sorrow, negative prevailing circumstances. The pain may be real, and the battle may be fierce, but Jehovah is greater, and His word of victory will put us over. Therefore, we must repeat that word of victory, take authority over the circumstances, and rebuke the storms.

We must employ the faith-filled word of God at all times. The word must never depart from our mouths. We must boldly proclaim, no matter the battles we face, that we are more than conquerors (Romans 8:37). We are born of God, and so we overcome the world (1 John 5:4-5). Greater is He that is in us than he that is in the world (1 John 4:4). We overcome Satan by the blood of the Lamb and by the word of our testimony (Revelation 12:11).

Faith must take what the grace of God makes available from His throne room, the ultimate Command Centre. From the throne room, God gives, releases, or dispatches His infallible word. He has exalted His word above all his titles. There is authority and power in the word. It is forever settled in the heavens. All things, circumstances and situations are subject to the highest authority of the word of God. Negative situations will be subdued and will line up with the word when we declare and boldly proclaim it with authority.

We must therefore take hold of the promises of God in our hearts by faith. They belong to us. Through faith and patience, we inherit them. We need to meditate on them, and feed them to our minds, souls, emotions and spirits until the life within them revitalizes our entire being and existence. That is when the word takes root and residence in our hearts.

The saints of God must consistently exercise and proclaim boldly their redemptive rights and privileges, and superimpose them on adverse or contradictory circumstances in life to change those situations to bring the blessings of God. We must say continually that we are the redeemed of the Lord, that we are the saved of the Lord, that we are the healed of the Lord, that we are the delivered of the Lord, that we are the prospered of the Lord, that we are the Jubilee of the Lord.

The Church needs to wake up to the glorious power, majesty and boldness of Jesus Messiah who has commissioned us for this ministry. He has given us the same authority and power to trample over snakes and scorpions, and to overcome all the power of the enemy, and He has declared that nothing shall by any means hurt us (Luke 10:19). The Church must therefore be relentless in prayer and in the proclamation of the gospel of peace.

Be bold and put the devil in his place. Be bold and preach the gospel. Boldly enter the throne room of grace. Boldly proclaim that which the Lord Himself has said; for His word will not return to Him void.

# Chapter 30

## JUBILEE MANDATE KEYS – UNITY IN THE CHURCH

Unity is that quality that is released when multiple strands of people come together, become single-minded, function as one, and blend beautifully like a symphony of chords.

Unity in the body of Christ is so dear to the heart of Jesus. It is a central key to enjoying and fulfilling the fullness of the Jubilee Mandate that He has given to His people. The Spirit-filled Church of today, and the Church that desires to experience the unprecedented move of the glory of God, must be principled and adhere to the dynamic precepts which govern unity in the House of God. Simply put, the Church must maintain Bible ways to get Bible results.

- **Unity in the Godhead**

Before Jesus' crucifixion, He taught the disciples about unity. He, the author and finisher of our faith, prayed that the Father would make His followers one in the same way that the Godhead demonstrates oneness.

"Neither pray I for these alone, but for them also which shall believe on me through their word; That they all may be one; as thou, Father, art in me, and I in thee, that they also may be one in us: that the world may believe that thou hast sent me." John 17:20-21

Unity is an eternal characteristic of the inner workings of divinity. None amongst the Godhead operates by themselves. The Trinity works in perfect "permanent synchronization." In the beginning, God (Elohim - <u>Father, Word, Holy Spirit</u>) created the heavens and the earth. (Genesis 1:1). God said, "Let <u>us</u> make man in <u>our</u> image and likeness" (Genesis 1:26).

The Godhead demonstrates excellent unity in every move. The unleashing of power in creation and in all existence, the perfection of beauty in creation, the release of limitless possibilities in every situation, circumstance or condition, and the release of effective and fruitful ministry, are all the by-products of perfect unity in the Godhead.

That unity did not cease when Jesus came to earth. He was anointed by the Holy Spirit and was also in constant coalition with the Father. The Father was in Him, and He was in the Father. He did whatever He saw the Father do (John 14:10). "How <u>God</u> anointed <u>Jesus</u> of Nazareth with the <u>Holy Spirit</u> and with power who went about doing good and healing all who were oppressed of the devil, for God was with him" (Acts 10:38). The Father did the anointing, Jesus the Son (Word) received the anointing, and the anointing was the flow or manifest power of the Holy Spirit.

If the Godhead so values and operates in unity, how much more the Church that Jesus gave His life for, which God foreknew, called, justified and predestinated to be conformed to the image and likeness of Jesus? (Romans 8:29-30). We can do no less but conform to that which the Godhead does.

The agreement or unity of two or more (such as a married couple, a family, the Church, or a nation), generates unstoppable power and energy to accomplish whatever they believe for, work for, and imagine to do. When Nimrod and his team united and sought to build a tower that would reach the heavens, God acknowledged that when a people become one, they can accomplish whatever they imagine to do.

Unity brings the visitation of God. If the union advances His will, He will bless it. If the purpose of the union is evil, He moves to destroy that purpose. In Nimrod's case where the people sought to build the tower of Babel, God intervened, confused their language, and scattered them abroad (Genesis 11:6-9).

Surely, the Lord God will come down to visit His people who unite to fulfill His will in the earth. He will move to bless those who pattern their existence after the Godhead, and seek to expand and promote the kingdom of God. He will come in all of His power and might to make a living reality, any dream or aspiration of the body of believers who are united in one purpose and one goal to advance God's kingdom.

- **Division in the Church**

A foundational truth of the Christian Faith is that everyone who has received Jesus as Lord and Savior and is born again of the Spirit and the Word, belongs to one body, no matter who, what, and where they are in the world.

"There is one body, and one Spirit, even as ye are called in one hope of your calling; One Lord, one faith, one baptism, One God and Father of all, who is above all, and through all, and in you all." Ephesians 4:4-6

Reinforcing this unity, the apostle Paul refers to the Church, the corporate and entire body of Christ, as one great house being built. The strength, beauty and architectural majesty of any great house depends on the kind of foundation on which it is built. The Church of Christ is not built on human ideas or the philosophies of men. It is built on the leadership, work, and the spiritual and scriptural precepts and guidance of the New Testament apostles and prophets, with Jesus Christ Himself as the chief corner stone.

"Now therefore ye are no more strangers and foreigners, but fellow citizens with the saints, and of the household of God. And are built upon the foundation of the apostles and prophets, Jesus Christ himself being the chief corner stone; In whom all the building fitly framed together groweth unto an holy temple in the Lord: In whom ye also are builded together for an habitation of God through the Spirit." Ephesians 2:19-22

Jesus Christ is the Rock on which the Church is built (Matthew 16:18). He is the chief corner stone who raised up apostles and prophets during His ministry and when He ascended on high (Ephesians 4:8-14). He, together with these apostles and prophets, make up the majestic solid foundation of the Church, and there is no foundation that anyone can lay other than that which is laid, which is Jesus Christ (1 Corinthians 3:11).

As the foundation of the Church, the work of the apostles and prophets in the narratives of the New Testament - the Book of Acts, the Epistles and Revelation - sets the parameters for, and defines, the functions and mandate of both the historical and the contemporary Church.

However, this majestic and glorious building of the Church has come under serious attack and shows increasing signs of cracks, fissures, breaks and instability. Most of the Church world is plagued by splits, divisions and confusion. There are so many permutations and expressions of this. For example, disgruntled persons and groups break away; ambitious persons fight to reallocate power, money, resources and opportunities and cause confusion; factions are created within the body; some people are incited by divisive persons to leave; others are simply manipulated and deceived into severing ties.

Let us be crystal clear - God is not the author of confusion; He is the God of peace, and He seeks peace in the body of Christ. Division originates from Satan (Lucifer). The activity of divisiveness is his device to weaken the Church and to cause it to derail from its assignment and focus. That should come as no surprise as that has been his modus operandi from the beginning, and is familiar terrain to him. He sinned from the beginning; he rebelled against God and persuaded a third of the angels in heaven to break away with him and follow him (Revelation 12:4, 9; Ezekiel 28:11-19; Isaiah 14:12-23).

He had the finest position among the archangels in heaven. He was very beautiful to behold, intricately made with an assortment of beautiful precious stones, and he was a walking orchestra, endowed with the blessed giftings of music and worship. With all that God gave him and placed within him, however, he was still displeased and dissatisfied, and the mystery of iniquity was found in him. By his act of iniquity or extreme wickedness, desiring the place of God and wanting to establish his own throne above God's, he brought about division in heaven.

Division amongst brethren is an act of witchcraft, and is based on manipulation, deception and control. Divisive people crave and feed off the support of others, and they go around with a barrage of lies accusing their leaders and compatriots falsely, and promising like-minded persons or innocent, vulnerable and gullible followers or both, a better life in their personal empire or kingdom they plan to build. With their enticing silver tongues, they lure and sweep away the innocent and vulnerable who have been planted by God in their respective local Churches, who are serving the Lord, and who had no pre-existing intention to leave their Churches.

A common but dangerous phenomenon that recurs is that congregation members are sympathetic to those who engender division. That is because those persons spell out a litany of "evils" the organization or leadership has done to them, in order to justify and validate their divisive actions. Any such sympathies from the congregation are misplaced because they encourage and give more impetus to those dividers to do that which is gravely injurious to the Church as a whole.

Even in the best case scenario where such grievances are legitimate, the division of the Church is never an option to deal with it; rather, there must be godly efforts to rectify the situation. More often than not, however, there is absolutely no basis for the division. Hear this well - God did not do anything wrong to Lucifer for him to do what he did. It is just that divisive people are never satisfied and will create problems even where none exist. The devil fills their hearts with pride, and they come to a place where they, like the devil, kick against leadership and authority. They reject the idea of submission to God's ordained leadership, and think of themselves and their aptitudes and giftings as superior to those who put them in their positions.

They feel that they are more deserving of authority and adulation, and must be in charge instead of the set leadership.

Many local assemblies have suffered hurts and wounds because of such division. Great visions of wonderful Churches have been shattered. The momentum and advancement of Churches have been interrupted and stalled. Pastors whose work became casualties to these nefarious actions of Church dividers have become discouraged, broken and embittered because of the betrayal and manipulation of the agents of Lucifer.

Some Christians have become discouraged and disappointed, and others feel abused because of the greed and deception of divisive people. And many are uprooted from the place where they were divinely planted by the sovereign dealings of God through the seductions of divisive people, thus disrupting or even wrecking their spiritual destiny.

There is a need for the people of God to wake up and draw a clear line of demarcation between those who are truly serving God and those who are serving their own interests, between those who promote unity and those who promote Lucifer's acts of division.

Any person who does not uphold, honor, promote and maintain the unity of the body Christ is NOT serving God's purpose, but the devil's agenda. It does not matter how persuasive such divisive agents are in justifying offence. It also does not matter how powerfully they may preach, prophesy or work miracles. Neither does it matter how seemingly successful they are or become. Their agenda is to satisfy their stomachs because their own belly is their god, as the apostle Paul explains. They seek recognition, fame and fortune at the expense of the unity of

God's people and the expansion of God's work. Therefore, no matter what it looks like at face value, these divisive persons are not interested in building and advancing God's work.

Many who are lured and deceived into leaving one local assembly to join with a person who divides the Church tend to buy into certain techniques of neutralization. They think that it is still the same body of Christ being served, and that the newly-formed organization is not preaching anything contrary to the word of God, and so that is okay. That is a false premise. It is not okay.

It is time for the people of God to be discerning to see through the wickedness that divisive people inflict on the body of Christ. They must not be blinded by the falsehoods of Satan, and must not become emotionally entangled or involved in what divisive and discordant people do. That they claim to be your "messiah" and manipulate you into thinking that unless you follow them, you are doomed, should not keep you bound to them. Break free from their controlling witchcraft powers now! May your eyes be opened to walk in the light of God's word, and may you reconnect with the place that God planted you to fulfill your spiritual destiny.

Every Christian must take a stand to maintain the unity of the Spirit in the bond of peace, and avoid agents of the enemy who rise up to promote offence and division in the body of Christ. Among the seven abominable things that God hates are a false witness that speaks lies, and sowing discord among brethren (Proverbs 6:16-19).

The only way out for these representatives of evil is for them to come to the place of true repentance and to bear the fruits of repentance. If they do not, the Bible says they should be "marked" and "avoided." No one should be a partaker of their sins.

"Now I beseech you, brethren, mark them which cause divisions and offences contrary to the doctrine which ye have learned; and avoid them. For they that are such serve not our Lord Jesus Christ, but their own belly; and good words and fair speeches deceive the heart of the simple." Romans 16:17-18

May God deliver His Church from such unreasonable and wicked persons who have no faith. May we, in the contemporary Church, allow the Spirit to crush our egos and superiority complexes, and flush out greed and any ungodly cravings of fame and fortune which stir up dissension, discord, contention and endless controversies. May our faithful God establish and build His Church, and keep His people from evil (2 Thessalonians 3:1-3).

- **Release of "Great Power" and "Great Grace" through Unity**

Unity unlocks "great power", and also, "great grace" upon the Church. Power (the explosive ability of God) and grace (the unmerited or undeserved favor of God) are the vectors that propel the effective enjoyment and transmission of the Jubilee Mandate.

The early Church functioned in the spirit of unity. During the times of the early apostles, there were thousands of believers who were part of the local Church in Jerusalem. The record shows that they were united in heart and soul, and in spirit and mind to the point that they had all things in common. The possession of each one was the possession of all.

"And the multitude of them that believed were of one heart and of one soul: neither said any of them that ought of the things which he possessed was his own; but they had all things common. And with great power gave the apostles witness of the resurrection of the Lord Jesus; and great grace was upon them all." Acts 4:32-33

The whole Church saw themselves as one, with one goal, one purpose and one dream to worship God, live for Christ, live for others, preach the gospel and advance the kingdom of God. They knew that unity was the key to open the treasure box of God's power and grace, and that, if they could fuse their spirits and souls together as one, God would show up. He would come down and visit them with His glorious presence, proving Himself mighty and strong on their behalf.

God is attracted to the unity of His people. Seeing their union, communion, fellowship of spirit, faith and vision, He descended on them and endowed them with great power to be witnesses of the living, resurrected Messiah. That denotes the release of boldness, a tremendous impact on the spiritual climate, and the tangible demonstration of mighty signs and wonders that advertised the kingdom of God.

The saints did not only experience great power, but also received God's outpouring of great grace, that is, unmerited favor, on them all. In other words, through the unity they exuded, they became a living expression of the excessive joy of the Jubilee, which is the year of the Lord's favor, and a conduit for its transmission to the world they witnessed to.

O, the depths of grace and power that would be unlocked from the yet untapped reservoirs of the chambers of Jehovah, which, like a flash flood, would clear away the debris of sin and satanic resistance, and dial in awakenings, revivals, salvation and the healing of innumerable multitudes in this generation and beyond!

May the Church unite around the purity of the Messiah and be one, to show the world that we are indeed His disciples. And may we give witness of our Messiah in great power, and with great grace upon us!

- **A Beautiful Analogy of Unity: Mount Hermon and Mount Zion**

Wherever there is unity, there is sweet fellowship, friendship and communion. Positive energy, strength, ideas and resources flow across the board. The strong strengthen the weak, and those who have more help the needy. No one falls through the cracks, no one is overlooked, no one is sidelined, and no one is left behind. The equitable distribution of gifts, skills, resources, thoughts and inspiration in a group where members are in harmony with each other translates into progress, success and advancement to all. The psalmist says:

"Behold, how good and how pleasant it is for brethren to dwell together in unity! It is like the precious ointment upon the head, that ran down upon the beard, even Aaron's beard: that went down to the skirts of his garments; As the dew of Hermon, and as the dew that descended upon the mountains of Zion: for there the LORD commanded the blessing, even life for evermore." Psalm 133

The unity of the brethren is likened to the pouring of precious ointment upon the High Priest Aaron's head. The precious ointment here refers to the anointing oil that was poured on the priesthood in consecration (Leviticus 8:1-12).

That oil was itself a picture of perfect unity at work as it was a mixture of four spices in olive oil – myrrh, cinnamon, cane and cassia – to make a holy oil (Exodus 30:23-25, 30). The mixture of the different components according to God's directions is what made the oil holy and sacred.

The flowing precious ointment is a depiction of the Spirit of God and the unity of the Godhead in the outpouring of His anointing upon His people. This oil pours profusely, flowing from Aaron's head, down his beard, and to his skirts.

Aaron's head is a type of Christ, who is the Head of the Church (Ephesians 5:23, 1 Corinthians 11:3, Colossians 1:18). Christ was anointed by God with the Spirit without measure.

Aaron's beard is also significant as the oil runs down it. The beard is made up of numerous different strands of hair coming out of different follicles, and this presents a picture of the diversity of the Church, which is made up of all types of persons, different people from every nation, race, kindred and tongue, who are nevertheless united and connected to the Head, even Christ. That same Spirit without measure on the Head (Christ) therefore pours onto the different strands of people who make up the Church.

The oil runs down the skirts of Aaron's garments. The skirts typify the body of Christ, which is the Church. God, in His love, has spread His skirt over us, making us His very own, His bride, and taking us under His care and protection (Ruth 3). As Boaz spread His skirt over Ruth and made her his bride, so has the Lord stretched out His pavilion over us and made us His own.

Jesus, our eternal High Priest, opens the tap of the anointing of the Spirit upon the body of Christ, His Church, when the Church maintains unity. In other words, the only setting in which believers can participate in this corporate anointing of the Spirit dished out by Jesus is within the atmosphere of sweet fellowship and oneness. Dwelling together in unity propels the flow of the anointing of God, and equips the people of God to walk in great power and great grace to fulfill their call and destiny.

That anointing is like the dew on Mount Hermon and Mount Zion. Mount Hermon was the highest peak in Palestine, referencing God's throne that is above all else. Geospatially, Mount Hermon, in the north, was never dry but blessed with fresh heavy dew which, at times, would even appear like rain or snow covering those mountains. This depicts the inexhaustible supply, and the refreshing and renewal, of the Holy Spirit from the presence of the Lord.

Zion is the picture of the Church. The peak of Mount Zion, in the south, was normally dry, and generally did not experience dew like Mount Hermon. However, the choice dew upon Mount Hermon (the Head) somehow perceptibly descended on Mount Zion as well.

The psalmist was trying to convey a deep truth, that there is something unique, a distinctive occurrence, that is able to supernaturally change the qualities and properties of that dry Mount Zion to make it vibrant.

The unity of the brethren is that supernatural agent. Unity imparts and transports to the dry patches of Zion, Hermon's life-giving dew, rain and snow. This means that, with unity at work, God's people will never be dry; they will receive the showers of blessing, seasons of refreshing, and restoration from the very presence of the Lord. That is great news!

Dew is distilled water, and water is a symbol of life. Dew and water invigorate the vegetation, and yield fruitfulness and a bounty harvest. The unity of the Church draws the fresh dew of heaven. The resultant is that it becomes full of life and begins to experience the gifts of the Spirit and the bountiful harvest of souls. God commands, imparts, transmits, and releases the blessings of life on His people as the dew of heaven, and the outpouring of the Holy Spirit brings the refreshing. His glory would be shown again and again in Zion, His Church.

Another result of unity among the brethren is that God commands life forevermore. This is the eternal life that Jesus has secured for us, salvation from eternal death or damnation. He came that we might have life, and life more abundantly. Hallelujah!

Jehovah causes that which is dead to come to life by the refreshing of the heavenly dew; that which is weak to become strong; that which is broken to be bound up; that which is bound to be set free; that which is out of joint to be aligned; and that which is lost to be restored by the supply of the Spirit and the abounding grace of God Almighty. That is the Jubilee message! Glory to God!

Let the people of God arise and be willing to pick up the Jubilee Mandate to proclaim freedom and liberty to a lost and dying world. It is the day of the Lord's favor!

# Chapter 31

## THE JUBILEE MANDATE - YOURS TO ENJOY, ENFORCE AND TRANSMIT FOREVER!

Jubilee is in open season. It is now in full bloom and upon all children of God who have come to Jesus. In receiving Jesus as our Lord and Savior, we have become born again, the New Creation.

Jesus (Immanuel) is now with us; He dwells eternally in us. And Jesus is the Jubilee in person. If so, then it is Jubilee that dwells in us. He is in us, and with us, and for us, always. Our very being has been recreated and infused with Jubilee, the person, and with Jubilee, as an experiential conception.

This means we do not have to wait out the 50-year cycle in order to celebrate the full benefits, rights and privileges of our redemption. Jesus, the Jubilee, is very present with us every minute of every day, and every moment. Hallelujah!

Jesus, in our hearts and lives, opens us up to the present, future, and eternal supplies of the Jubilee, so we can confidently enforce and enjoy the freedoms that the Father has made available through the Son.

Jesus brings Jubilee to all who believe in His saving grace, and we have received so much of this indescribable benefit. Having personally experienced the Jubilee - the salvation, deliverance and favor of the Lord – the question is this: What is our reasonable response to God?

Our response, as believers, cannot be disparate. It must be proportional to, and commensurate with, the magnitude of what we have received.

This is the reality of our world – that countless others are yet to be reached with the Jubilee message. Jesus' heart beats for the lost. He was moved with compassion for the multitudes who were scattered abroad as sheep without a shepherd. "The harvest is plenteous, but the laborers are few," He said.

This is the Jubilee Mandate – that every one of us who has been touched by Jubilee must share in this burden for the lost. In appreciation for what we have received from the Lord, we must also break out in the Spirit and fire of Jubilee and register emancipation in the hearts and souls of humanity. We must be at the forefront of the battle to bring in the harvest of souls, and must lift earnest prayer for God to raise up laborers to go into the harvest fields (Matthew 9:35-38).

The Jubilee Mandate, mantle, unction and authority has been passed on to every believer, and every saint is an evangel who must go out and proclaim the Jubilee.

"And he said unto them, Go ye into all the world, and preach the gospel to every creature. He that believeth and is baptized shall be saved; but he that believeth not shall be damned. And these signs shall follow them that believe; In my name shall they cast out devils; they shall speak with new tongues; They shall take up serpents; and if they drink any deadly thing, it shall not hurt them; they shall lay hands on the sick, and they shall recover." Mark 16:15-18

Every believer has been equipped with the full scope of the power and anointing to carry out the Jubilee Mandate.

We have Jesus' full permission to ensure that His will, plan, purpose and design on earth is enforced and maintained. All things of the Father God have been given to Him, and He has all power in heaven and on earth (Matthew 28:18-20). He has transferred the fullness of this power and authority to the body of believers.

We have His name, and Jehovah God has lodged within the name of Jesus, the treasures, glory, authority and powers of the Godhead (Colossians 1:19, 2:9-10; Isaiah 9:6). That beautiful name is as sweet ointment poured forth upon those who hurt, and is a strong tower to all who run into it. In this name shall the sick be healed, the dead raised, lepers cleansed, and devils cast out. It is the name that is above every other name; at the mention of this name, every knee bows, of beings in heaven, beings on earth and beings under the earth.

We have also been engrafted into, and entrenched in, the kingdom of God as first-class citizens, and are no longer afar off, neither are we aliens. The kingdom of God holds the highest authority and power, which transcends and supersedes all others. Jesus is this kingdom, and He came to proclaim this kingdom, to superimpose it on the kingdom of darkness, and to dispel that darkness with His glorious light, to disarm every principality and power, and to announce freedom and liberty to the captives. He holds the keys to this kingdom, and He has given us those keys:

"And I will give unto thee the keys of the kingdom of heaven: and whatsoever thou shalt bind on earth shall be bound in heaven: and whatsoever thou shalt loose on earth shall be loosed in heaven." Matthew 16:19

In addition, God has poured out His Spirit upon us in these last days, and we have the heavier weight of the Spirit and glory of God resting on us, even the overpowering, overcoming increase of the anointing that tears down satanic bondages and falsehoods and brings Jubilee to all who believe.

Let us be deeply connected to Jesus, to know who He is and understand His heart, mission and passion. And let our hearts be set ablaze and aflame with the Spirit's fire to carry out the great commission to go from house to house, street to street, visiting communities, parks, crevices, school campuses, villages, towns, cities, prisons, hospitals and literally, any place that souls can be found.

May God's holy fire roll away the Church's cloak of complacency and apathy! May our dry eyes be wet with tears of compassion to see a world in bondage, enslaved by sin, racked by diseases, soaked in all forms of addiction, oppressed by satanic schemes, tormented and afflicted by demonic power, deceived by false prophets and religions, and marching helplessly into eternal damnation in hell and the lake of fire! May our hearts feel the pain of the lost and dying world once again! And may we, again and again, turn that key of freedom which we hold, by presenting incessantly, Jesus Messiah, the Lamb of God who takes away the sin of the world.

"Thy people shall be willing in the day of thy power, in the beauties of holiness from the womb of the morning: thou hast the dew of thy youth." Psalm 110:3

We are willing, O God, for this is the day of your power. This is the day of the unprecedented outpouring of the Holy Spirit, the very dew of heaven. It is the day of soul-winning, and of bringing the harvest of souls into the local assembly. It is the day of preaching the gospel in and through every forum, from house to house, in public gatherings, at holy convocations, at impactful gospel campaigns, through the media, and through the airwaves. This is the day of the release of true apostolic and prophetic ministry at local levels, and also at major national apostolic and prophetic gatherings. This is the day of the demonstration of diverse gifts of the Holy Spirit.

The harvest is ripe. The world waits in suspense and expectancy for good news. Hark! Hear countless united and purpose-driven heels tapping, and the sound of the believers moving all over the globe spreading Jubilee in miracles, signs and wonders, working tirelessly in season and out of season, and filling the whole earth with God's greater glory and power!

And O! Hear the jubilation, the exceeding and surpassing joyful sound of lives set free, multitudes and multitudes breaking out with songs of deliverance and shouts of joy!

Today is the day of salvation! It is the year of the Lord's favor! It is the Jubilee that never ends! The Jubilee Mandate is truly here! As the Lord has said, so shall we also boldly, zealously and prayerfully say:

"The Spirit of the Lord is upon me, because he hath anointed me to preach the gospel to the poor; he hath sent me to heal the brokenhearted, to preach deliverance to the captives, and recovering of sight to the blind, to set at liberty them that are bruised, To preach the acceptable year of the Lord." Luke 4:18-19

# PRAYER FOR SALVATION

Heavenly Father, creator of heaven and earth and all things in existence, I come to You today having heard Your word. You loved the world so much that You gave Your only begotten Son, Jesus, that whosoever believes in Him should not perish, but have everlasting life. Your word reveals that the wages of sin is death, but the free gift of God is eternal life through Christ Jesus.

I believe that Jesus died for my sins. Cleanse me from every sin through the blood that He shed for me. I believe in my heart that God raised Him from the dead, and I confess with my mouth that He is Lord. I receive Him as my Lord and personal Savior. I receive the new birth. I am a New Creation in Christ Jesus. Write my name in heaven in the lamb's book of life. Thank you, Father God, for saving me, in Jesus mighty name. Amen.

# AUTHOR'S PROFILE

Andrew D. Asare is the Pioneer and Presiding Apostle of OMEGA CHURCHES (formerly Faith Foundation International). He is ordained and licensed with the Christian International Network of Churches, under Dr. Bill Hamon. He has been active in Christian leadership for almost four decades and is well-studied with a solid background in Biblical Studies, Theology, and Christian Counselling.

From his teenage years to the present, Andrew has functioned in diverse and increasingly responsible roles in the body of Christ. He has been involved in youth ministries, miracle crusades, capacity-building, and church planting. He is passionate about evangelism and soul-winning, and his heart is to establish the people of God in the fundamental tenets of the faith to bring them to the place of maturity, stability and fruitfulness. His voice is one that encourages the recognition of spiritual authority and the maintenance of order within the body of Christ. He has mentored many Christian Ministers and Leaders who are thriving in ministry around the world. He believes in the flow of the greater glory of the latter house in miracles, signs and wonders.

# SUMMARY/SYNOPSIS OF THE JUBILEE MANDATE

Adam, the first man, disobeyed God's command not to eat of the fruit of the tree in the midst of the Garden of Eden. That act of disobedience alienated him from God, his maker, and subjected him and all of humanity after him to the dominion of Satan. The world came into bondage to sin, and to the horrors of eternal condemnation and spiritual death.

But God, responding to the fall of man, initiated the redemptive process. He incrementally unveiled it in the Old Testament narratives in images, types and shadows through the institution of the Sabbath observance (culminating in the Jubilee), the celebration of the appointed Feasts of Israel, and the revelation of Jehovah God in His redemptive names.

Fast forward many centuries later, and we see Jesus, the Son of God, coming to the synagogue in Nazareth, on a glorious Sabbath day. He reads a profound scripture from the Book of Isaiah on the Jubilee, the acceptable year of the Lord, and follows it with an astounding, self-referential and self-invoking declaration: **"This day is this scripture fulfilled in your ears."** (Luke 4:16-21). Hallelujah! Jesus has come to fulfil the Jubilee through and through!

It is altogether fascinating and intriguing how Jesus emerges in the New Testament scripts as the Mega Star - the eminently qualified Lord of the Sabbath, the personification of the Feasts of Israel, and the composite expression of all the redemptive names of Jehovah, the name which is above every name and which holds all the glory, authority, power and majesty of God.

"The Jubilee Mandate" is prayerfully crafted to showcase Jesus as God's anointed One, chosen before the foundation of the world to fulfil every detail of the Old Testament types and shadows with precision and accuracy. He brings to all who are bound by the shackles of sin, satanic oppression, sickness, poverty, premature death and eternal condemnation, FREEDOM and JUBILEE.

This is the Jubilee Mandate: Jesus completely obeyed the Father's Mandate; with zeal, compassion, power and the anointing of the Holy Spirit, He proclaimed the Jubilee that sets the captives free. And then He declared that, as the Father sent Him, so has He sent us, His body.

The Church, then, has the same Mandate of Jesus, even the Jubilee Mandate, to go into all the world, proclaiming salvation, healing the sick, casting out devils, demonstrating the power of God, and setting humanity free in Jubilee.

This book encourages the Church to tap into the treasures and spiritual assets of the Jubilee, and to intentionally and strategically transition into the "greater works" mode. May our passion for the lost be rekindled and our hearts set aflame by Holy Ghost fire to snatch the multitudes of lost souls from eternal damnation and purposefully shepherd them into the kingdom of God. The hour to do the works of God is now! The move of God is now! Jubilee is now!

www.ingramcontent.com/pod-product-compliance
Lightning Source LLC
Chambersburg PA
CBHW060106170426
43198CB00010B/791